THE PRIVATISATION OF
JAPANESE NATIONAL RAILWAYS

The Privatisation of Japanese National Railways

TATSUJIRO ISHIKAWA
and
MITSUHIDE IMASHIRO

THE ATHLONE PRESS
LONDON AND NEW BRUNSWICK N.J.

First published 1998 by
THE ATHLONE PRESS
1 Park Drive, London NW11 7SG
and New Brunswick, New Jersey

© Tatsujiro Ishikawa and Mitsuhide Imashiro 1998

British Library Cataloguing in Publication Data
*A catalogue record for this book is available
from the British Library*

ISBN 0 485 11452 6 hb

Library of Congress Cataloging-in-Publication Data

Imashiro, Mitsuhide, 1949–
    The privatisation of Japanese national railways : railway
management, market and policy / Tatsujiro Ishikawa and Mitsuhide
Imashiro.
        p. cm.
    Includes bibliographical references and index.
    ISBN 0-485-11452-6
    1. Nihon Kokuyū Tetsudō. 2. Railroads—Deregulation—Japan.
3. Privatisation—Japan—Case studies. 4. Railroads and state—
Japan. I. Ishikawa, Tatsujiro, 1921– . II. Title.
HE3360.N5145 1998
385'.1—dc21   98–5775
                                                                                               CIP

Distributed in the United States, Canada and South America by
Transaction Publishers
390 Campus Drive
Somerset, New Jersey 08873

Typeset by Ensystems, Saffron Walden

Printed and bound in Great Britain by
Cambridge University Press

Contents

Preface

Japanese National Railways have, under the 'public corporation' system, recovered from the damage suffered during the Second World War, and brought about a golden age of railway transportation in Japan. Under the same 'public corporation' system, however, it went into decline, and moved towards privatisation and its break-up into divisions.

I joined the national railway in autumn 1945, just after the Second World War. In those days, the organization was called the Ministry of Transport Railways Bureau [Tetsudo Sokyoku], and was operated by the government. The change to the public corporation, 'Japanese National Railways', came four years later.

Since then, I spent thirty years with JNR, with opportunities to participate in its various fields of business operation, both directly and indirectly. After retiring from JNR, I was able to spend another twenty years in a position where I could observe the operation of the railways by being a member of research institutes specialising in transport matters.

Within a 114 year history, it was only since 1981 that the national railways in Japan went into the red, in other words, failed to fund its operating costs from its revenue from fares. JNR had provided one hundred years of service in meeting the needs of the economy and the general public, as well as contributing to their development and progress, without receiving any financial support from government.

The root of the problem facing the railway industry in many countries was that the railways had come as the earliest means of transport. Initially, railways were expected to function as a major mode of transportation and railway networks extended to even the most remote places. As times changed and it became possible to choose between various means of transport, the need arose for railways to make adjustments with rival means of transport. Railways, in its search for survival, should take advantage of its special characteristics by focusing on mass transport. In the field of small-scale light traffic, railways should hand the task over to motor vehicles. Reviewing the functions of railways as well as reorganizing the railway network is more or less inevitable in almost any country; however, the difficulty in implementing change differs from country to country, with differing conditions.

JNR was privatised and broken up in 1987. It looks as though each of the new companies has set off to a good start. Nevertheless, not all the issues which led to JNR's decline have been solved.

This volume is a collection of essays written with the aim of clarifying the fundamental problems faced by JNR, and to deepen the general public's understanding of this subject. This has been achieved with the co-operation of Professor Mitsuhide Imashiro. The major part is made up of articles of mine entitled 'Nichiyo Hyoron' [The Sunday Column] which appeared every week in Kotsu Shinbun – a newspaper specialising in transport matters – for nearly seven years, up until a few months before JNR was transferred to JR. As a collection of newspaper columns, the issues are not presented systematically, but I feel, nonetheless, that by reading this material, people will be better able to grasp the nature of the problems that were present for JNR, some of which will perhaps persist for some time to come.

July, 1998
Tatsujiro Ishikawa

Acknowledgements

The chapters in this book are revised and modified versions of the following essays and articles. The Japanese titles are shown for the pieces of work which were originally written in Japanese.

Chapter 1: Imashiro, M   Restructuring of the Japanese National Railways and its Problems, *Modern Business and Management: Some Aspects of Japanese Enterprise*, Institute of Business Research, Daito Bunka University March, 1992.

Chapter 2: Imashiro, M   *Outcome of the Privatisation of the Japanese National Railways*, Research Papers No. 12, Institute of Business Research, Daito Bunka University March 1991.

Chapter 3: Ishikawa, T   Kyodai Soshiki no Kokufuku: Kokutetsu ni Okeru Bunken Kanri no Keiken, *Unyu to Keizai* (Transportation and Economics), Vol. 43, No. 3, March, 1983.

Chapter 4: Imashiro, M   *Provincial Railway Policy and the Third Sector Railways in Japan*, Research Papers No. 17, Institute of Business Research, Daito Bunka University March, 1993.

Chapter 5: Ishikawa, T   Henka e no Taio, *Unyu to Keizai*, Vol. 48, No. 10, October, 1988. Imashiro, M   Keiei no Shin-Kyokumen to Toumen no Syokadai, Unyu to Keizai, Vol. 48, No. 10, October, 1988.

Chapter 6: Ishikawa, T   Nichiyo Hyoron, *Kotsu Shinbun*, 1980–1986.

Many people have helped in getting this book published – in particular, Fumiko Ishii, Ryoko Ishikawa, Kathrin Köster, Hanae Kudo, Ian Smith, and Akiko Yamada. Without the support of Kotsu Tokei Kenkyujyo (Institute of Transportation Statistics) it would have been impossible to get the book completed. Brian

Southam of The Athone Press waited patiently for the completion of the English manuscript. I wish to express my great appreciation to all these people.

Policies concerning railways in Japan are still in the course of change. This book discusses several issues regarding the fundamentals of railway operation. If readers have questions on problems which have arisen or may arise in the future, please contact Kotsu Tokei Kenkyujyo. We would like to answer them as far as we can.

July, 1998
Mitsuhide Imashiro

1

Restructuring of the Japanese National Railways and its Problems

1. INTRODUCTION

In April 1987, the JNR (Japanese National Railways) was privatised and reorganized into nine corporations, two special corporations and one foundation.

For more than a century, railways had been the backbone of domestic transport in Japan. With their vast size, they dominated the transport market. After the 1960s, however, the development of auto-transport quickly eroded their dominance. In the process, internal and external problems such as JNR's large debt, the decline of rural railway systems, the stagnant demand for rail freight services and restrictive government regulations bedeviled the railways.

On the other hand, while railways are no longer the supreme transportation method of our time, they are still the leader in urban and inter-city transportation, and here there is a need for more capacity and flexibility. Whether railways can fully exploit the advantages of their system in order to survive in a competitive market, will depend upon the effectiveness of JNR's new restructure along with both other policies of deregulation.

2. PRIVATISATION AND BREAK-UP OF JNR AND DEREGULATION

The eight Acts for the privatisation and break-up of JNR provided for the deregulation of the entire railway system including private railways. JNR was initially meant to provide for the welfare of the general public and the Railway Nationalisation Act denoted railways as 'the property of the nation'. JNR was a special public corporation (Tokushu houjin) established by the government, but to all intent and purpose it was the government itself or its alter ego.[1]

The restructuring of JNR changed this special nature of JNR, and the notion of a 'national' railway system was scrapped. The JNR Restructuring Act of 1986 (The 87th law), states its purpose as follows: 'The railway and related operations of JNR being out of control and the current management of the entire national system by a public corporation no longer assuring the appropriate and healthy operation of the business, it is vital to establish a new management system which is responsive to need. It is also vital that under this management JNR should fulfil the role of the basic method of transport in Japan, for it is imperative to stabilize the life and economy of our people. With this in mind, this law sets out the basic elements for the radical restructuring of JNR so as to create an effective and responsive manangement'.

'Improving the welfare of the general public' was replaced by 'responding to market needs and establishing effective management'. Another act was the Application Act of 1986 (93rd law). This repealed the JNR Act, the Railway Construction Act and the JNR Fare Act. The government's responsibility for constructing the rural railway system came to an end, and likewise the procedure about fares that involved the legislature (although spending on the construction of rural railways by the Railway Construction Act had been frozen since 1980). Even the procedure on fares was already less rigid after the revision of JNR Fare Act in December, 1977: however, JNR still had to obtain the approval of the Minister of Transport on fares and there was some limit on the fares it could propose.

Another of the restructuring acts was the Railway Business Act (the 92nd law) which repealed the Local Railway Act relating to private railways. The Act distinguished between those doing business with railways constructed or owned by themselves (first-class sectors), those doing business with railways owned by a third party (second-class), and those building railways with the purpose of selling them or providing the rights for their own use (third-class). Railways entail large amounts of track cost, and this lengthens the lead time of investment. This law expanded the scope for business enterprise by separating the track cost from the cost of running train services.

Most railways of the past were in the first-class category but Nihon Kamotsu Tetsudo (Japan Freight Railway) will be second-class. Tetsudo Kodan (Japan Railway Construction Corporation) and Hon-shi Kodan (Honshu-Shikoku Bridge Construction Corporation) would be third-class though they are exempt from the classification by law. The Railway Business Act also drastically simplified the rules of the Local Railway Act. The new Plan Manager System enabled qualified business personnel to carry out inspections in place of government or JNR personnel. The Railway Operating Act (Tetsudo Eigyo Ho) remained so that railways would then be governed by this Act and the Railway Business Acts.

3. FROM MONOPOLY TO COMPETITION

3.1 *The Collapse of JNR Finance*

The immediate reason that led to the privatisation and break-up of JNR was its massive deficit which stemmed from the rapid erosion of the monopoly JNR enjoyed. It was after 1964 that the financial condition of JNR got worse. A deficit of 30 billion yen that year was financed out of reserves, and could have been temporary. However, the deficit kept on growing and by 1966 the reserves had been used up.

In 1971, there was a huge operating loss of 234 billion yen and after the oil crisis deficits of about one trillion yen were regularly incurred. These were financed by borrowing. Funds for capital projects were also raised by borrowing, and long-term liabilities mounted. Because the ways of raising funds were limited, dependence on debt increased, and interest payments became a problem for JNR's management. The government suspended these interest payments in 1976 and in 1980, but this provided only temporary relief.

Meanwhile, three attempts to rescue JNR were made including a special act for JNR's financial recovery (JNR Rehabilitation Act). These included capital investment projects based on plans drawn up several years previously. The basic thinking was to invest for modernisation and bring costs down while improving the level of service to increase the volume of rail use. In the event, inflation and increasing labour costs pushed up total costs, growth in transport volume remained weak and competition from road and air services got fiercer.

Continuing with much the same capital investment during the 1970s as the way to recovery made things worse. JNR failed to adjust to the changing economic environment and stuck to expansion while most private companies were cutting back their operations. Another problem was that the investment plans were fragmented; there was no strategy of investing in fields which could exploit the specific advantages of railways.

From 1980, a new rescue plan – backed by the JNR Recovery Act and called the Management Improvement Plan – was launched. Unprofitable services such as rural lines were to be trimmed, discount fares introduced and the freight yard-system scaled down. This recovery plan was quite different from previous plans but still lacked the vision to revive the railway system as a whole.

Figure 1 shows the income expenditure outcome for 1985. The net loss was 1,850 billion yen, a staggering 5 billion yen per day. The outgoings include special labour costs and the Tohoku & Joetsu Shinkansen capital investment which were not the responsibility of JNR management: excluding these, the loss shrinks to 300 billion yen. The special labour cost was incurred by the JNR having to take on the former Colonial Railways employees, and the Shinkansen capital investment was one not sanctioned by JNR. These outlays were approved by the government though it is not clear if JNR can claim to be free of all the responsibility for them. The Special account in Figure 1 relates to past borrowings, the interest payment of 350 billion yen having an equivalent government subsidy.

Figure 2 shows the balance sheet for 1985. Long-term debt accounted for 88 per cent of the total liability, the result of financing not only the operating loss but also most of the investments. Paid-up capital was a small part of total liability for the government had been reluctant to provide any financial aid to JNR. The accumulated loss (including past debt) had reached 14,100 billion yen and long-term liabilities 23,600 billion yen. This meant that out of over 23 trillion yen of debt 14 trillion had already been used up to pay off losses; only the remaining 9 trillion represented real capital stock.

3.2 *Unprofitable Operations and the Source of Loss*
To see which operation caused the losses in 1985, Figure 3 shows the results of mainline, local and automative divisions. Main-line railways operate in and between major cities, comprising in length about half of the whole rail network and 90 per cent of the total

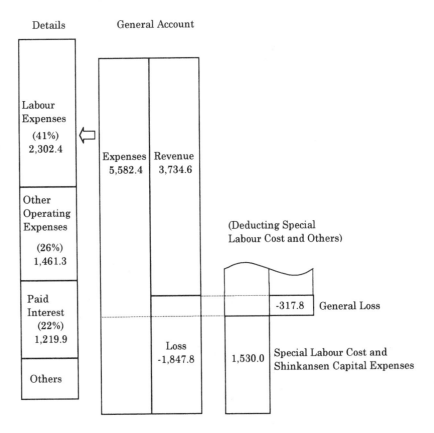

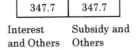

Figure 1: Overall Balance (billion yen)

volume of rail transport. While these are well placed to take advantage of the rail system, it is otherwise for local railways with their low transport density. This classification highlights the divisional differences and serves to indicate what needs to be done in running the railway system.

General Account

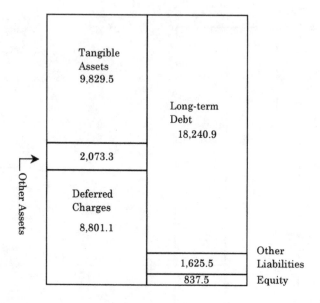

Figure 2: Balance Sheet (billion yen)

The absolute amount of loss is bigger with main-line railways but the proportion of the total loss is bigger in local railways. Excluding special labour costs, main-line railways can even generate an operating profit. The budgeted balance for main-line railways that was intended by the Management Improvement Plan was reached ahead of time and exceeded the financial goal. Contrary to the general belief that the plan's goal was unrealistic in view of past failures, JNR management undertook a determined attempt to rationalise its work. Local railways were up against a falling volume of transport and revenue fell more than

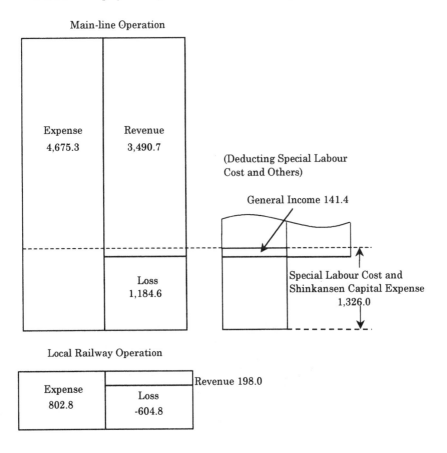

Figure 3:   Railways Income (billion yen)

the cost-cutting effects of the rationalisation programme. In previous years, the loss incurred by local railways accounted for
about 30 per cent of the total loss. The decline in the volume of
transport in this sector was caused in part by the rapid growth and
development of bus transport, but more so by the spread in the
use of automobiles that began in the 1960s. Mass production

reduced the relative price of cars and trucks which quickly spread into rural areas. Multi-vehicle households were not uncommon and price competition between manufacturers contributed to the popularity of motorbikes.

Railways and other public transport can not match the convenience of cars particularly in serving local needs. Vehicle owners generated the revenue to finance road construction, and thereby helped to create an automobile society. The monopoly that railways enjoyed all but disappeared. The change affected JNR, private railways and buses. Public transport was left to provide for poorer people, but even they had government subsidized alternatives such as school and hospital buses.

Deprived of its monopoly, local railways could not even make economies on account of the nation-wide unified fare system and ineffective management control. On the other hand, private railways survived for they switched some of their operations to buses at an early stage, and they could also vary their fares in different parts of the country.

Another loss-making service is freight. Separate financial results are made for passenger and freight services as shown in Figure 4 for 1985. (The figures are not 'Divisional' so the total is not the same as for JNR as a whole). Total expense is divided into passenger and freight operations along with 'common expense' which is then apportioned to passenger/freight expense. It will be seen in Figure 4 that neither passenger nor freight operations cover costs, and that freight cannot even cover its own proprietary costs.

Balancing the revenue and this proprietary expense was one objective of the Management Improvement Plan. It is of little significance that revenue should offset proprietary expense, given that this is only a part of the total expense, but that the revenue cannot even cover part of the expense tells how seriously unprofitable that operation was.

JNR used to dominate the market for domestic freight. Right after the war, with the shipping industry almost completely destroyed, railways were crucially important and it was put on the priority list of industrial development by the government along with coal and steel. With the recovery of shipping, the market for large-volume long-distance freight returned to it. The balance between shipping and land transport settled with each industry's

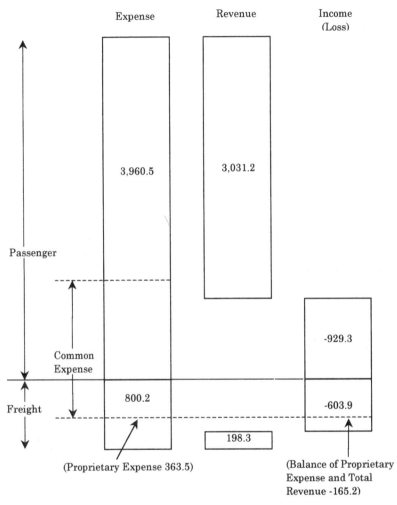

Figure 4: Income of Passenger/Freight Operation (billion yen)

share of the business set by the distance of freight markets. JNR still enjoyed leadership in the overland transport markets. However, once the economy started to grow rapidly, it did not have the capacity to deal with the sudden growth of freight, resulting in stocks piling up in rail-yards.

This dominance came to an end when private companies began

to provide scheduled truck services and road construction began to take off. Since the truck transport business required only small amounts of capital, a highly competitive situation emerged. JNR freight based on a dominant market position, had little or no chance against the new type of service. Some counter-measures were taken but their competitiveness remained weak. Rail freight operations became unprofitable and shrank in size.

Rail passenger operations did not become unprofitable, but in inter-city transport monopoly gave way to competition. Rail dominance diminished as the domestic airline system and long-distance bus services flourished. A market in which railways are mainly dominant is limited to major cities. Cross-subsidization between profitable and unprofitable operations and between operations with market dominance and without, is now recognised as a problem for management.[2]

4. THE PROCESS OF JNR RESTRUCTURING

4.1 *Nationalisation and Reformation After the War*

The Government Railway, later renamed JNR, had been in existence for 114 years since the first railway was built. Then railways were not seen as the property of government and private as well as governmental railways were built and managed separately. The basic structure of JNR was established in 1906–07 when the railways were nationalised. It was government railway officials such as Masaru Inoue who stressed the need to integrate the railway system. The idea was to rationalise rail transport to achieve economies of scale and thereby lower costs and fares. The goal was to achieve greater efficiency, along with an expansion of the railway system.

The military authorities were also in favour of nationalisation, but their support was something akin to the Treasury supporting any plan that raises revenue rather than for any other reason. Among businesses, the Mitsubishi group opposed nationalisation and the Foreign Affairs Minister, Takaaki Kato, son-in-law of Mitsubishi's leader, Yatarou Iwasaki, resigned from the Cabinet in protest. Eiichi Shibusawa, the famous businessman in the Meiji era, also had reservations about nationalisation as it implied helping private companies.

However, the government was under pressure to reduce transport costs and hence export costs in order to improve the post-war overseas balance of payments with Russia. Mitsui group, another business group, recognized this need, and later on Shibu-sawa and others went along with nationalisation.

The price paid for the seventeen railway companies which were nationalised was quite high (though the proceeds were reinvested in electric utilities, in some of the heavy and other industries). Interest payments on the bonds issued for the purchase of the railway companies proved to be a heavy burden for the nationali-sed railways. At this stage Tetsudoin (Railway Agency) was created; Railway Accounting was separated from Government General Accounting under the Imperial Railway Accounting Act of 1909, and the basic structure of JNR was thereby established.

This accounting independence was threatened when the railway authority had to forfeit special military expenses during the Sec-ond World War. This expenditure along with the overloading of the system during and after the war as well as the damaged caused by bombing, brought several problems to JNR management after the war. At that time, institutions such as Mitsubishi Research Institute proposed to sell off JNR to the public but not enough support was forthcoming. A self-supporting plan similar to one in the Soviet Union and, reflecting the views of JNR officials, called for the financial independence which had been undermined by the special military expense. The idea of the plan was already incor-porated and assured in the revision of the Imperial Railway Accounting Act and was continued in the debate concerning the conversion of JNR into a public corporation. (It had an effect outside JNR and was adopted in the internal management of the automotive industry).

Changes to the railways after the war were required in conjunc-tion with the need to reorganize the Ministry of Transport of which the Bureau of Railways was one of the branch offices. In 1948 General MacArthur proposed that the railways, along with the salt and tobacco businesses, be managed as a public corpor-ation. The concept of the public corporation was introduced in the 1920s in the U.K., and the New Deal policy in the U.S.A. took up the idea. The independence movement in Germany after the First World War and Trusts in the Soviet Union also held similar ideas of organization, albeit under different names.[3]

The experience in other countries helped to shape the concept and form of the public corporation in Japan. Its aim was to improve the efficiency of management by giving the organisation autonomy and excluding any direct involvement by politicians and government. For example, allowing management to make decisions on wage and labour conditions without involving the government. Separating ownership and management as in private companies, was to be attempted in the public sector.

However, in reality the public corporation in Japan was introduced so as to preserve the Japanese bureaucracy that existed before the war. Government structures were maintained and little effort made to change the old bureaucracy. The Japanese public corporation that was created did not have all that much autonomy and this gave rise to a series of problems for JNR.

4.2 *From the Rincho Report to Supervisory Committee's 'Opinion'*

It was at the end of 1980 when the second Rincho (Special Government Inspection Committee) was organized. It was formed to reduce spending because the government's budget was in trouble. Its promoters included Treasury staff, the head of the Government Management Agency (Gyosei Kanri Cho) Nakasone and business representatives who feared an increase in corporate tax. Each of them had differing interests but after the attempt to introduce a general sales tax failed (under the Ohira Administration), government reform became the big political issue of the time.

It was obvious that merely to reduce spending could not balance the budget. Though the business slogan of 'saving the budget without tax increases' was a popular one, it was impossible to do so without some kind of new tax. To balance the budget, a cut had to be made in the appropriation amounts which had kept on rising since 1965. The increased public investment that was meant to offset the recession of 1965 led to the issue of bonds to cover the interest payments. Issuing bonds to finance public investment to create jobs in recession and to recall bonds when the economy picks up can be held to be a basic function of government finance. In reality, public investment and subsidies are difficult to control.

Subsidies to specific areas or industries led to the formation of voting groups to elect Diet (Congress) members who would protect these subsidies. Diet was criticized for becoming a platform for its members simply to further special interests. This problem of representative democracy is not peculiar to Japan.

Rincho – with its business representatives – could not abolish subsidies. Though its chairman was a respected and popular businessman, he did not do anything that would harm his business nor could he. On the other hand, the Prime Minister (and ruling party leader), had to do something to convince the public of his commitment to reform. It was against this background that the ailing finances of JNR moved into the political limelight.

The national budget deficit was attributed to the three K's: (Kokutetsu=JNR, Kenpo=Health Care System, Kome=Food Management Law). Of these, JNR was the most attractive on account of its size and the public sentiment hostile to it. The privatisation and break-up of JNR became the biggest topic of the Rincho report.

When the restructuring of three public corporations, JNR, NTT (Nippon Telegraph & Telephone) and Tobacco & Salt Corp., was proposed, NTT was the first to accept privatisation while avoiding being broken up. The Tobacco & Salt Corp. did not resist privatisation either. JNR, however, resisted privatisation – in part to protect the interests of some party members.

Nevertheless, the JNR Restructuring Supervisory Committee – which was in charge of carrying out the wishes of Rincho – was set up. The committee was totally independent of JNR and worked under the guidance of the Ministry of Transport. In July 1985, it submitted a recommendation on privatisation/break up (Opinion on the Restructuring of JNR) similar to that of Rincho. For its part, JNR published its own reorganization plan (Basic Policy for Management Restructuring) in January 1985.

The JNR plan accepted the privatisation proposals but rejected the breaking up of the organization. Prime Minister Nakasone fired the JNR chairman, Nisugi, reshuffled more than half of the top officials at JNR and put Sugiura, a bureaucrat of the Ministry of Transport, in as Chairman. This altered the balance of power between JNR and the Ministry of Transport, and privatisation/ break up went ahead.

Even if all the deficit of the 'three K's' were to disappear, the government budget could still not be balanced. Eliminating the loss of JNR would not alone balance the budget. The appropriate way to balance the budget would have been to examine the

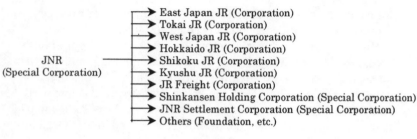

JNR
(Special Corporation)

→ East Japan JR (Corporation)
→ Tokai JR (Corporation)
→ West Japan JR (Corporation)
→ Hokkaido JR (Corporation)
→ Shikoku JR (Corporation)
→ Kyushu JR (Corporation)
→ JR Freight (Corporation)
→ Shinkansen Holding Corporation (Special Corporation)
→ JNR Settlement Corporation (Special Corporation)
→ Others (Foundation, etc.)

Chart 1:   Break-up of JNR

subsidy system. Instead, JNR became the scapegoat. It was akin to corporations talking the blame for the oil crisis in the 1970s.

JNR was attacked more directly, and lax office procedures and bureaucratic management provided the media with plenty of material to criticize. The issue won the support of the public who were unhappy with the amateurish attitude towards customer services and the JNR's relatively expensive fares in comparison with private railways.

4.3 *Outline and Problems of Restructuring*

The break-up was meant to solve the problems arising from the nationally unified system which was incapable of properly managing such a scale of operation and which led to unsound arrangements between its subdivisions. Privatisation was meant to cope with the defects of the public corporation structure. Six companies were to be created, three from Honshu Island and other three from the remaining three islands, each company becoming a corporation in which all of its shares would initially be in the hands of the government. The initial plan described in the 'Opinion' is shown in Chart 1 and Figure 5.

Why did JNR have to be broken up? What about just giving autonomy to each of its divisions? Is breaking up to six parts the only way? Can the problem not be solved by correcting the deficiencies of the public corporation structure? The 'Opinion' answered all these questions but its answers were not convincing. Essentially, we were at the stage of having to do something in order to make a proper break-through.

Breaking up JNR does not, by itself, reduce the deficit. What is necessary to reduce the deficit is to increase competitiveness and

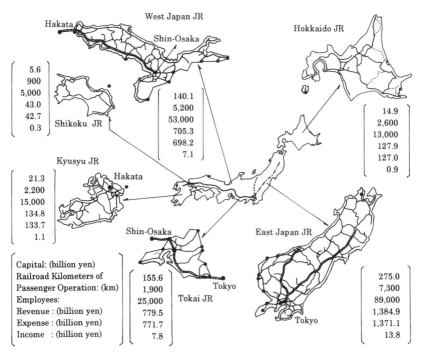

Figure 5: The Six JR's after the Break-up
(Source: Kato, J. (1985). Kokutetsu Saiken wa Kounarau, pp. 8–9)

to cut costs. That is what JNR in its current form was doing as shown in the improved finances of its main-line railways. Transport demand in this country differs from one region to another quite a lot. While the Tokai Corridor (Tokaido) is the busiest route, other markets have entirely different demands. For example, the Tokaido & Sanyo Shinkansen (bullet-train system) carried 35,200,000 passengers per kilometre in 1984 but Joetsu Shinkansen carried only about one-fifth of that number. Even within the same railways, Sanin-Honsen carried a mere fifteenth of Takasakisen's passengers. This difference is reflected in varying levels of profitability amongst the railways (Figure 6).

In breaking up JNR, the 'Opinion' tried to balance these descrepancies with two measures. One was to separate the parts in such a way as to maintain as much parity as possible in terms of profitability. Another was the profit adjustment measure which is

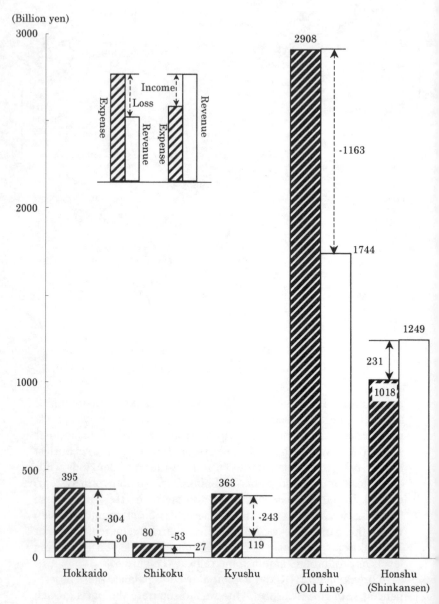

Figure 6:   Operating Income by Region (Fiscal 1985)
(Source: Report of JNR Audit)

represented by the Shinkansen leasing system and the Three-Island Companies Fund (Management Stability Fund).

Shinkansen leasing means that the whole Shinkansen system is to be transferred to an independent special corporation from which all JR parts of JNR could lease and operate the system. The aim is to offset the losses of unprofitable parts such as Tohoku or Joetsu with the profitable Tokaido Shinkansen. Whether offsetting the regional discrepancies in this manner is a good measure or not remains to be seen: now that the construction of the Seibi Shinkansen (Planned Shinkansen) is getting the go-ahead, this internal subsidy may be a matter of controversy in the future.

The Three-Island Companies Fund was designed to help the railway operations of Hokkaido JR, Shikoku JR and Kyusyu JR – which have markets in which it is extremely difficult to make profits – with the fund's investment profits. The argument was that the fund would be more advantageous than a subsidy but it is really nothing more than consolation money. Even though the amount of the fund has been increased, it might not be enough. The Three-Island companies will have the fund but will assume no long-term liabilities.

Local railways will be maintained using the profits of main-line railways, some of them having already changed over to bus services. Local lines which escaped closure are also the subject of subsidies, but they should be better financed with other sources of income.

Another issue of JNR restructuring concerns surplus workers. The number of employees which once reached 420,000 is to fall to 270,000. Since the new JNR companies would accept only 215,000, 60,000 will be made redundant. It was assumed that 20,000 of them will retire and 40,000 will join the JNR Settlement Corporation (Kokutetsu Seisan Jigyodan) and wait for new jobs. The surplus work force is concentrated in rural areas where transport demand is weak. For example, one out of two JNR workers is said to be excess to requirements in Hokkaido, one of the regions with least job opportunities. Since the plans were drawn up, however, more workers than previously expected have retired and there are fewer workers out of a job, not that this makes it less painful for them.

4.4. *New Companies and Inter-city Transport*
It is obvious that railways have an advantage within major cities but are not suitable as a mass transit system in rural areas. The

	Passenger							Freight	Remarks
	Hokkai-do	East-Japan	Tokai	West-Japan	Shikoku	Kyushu	Total		
No. of Employees (×1000)	13.0	89.5	25.2	53.4	4.9	15.0	201.0	12.5	
Operating Kilometers (×1000)	2.5	7.5	2.0	5.1	0.8	2.1	20.0	9.9	
Volume (100 million passenger kilometers/million ton kilometers)	36	994	384	453	15	69	1,952	54	
Assets (billion yen)	293.2	3870.5	548.5	1312.2	114.4	349.1	6487.9	163.2	
Accepted Liability (billion yen)	-	3298.7	319.2	1015.9	-	-	4633.8	94.4	
Initial Fund (billion yen)	682.2	-	-	-	208.2	387.7	1278.1	-	
Capital (billion yen)	15.2	296.6	165.5	155.0	5.7	23.9	661.9	34.3	
Operating Revenues (billion yen)	86.1	1472.2	825.3	772.5	30.8	118.4	3305.3	171.5	
Operating Income (billion yen)	-49.5	248.4	26.4	80.5	-14.8	-27.0	264.0	8.2	Forecast for 1987
Net Income (billion yen)	0.9	14.8	8.3	7.8	0.3	1.2	33.3	1.7	

Chart 2:   Outline of JNR Spin-offs (JR) (Part1)

question is whether they can succeed in the inter-city market where they compete with highways and air transport. Since 1970 with the construction of new highways and the improvements to local airports to accommodate jets, rivals to the railways are getting more and more competitive. Between Shinkansen and highways, the former (railway) still has a lead but between local railways and highways, the former is not competitive at all. The most critical area for the new railways management is where main-line railways are in competition with highway transport.

As highways can be built faster than new Shinkansen lines, the competition between main-line railways and highway transport will become much more widespread. While there is a speed limit on highways, the main-line railways can reach speeds of up to 160km/hour using the same track. Speed is one way to a better service and lower cost. On highways, scheduled bus services are being introduced, with low fares as a powerful attraction. With airlines, railways will have a more co-operative relationship.

Chart 2 relates to the new railway companies. Six JRs and the freight company are all special corporations. They will become private companies when their shares are offered to the public; they are government companies for the time being. As Chart 2 shows Higashi-Nihon (East Japan) JR is the largest in size with an operating revenue for the first year put at 1,472.2 billion yen. This amount represents twice the revenue of Tokai (Central Japan) JR or Nishi-Nihon (West Japan) JR. In terms of operating revenue, the Three Island Companies have only 2 to 8 per cent of the amount of Higashi-Nihon JR.

In comparison with other corporations, Higashi-Nihon JR's projected revenue (for 1987) is lower than Shin Nippon Seitetsu (Nippon Steel)'s 2,200 billion yen but close to Mitsubishi Heavy Industry's 1,800 billion yen and considerably larger than Japan Air Line's 870 billion yen. Assets-wise, it is about the same as Nippon Steel's 3,560 billion yen.

For 1987, the Three Island Companies are expected to operate at a loss while three JRs of Honshu Island origin are expected to make sizeable profits. In comparison to about 20 billion yen of operating profit of most private railways, Higashi-Nihon JR's profit will be 248 billion yen. On a net basis, the Three Island Companies will break even with their subsidies. Tokai JR and Nishi-Nohon JR will make profits comparable to those of major private railways and Higashi-Nihon JR will make twice as much profit. All the new JR companies issued projected earnings for the next five years, and according to these figures, Higashi-Nihon JR's net income for 1991 will be 36.7 billion yen.

Three Island Companies will still have operating losses. The freight company is expected to have a net income of 1.7 billion yen and to maintain that level of profit for five years. The transport volume during this period is assumed to remain flat.

Higashi-Nihon will try to strengthen its transport network within the Tokyo area and between the capital and the Tohoku area. Nishi-Nihon has to secure its lead and regain its market share in the Keihanshin Area where competition with private railways is fierce. Tokai has to maintain the superiority of the Tokaido Shinkansen and increase the volume of transport in Nagoya and Shizuoka. The Three Island Companies would have to find a market in intra-city transport. The freight company should try to balance its budget and convert itself into a properly integrated distribution business. The entity that owns the Shinkansens, the Shinkansen Holding Corporation and the Settlement

	Shinkansen Holding Corporation	Railway Communications	Railway Information Systems	Laboratory for Integrated Railway Technology	JNR Settlement Corporation
Status	Special Corporation	Corporation	Corporation	Foundation	Special Corporation
Employees (×100)	0.6	5.7	2.8	5.5	410
Assets (billion yen)	5700	41	18	...	...
Accepted Liability (billion yen)	5700	37	16	-	23,100
Capital (billion yen)	...	3	1	-	...

Chart 3:   Outline of JNR Spin-offs (JR) (Part2)

Corporation (which will inherit the legal status of JNR) will both be special corporations. (Chart 3)[4]

JNR's Information & Communication business, is not to be broken up but will be handled by yet another company.

NOTES

1 Yamaguchi, M. (1985). Unyu Hosei Tsusoku no Kenkyu, Kotsu-Kyo-ryoku-kai, pp. 245–6.
2 Imashiro, M. (1986). Kokutetsu Kaikaku no Kadai to Shiten. *Chiri* number 11 of 31st issue.
3 Urabe, K. (1986). Kokyo Kigyo Tai Ron, Moriyama Shoten.
4 The amount of accepted liability and others are subject to changes in external factors.

2

Outcome of the Privatisation of the Japanese National Railways

1. INTRODUCTION

By the third year since the privatisation of JNR (which took place in April 1987), the newly-formed Japan Railways (JR) companies have been able to record better-than-predicted results but this has been during a period of economic prosperity. The only previous example of a country privatising a national railway system with a large debt is Chile, and many countries will observe the current success of the privatisation of the JNR with considerable interest.

Which of the problems that troubled the JNR have been solved, and which still remain to be resolved? Privatisation itself has created some new problems. JNR has been converted from a public corporation to a limited company the stock of which is wholly owned by the JNR Settlement Corporation, a public company. From the point of view of ownership, therefore, the JR companies are still public enterprises. The privatisation process will be completed with the flotation of their shares.

2. THE FINANCIAL STRUCTURE OF THE JNR

The way in which the JNR was privatised and broken up and its timing, were decided at a Cabinet Meeting held in October 1985. This Cabinet decision was based upon a report by the JNR Restructuring Supervisory Committee which was prepared three months earlier, in July 1985. The supervisory committee had five members and an office staff and was set up in June 1983 under the auspices of the Prime Minister's Office. There were no JNR representatives on the committee and it was therefore independent of the JNR. The committee members and the office staff were either people who had been involved in the 'Second Government Inspection Committee', or civil servants from the office within the Ministry of Transport which supervised the JNR.

The committee's report included their views on how the railways should be managed, how the long-term debts should be paid off, and recommended that it should be done with all possible speed. In respect of the report, the Prime Minister was obliged to implement its proposals. The committee had considerable authority over the JNR and also within the government; it had the right to make 'recommendations' and to make pronouncements about the JNR budget.

At first the JNR was reluctant to co-operate with the committee. The committee announced their policy of breaking up and privatising the JNR in August 1984. The JNR Management's reply was to publish, in January 1985, its own 'Basic Policy for Management Restructuring', in which it was proposed that JNR should not be broken up, and that privatisation should be a much more gradual process. The response of Prime Minister Nakasone was to remove, in June 1985, all the top management of the JNR, including the President, who was replaced by a civil servant from the Ministry of Transport. After this, progress towards reform was rapid. In the following month, July, the committee published its 'Opinion', from which point the reform of the JNR began in earnest. The financial results of the reforms became apparent in the figures for 1986.

The eight laws necessary for the reforms were passed in December 1986, though by this stage, the reforms were already under way; once the government had made a decision it was not felt necessary to wait for the Diet's approval. Initial preparations were made in the latter part of 1985, implementation began in 1986, and management was delegated to the new companies in 1987.

Looking at JNR's last ten years, we find that although there was a slight fall in 1982, the number of passenger-kilometres remained steady at just under two hundred trillion for the whole of the period. A breakdown for the different sectors within the national railway system, however, reveals that the situation was changing. The number of passengers on the Shinkansen lines was increasing, the number excluding season ticket holders on other lines was decreasing, and the number of season ticket holders (i.e. commuters) gradually increasing. During these ten years fares were raised every year except 1977 and 1983, with an average increase of 6.7 per cent over the previous years. In 1985, for the first time, the combined revenue from Shinkansen lines was greater than from the combined revenue from other lines (excluding the revenue from season tickets for the latter). From 1979 onwards the amount of freight carried by the national railways decreased rapidly, halving in the space of seven years. This was because they reduced the number of 'complete wagon-load goods' (which are costly to transport), although container freight was increasing. The revenue from freight decreased sharply; it represented a mere 5.4 per cent of the revenue from passenger services in 1986 (and has stayed about the same since). A breakdown of sources of revenue shows that 84 per cent was from the passenger fares, 4.6 per cent from freight, and 6.2 per cent was miscellaneous revenues; 5.2 per cent was from grants. Miscellaneous revenues increased rapidly as more shops and restaurants were run by the railways, but it remained a small amount in relation to the total.

The type of grants involved were the 'grant in support of operations', the 'grant for constructions costs', and the 'special account grant', which was created in 1976 due to the severe pressure the JNR was under as a result of its long-term debts. The repayment of a part of the long-term debts was deferred, and the government grant was used to pay the interest on it. This step was taken again in 1980. About half of the total grant received was used for the special account and most of the remainder to subsidise the profit and loss account; very little went into the capital account. The profit and loss subsidies were for the cost of repairs, for provincial services, and for special retirement allowances. As can be seen in Figure 1, the total amount of the grants decreased from 1981 onwards.

Figure 2 shows the fluctuations in net losses. The total decreased a lot in 1986, reflecting improved management practices. 'General losses' improved in real terms from 1984 onwards. By 'general losses' is meant the remainder after the losses incurred as a result of factors for which the JNR was not held responsible – payment of special retirement allowances, special pensions, and the constructions costs of the Tohoku and Joetsu Shinkansen lines – were subtracted from net losses. The special retirement allowances and special pensions were payments to railway workers from Japan's former colonies who had been brought over to work for the JNR after World War II. Private companies also brought

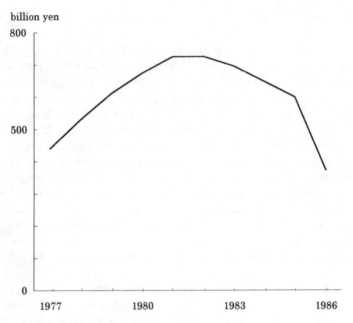

billion yen

Figure 1: Fluctuations in the Amount of Grants to the JNR[1]

workers over from the colonies. The government had refused to let the JNR set up a 'reserve fund for retirement allowances' for these workers, so the responsibility for these costs was indeed the government's.

As for the construction of the Tohoku and Joetsu Shinkansen lines, the government recognized that the burden would be too great for the JNR, and accepted that JNR would not be responsible for them.

Allowing for these, the accounts for the JNR's final year, 1986, show a considerable improvement. Figure 3 shows a simplified Profit and Loss Statement for that year. The special account grant has already decreased. The ratio of labour costs to revenue has decreased to 58 per cent, reflecting the improvement in the structure of JNR. However, the ratio of interest payments to revenue is high, at 36.8 per cent, and the most pressing task at this time was to free the railways from the pressure of interest payments. The government, however, was not prepared to defer payment of these debts as in the past.

(Unit : billion yen)

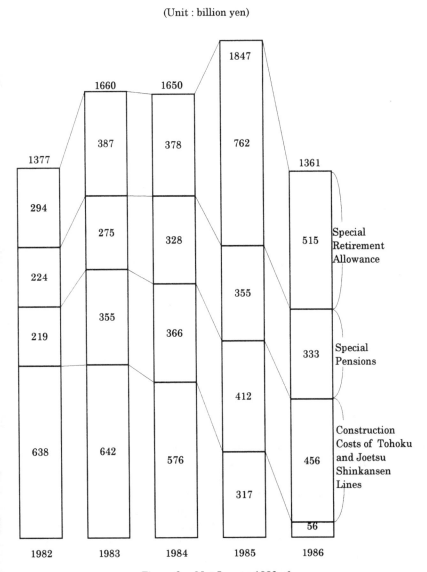

Figure 2: Net Losses 1982–6

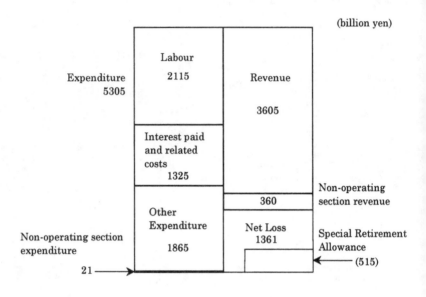

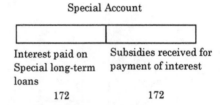

Special Account

Figure 3:   The Final Profit and loss Statement of the JNR
(April 1st 1986–March 31st 1987)

Their intention was to have them paid off in conjunction with the privatisation process.

The reason that interest payments had become such a burden was that the JNR was severely restricted in its means of raising capital, and came to be dependent upon long-term loans. Figure 4 shows the liquidation balance sheet for JNR's final year. We can see that the long-term debts were virtually equal to the combined total for the fixed assets and losses carried forward. Long-term debts accounted for a staggering 82.7 per cent of the total capital debt. The figure for long-term debts (with the special account included) was 25 trillion yen.

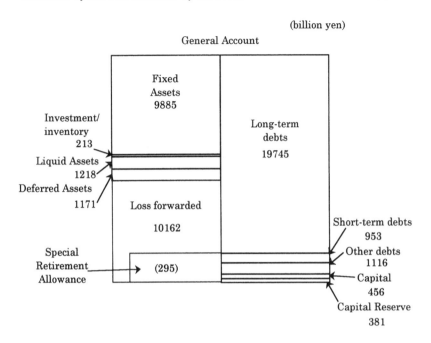

Figure 4: Liquidation Balance Sheet for the JNR
(March 31st 1987)

3. PAYMENT OF DEBTS THROUGH PRIVATISATION

Long-term debts amounted to 25 trillion yen, but the total amount of debt which had to be repaid was calculated to be 37.2 trillion. A breakdown of the extra twelve trillion is shown in Figure 5. The debts of the Japan Railway Construction Public Corporation and the Honshu-Shikoku Bridge Authority were included, because the costs of the projects involved (such as the Aomori-

(Unit : trillion yen)

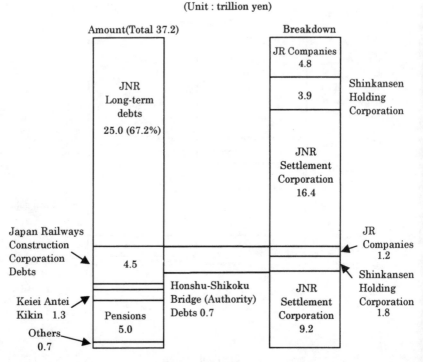

Figure 5:   Breakdown of Burden of Long-term Debts

Hakodate Tunnel and the Honshu-Shikoku Bridge) would normally be borne by the National Railways.

The *Keiei Antei Kikin* (literally Management Stability Fund) is a fund set up to support the running of passenger services on the three islands of Hokkaido, Shikoku and Kyushu, because the passenger lines there all ran at a loss. It was therefore decided that the interest from the fund should be used to meet the anticipated losses.

The expenditure for pensions, 5 trillion yen, is not an enormous amount; almost all of it was to meet the shortfall in accumulated pensions – the rest to cover the cost in finding employment for the JNR staff who were not taken on by the JNR companies or by the JNR Settlement Corporation.

In Figure 5, it will be seen that the three island JR companies, (Hokkaido, Shikoku and Kyushu) will not take over any of the debts. They will be shared by the Honshu JR companies. It was calculated that the latter would be able to operate smoothly with debts in the order of 4.8 trillion yen, the amount of long-term debt they have taken over from JNR. They will also pay the sum of 1.2 trillion yen to the Japan Railway Construction Public Corporation for the use of their facilities, and this will be used to repay the debts of the Corporation so that they will have direct debts of 5.9 trillion yen. The Shinkansen Holding Corporation took over 3.9 trillion yen of JNR's debts, the book value of the Tokaido, Sanyo and Tohoku Shinkansen lines' assets, as well as the Japan Railway Construction Public Corporation's 1.8 trillion yen debt for the Joetsu Shinkansen line. All the remaining debts, a total of 25.6 trillion yen were to be taken over by the JNR Settlement Corporation. To give some idea of the enormity of this figure, it is equal to the combined debts of the world's two leading debtor countries, Brazil and Mexico, in 1987.[1]

For the debts inherited by the Honshu JR companies, the Shinkansen Holding Corporation, and the JNR Settlement Corporation, Figure 6 shows how they would be paid off. The Honshu JR companies' share, 5.9 trillion yen would all be paid off from operating profits.

The revenue for the Shinkansen Holding Corporation's 5.7 trillion yen debts are the charges on the three Honshu JR companies for the use of the Shinkansen lines. These amount to 8.5 trillion yen, which is 2.9 trillion more than the Corporation's debts. This is because the 3.9 trillion yen debts inherited from JNR for the Tokaido, Sanyo and Tohoku Shinkansen lines were calculated at book value; calculated at current replacement cost the figure increases by 2.9 trillion. In other words the Shinkansen lines are being leased to the JR companies at current replacement cost, but the debts will be repaid at book value. Part of the extra revenue will be channelled, via the JNR Settlement Corporation, to the *Keiei Antei Kikin* which supports the operations of the three island JR companies.[2] Thus the profits from the Honshu Shinkansen lines will be used to stablise the loss-making railways of Hokkaido, Shikoku and Kyushu. The JR group of companies' main source of revenue will be the Shinkansen lines. There is the question whether it is appropriate to finance the fund from the profits of the Shinkansen lines.

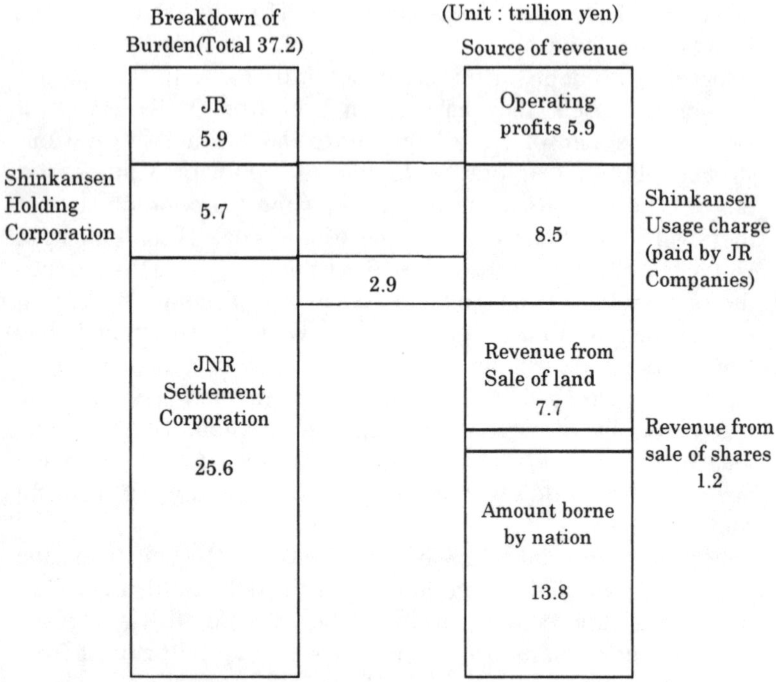

Breakdown of
Burden(Total 37.2)

(Unit : trillion yen)
Source of revenue

Figure 6:   Sources of Revenue for Payment of Long-term Debts

As well as the 2.9 trillion yen for the use of the Shinkansen lines, the JNR Settlement Corporation will obtain revenue to pay off its portion of the debts from the sale of land and shares. It will sell the 8,180 hectares (13 per cent of the total) of land it inherited from the JNR (The JR companies got possession of only the minimum amount of land necessary for them to operate their railway services). The Corporation currently holds all the shares in the JR companies and will sell all of them after the flotation. This flotation is currently the major target of both the JNR Settlement Corporation and the JR companies. The Corporation will also sell to the government its holding in the Teito Rapid Transit Authority (the Tokyo Underground). Although the revenue from these sales will be used to pay off part of the debts, the nation will still bear the burden of paying off the remaining 13.8 trillion yen, 37.1 per cent of the total debts.

4. THE AVERAGING OUT OF PROFITS BETWEEN THE JR COMPANIES

JNR was too big and unwieldy to be managed efficiently, and therefore had to be split up. However, because of the wide variations in profitability depending on the region and the type of service – freight or passenger – measures were required to ensure that each of the private companies would be able to operate independently.

By far the largest transportation market in Japan is the Tokaido region, the 550 kilometres between Tokyo and Osaka. This is not only because of the volume of travel between the two cities but that the area between these cities is also built-up and densely populated. The Tokaido Shinkansen line is extremely profitable, and is well able to compete with both road and air services. The suburban railways have a large share of the commuter market for Tokyo and Osaka. The roads are congested and parking difficult so that commuting by car is not the norm.

In other markets the railways are less dominant. The other main lines face fierce competition from both road and air services. Provincial lines have already lost the battle to the motor car. For freight the Tokaido region is again the most important market, but generally speaking freight is less profitable than passenger services.

It was realized that there would be big differences in the profitability of the various JR companies, since they serve different kinds of markets. The government was forced to accept measures in order to ensure that the companies would be able to stand on their own feet and that their debts could be paid off. Thus, the Shinkansen facilities were to be owned by a public company, the Shinkansen Holding Corporation, which would lease the Shinkansen lines to the three Honshu JR companies who would operate these lines.

The Honshu JR companies would pay the Corporation 8.5 trillion yen in 30 annual instalments (principal and interest in equal proportion), this amount representing the current replacement cost of these facilities. The East Japan JR Company would run the Tohoku and Joetsu Shinkansen lines, the Central Japan JR Company the Tokaido Shinkansen line, and the West Japan JR Company the Sanyo Shinkansen line. The proportions of the

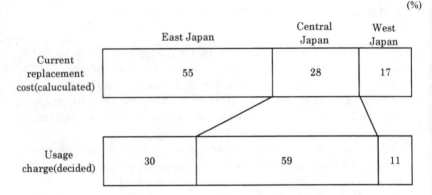

Figure 7:   The Shinkansen Usage Charges to be paid by the
three Honshu JR Companies[4]

current replacement cost to be borne by these three companies
are shown in Figure 7. The Central Japan company's share of the
usage charge is by far the largest; this was intentional, the aim
being to average out the profits of the companies, charging more
to the company most able to pay and reducing the burden for the
other two.

As well as giving the Central Japan Company an extra burden,
these measures created a new problem. Although the Corporation
owned the Shinkansen lines and leased them to the Honshu JR
companies, it was not responsble for the maintenance and renewal
of the fixed assets. This had to be done by the JR companies, so
although they had to spend on maintenance and renewal, no
depreciation fund was available to finance this expenditure, and
they would be forced to borrow the money.

The 30 year usage charge to the Shinkansen Holding Corporation is, in effect, a fixed cost. With an ordinary debt it is possible
to pay it off early, or have it renewed as conditions change, but in
this case there would be no such flexibility. This problem was
identified after the first part of the privatisation had taken place.
The government has since agreed to change the system from
leasing to one of purchase by instalments. Another basic element
of the 'profit adjustment measures' was the *Keiei Antei Kikin* to
cover the expected losses of the three island JR companies.

The total amount of this fund was to be 1.3 trillion yen – the principal was to be transferred to the three companies over a period of eight years – the fund to be financed by profits from the Honshu Shinkansen lines, particularly the Tokaido Shinkansen. Thus the Tokaido Shinkansen would play a critical role in the maintenance of the railway network for the whole of Japan. It was calculated that the fund would yield a return of 7.3 per cent, sufficient to meet the losses of the three companies. (The calculation was based on the yield from national bonds over the previous ten years). At the end of the eight years, the three island JR companies will have to manage the fund themselves. It is by no means certain they would be able to secure a yield of 7.3 per cent or more, so they could be saddled with a problem.

A minor element in the profit adjustment plan was the adjustment of freight and passenger service profits. Like the provincial lines, the freight sector in the days of the JNR ran at a loss. There were misgivings about whether a single company could run the whole of the freight sector successfully. The plan was therefore to improve the competitiveness of the freight sector and to change the accounting method to one of 'avoidable costs' – first used by British Rail – so as to reduce the burden of the freight company where transport costs were common to freight and passenger services. What was gained by the freight company would of course, be lost by the passenger side.

5. THE ACCOUNTS OF THE PRIVATISED COMPANIES/ JAPAN RAILWAYS

The JR companies performed much better than anticipated since privatisation. In the first year after privatisation their combined profits came to 151 billion yen, four times the government's forecast in its profit plan. Table 1 shows the results for the three Honshu passenger companies and the freight company, all of which made both an operating profit and an ordinary profit. All of them had much bigger profits from operating the railways than from other sources.

Table 2 shows the results for the three island JR companies. They had all taken over unprofitable passenger services, and they all made operating losses. They were also unable to make a profit in other areas, perhaps because they had only recently began to run businesses other than the railways. It was the profit from the

Company	Year	Operating Profit / Loss Section					Non-Operating Section Revenue	Non-Operating Section Expenses	Ordinary Profit	Net Profit
		Railways			Other Profits	Total Operating Profit				
		Revenue	Expenses	Profit						
East Japan	88	1,612	1,296	316	7	323	17	254	85	41
	89	1,672	1,395	277	3	281	20	198	103	57
Central Japan	88	965	864	101	0	102	16	24	94	35
	89	999	887	112	1	113	17	23	108	66
West Japan	88	747	676	70	0	70	8	71	8	20
	89	823	734	88	2	90	10	60	40	25
Freight	88	182	172	10	—	10	1	5	6	3
	89	192	182	9	—	9	1	5	6	2

(Amounts less than ¥1,000 million ignored)

Table 1: The Accounts of the three Honshu JR Companies and the JR Freight Company (Unit: 1,000,000,000 yen)

Company	Year	Operating Profit / Loss Section					Profit from Management of Keiei Antei Kikin	Ordinary Profit	Net Profit
		Railways			Other Profits	Total Operating Profit			
		Revenue	Expenses	Profit					
Hokkaido	88	81	132	-51	-1	-53	49	-1	1
	89	80	131	-50	-1	-52	49	0	0
Shikoku	88	40	50	-9	0	-10	15	5	1
	89	41	51	-10	-1	-11	15	6	3
Kyushu	88	129	152	-23	-5	-28	28	3	3
	89	135	163	-27	0	-28	28	3	1

(Amounts less than ¥1,000 million ignored)

Table 2: The Accounts of the three Island JR Companies (Unit: 1,000,000,000 yen)

Keiei Antei Kikin which made up for the financial losses of these companies. The ratio of profits from the fund to revenue from the railways was quite high, 60 per cent for Hokkaido, 37 per cent for Shikoku, and 21 per cent for Kyushu.

There are three reasons why these results were better than expected. The first, and the most significant was the extremely healthy state of the Japanese economy. The second was that they have been freed from the constant pressure they were under when they were part of the JNR, stemming from their inability to pay the interest on debts. The third was the reduction in labour costs.

For some these results are seen as the fruits of privatisation and show that privatisation has solved the many problems which plagued the JNR. However, the privatisation plan was so designed that these companies would be profit-making and these results could therefore be said to be pre-determined. There are some potential problems in these published figures.[3] The first is that the Shinkansen lines, which are such an important source of revenue to the JR companies, are susceptible to fluctuations in business conditions. (This is also true of old non-suburban lines.) Revenue is high and buoyant when the economy is booming but not so in a recession. The existing private railways which serve Tokyo and Osaka have a high proportion of season ticket holders, so that they are not so badly affected by recession. Of the JR companies, the only one of which the same can be said is the East Japan Company, having a large share of the commuter market in Tokyo. Figure 8 shows the breakdown of the revenue of the Honshu JR companies and the main existing private railway companies by type of passenger. We can see from it that the Central Japan and West Japan JR Companies receive a high proportion of their revenue from Shinkansen and from old non-suburban line passengers. Hence, their results may well deteriorate sharply if the economy were to stagnate. Figure 9 (taken from a paper by Takao Makido[4]), shows the strong correlation between the number of passengers using the Shinkansen and GNP. That this type of revenue is so susceptible to fluctuations in the economy on the one hand, and the inflexible nature of the railway costs on the other, means that the companies have a lot to fear from a recession.

Another problem concerns the management of the *Keiei Antei Kikin*, which may be described as the lifeline of the three island JR companies. In the near future they will have to manage this

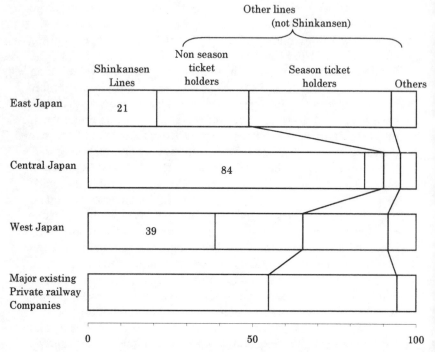

Figure 8:   Breakdown of Revenue Sources of Railway Companies[4]

fund themselves. Interest rates are not under their control and companies have to live with them; no matter how well the fund is managed, if interest rates rise it may not be possible to obtain the extra revenue which would then be required.

Take the Hokkaido Company which receives such a large part of its revenue from the fund. A one per cent fall in interest rates would mean a fall in revenue of 6.8 billion yen. The three island companies should be made to depend less on the fund. Figures 10 to 12 show the assets and debts of these three companies and highlight the importance of the fund to them at the time.

A further problem is the weakness in the financial structure of the Honshu passenger companies and the freight company. Take their balance sheets in Figures 13 to 16. The feature common to all of them is their low equity rates. What is more, the figures for the three passenger companies do not reflect the usage charge for the Shinkansen. When this is included, their equity rate is less

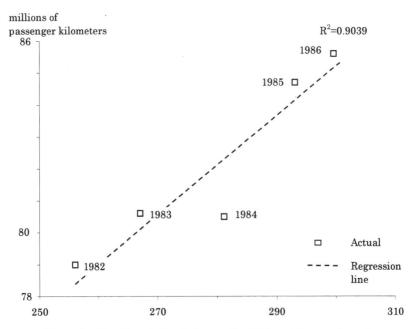

Figure 9: The Correlation between the GNP and the number of
Passengers on the Tokaido Shinkansen   See Note 4

than 10 per cent. Railway companies tend to have a lower equity
ratio than companies in other industries because they have a
higher level of fixed costs. However, the major existing private
railway companies' average equity ratio is 18 per cent, significantly
higher than the newly-privatised JR companies. The flotation of
shares will provide a new means of raising capital, and should
help improve the situation.

6. THE FLOTATION

The situation at first was that a public corporation was converted
to private companies but that shares were held by the JNR
Settlement Corporation. The corporation was a public company
owned by the government, so from the point of view of ownership
the new JR companies were still public companies. The next stage
in the privatisation process was the flotation of shares.

The flotation was to be initially only for the three Honshu and

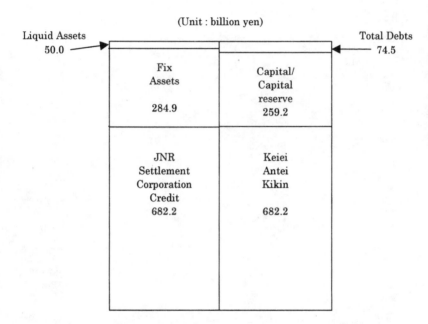

Figure 10:   Hokkaido JR Company Balance Sheet, March 31st 1988

freight companies. They had to satisfy criteria laid down by the Stock Exchange, hence their effort to raise their equity ratio in spite of the pressures of debt repayments and the fixed nature of their assets. The intention was for the Corporation to sell all the shares, so that the three companies would then become private companies in every sense. The East Japan Company and the Central Japan Company were very profitable companies, while the West Japan Company was rather less so.

The method of leasing the Shinkansen lines meant that these companies were unable to allow for depreciation: this problem was of particular significance for the Central Japan Company. The Ministry of Transport therefore formulated a new plan whereby the assets of the Shinkansen lines were revalued, and sold to the JR companies at the new value, namely 9.1 trillion yen, one trillion more than the usage charge. The payment was to be by instalments, but it did mean that when the JR companies gain possession of the Shinkansen lines, they will assume debts of 9.1 trillion yen. The book value, 5.7 trillion yen, was to be paid over

(Unit : billion yen)

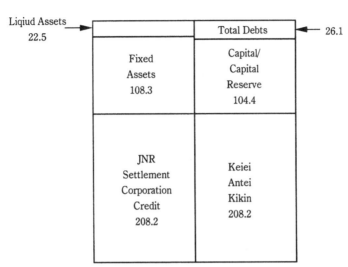

Figure 11:   Shikoku JR Company Balance Sheet, March 31st 1988

a period of 26 years, while a period of 100 years was considered for the payment of the remaining 3.4 trillion yen. The extra one trillion was to be a source of finance for the construction of extensions to the Shinkansen lines. These extensions were known as the 'Shinkansen Construction Plan', and local communities were keen to see this plan implemented. (Fig. 17).

The wisdom of burdening the three Honshu JR companies with a further trillion yen is questionable. Was it sensible to finance the Shinkansen Construction Plan from the profits of the existing Shinkansen lines? With a healthy economy the Central Japan Company was making good profits, but this is not to say that these profits should have been used as loans to the Honshu JR companies.[5]

The timing for the complete privatisation for the Honshu companies depended on the stock market situation but afterwards, these companies would not be completely independent of the rest of the JR group, including the three island companies whose shares will not have been put on the market. They would also continue to have dealings with the JNR Settlement Corporation, and the Railway Construction Corporation. The differences in the sizes of

(Unit : billion yen)

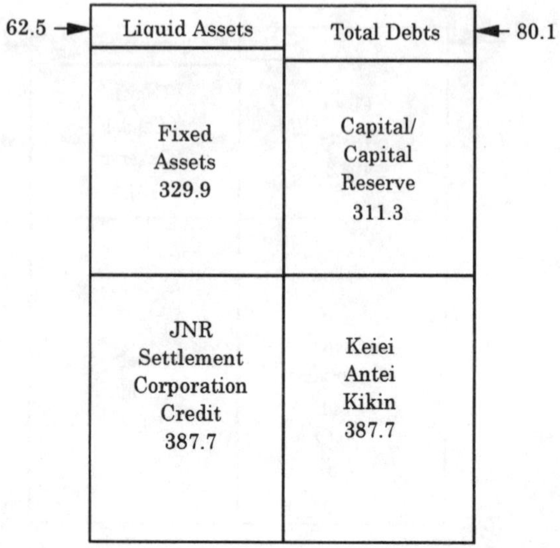

62.5 →	Liquid Assets	Total Debts	← 80.1
	Fixed Assets 329.9	Capital/ Capital Reserve 311.3	
	JNR Settlement Corporation Credit 387.7	Keiei Antei Kikin 387.7	

Figure 12:   Kyushu JR Company Balance Sheet, March 31st 1988

(Unit : billion yen)

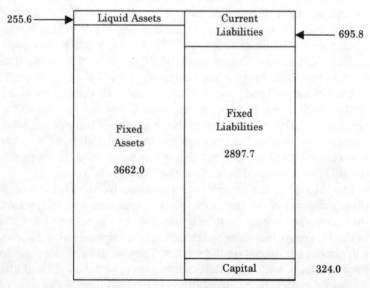

255.6 →	Liquid Assets	Current Liabilities	← 695.8
	Fixed Assets 3662.0	Fixed Liabilities 2897.7	
		Capital	324.0

Figure 13:   East Japan JR Company Balance Sheet, March 31st 1988

(Unit : billion yen)

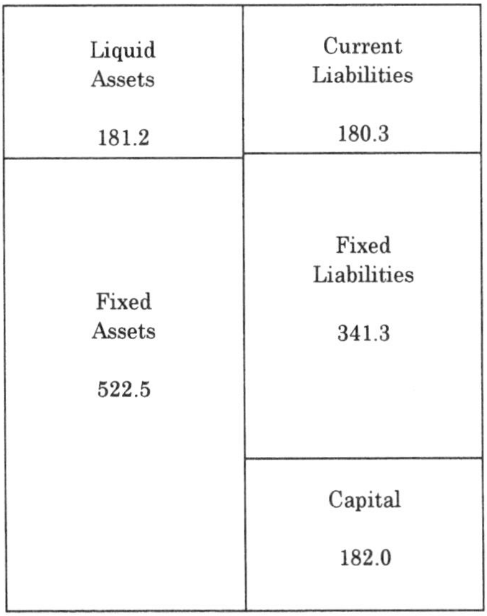

Liquid Assets 181.2	Current Liabilities 180.3
Fixed Assets 522.5	Fixed Liabilities 341.3
	Capital 182.0

Figure 14: Central Japan JR Company Balance Sheet, March 31st 1988

(Unit : billion yen)

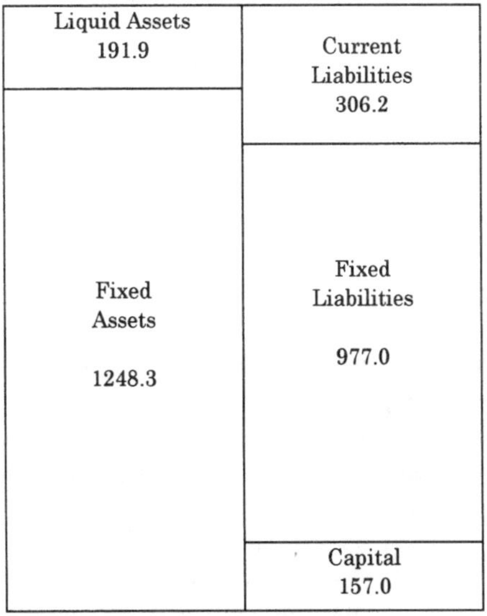

Liquid Assets 191.9	Current Liabilities 306.2
Fixed Assets 1248.3	Fixed Liabilities 977.0
	Capital 157.0

Figure 15: West Japan JR Company Balance Sheet, March 31st 1988

(Unit : billion yen)

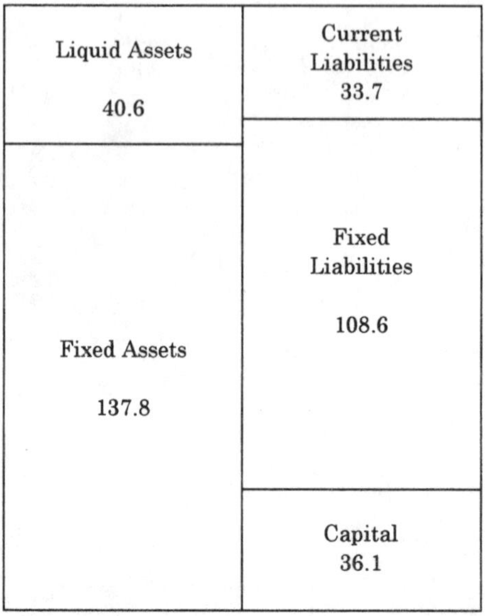

Liquid Assets 40.6	Current Liabilities 33.7
Fixed Assets 137.8	Fixed Liabilities 108.6
	Capital 36.1

Figure 16:   JR Freight Company Balance Sheet, March 31st 1988

the various companies' markets will widen, and the difference in their ability to raise capital will become increasingly apparent.

7. IN CONCLUSION

Reviewed here is the initial outcome of the privatisation of the JNR from the point of view of the finances of the railways. The privatisation process is not complete, and several problems have still to be resolved. One achievement at this stage is that the JNR's debt problems have been set apart from the management of the railways. Also, in the near future the three Honshu companies will be given new means of raising capital when their shares are issued. One of the reasons for the continued worsening of the financial position of the JNR was that it was restricted largely to long-term loans to raise capital.

The good results the JR has achieved so far do not mean that the basic situation facing the railways has been altered. The

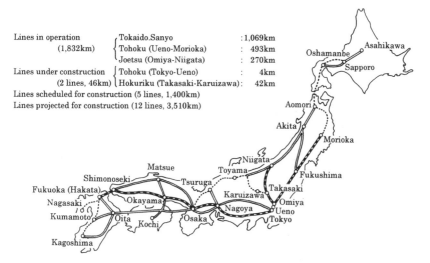

Lines in operation   Tokaido.Sanyo   : 1,069km
    (1,832km)   Tohoku (Ueno-Morioka)   : 493km
           Joetsu (Omiya-Niigata)   : 270km
Lines under construction   Tohoku (Tokyo-Ueno)   : 4km
    (2 lines, 46km)   Hokuriku (Takasaki-Karuizawa) : 42km
Lines scheduled for construction (5 lines, 1,400km)
Lines projected for construction (12 lines, 3,510km)

Figure 17:   Nationwide Shinkansen Network
Source: National Railways Reconstruction Promotion Headquarters.
Minister's Secretariat, Ministry of Transport

railways are still in a difficult position, facing fierce competition from road and air services, and this is likely to be the case for the foreseeable future.

An important aspect of privatisation concerns the measures taken to tackle problems with staff. One aspect of this has been the reduction in the number of staff in order to reduce labour costs; the other the growing need to examine policy towards the unions since there have been several serious disputes and unpleasant incidents.

(January, 1991)

NOTES

1 Yokobori, M. Kokutetsu Kaikaku no Saimu Shori, *Unyu to Keizai*, Vol. 48 No. 10 (1988). Regarding the JR companies first year in business, see Imashiro M. JR Kakusha Zaimu Bucho ni Kiku, *Unyu to Keizai*, also in Vol. 48 No. 10.

2 Tsuchiya H. Shinkansen Tetsudo Hoyukiko no Kino. *Unyu to Keizai*, Vol. 48 No. 10. (1988).

3 On the problems since privatisation see Ishikawa T. Henka e no Taio,

and Imashiro M. Keiei no Shinkyokumen to Tomen no Shokadai, both in *Unyu to Keizai*, Vol. 48 No. 10, Oct. (1988).

4　Makido T. JR no Kabushiki Jojo o Meguru Shomondai, *Kigyo Kaikei*, Vol. 42 No. 1. (1990).

5　Takao Makido pointed out that when the accounting was done for the purchase of the Shinkansen assets (from the Shinkansen Holding Corporation by the three Honshu JR companies) it would have been better to use the current replacement cost rather than the actual purchase price of the assets. Makido T., Sinkansen Shisan Kaitori ni Tomonau Kikei Shori, *Kigyo Kaikei*, Vol. 42 No. 10. (1990).

3

The Foundation of JNR's Reconstruction
The Problems of a Large Organization and Decentralized Control

INTRODUCTION

The operations of JNR, with its network of tracks of about 21,000 kilometres nationwide, were manned by an enormous labor force. The number of its employees once reached a peak of 610,000. Nor can railways run, not even a single train, without close co-operation among various work sites and sectors such as stations, conductors, engines, track maintenance, power supply, and so on. The scale and structure of the national railway businesses were not peculiar to Japan and were similar in other countries.

The so-called operational division system – developed in the United States as an arrangement to overcome inefficiencies of large-scale management – originated from the country's railway business. To organize hundreds of thousands of employees so that they work toward a single business goal is a substantial operation in itself.

JNR carried out major organizational changes several times which, in the final analysis, was a struggle with its large size. This was also a history of attempts, swinging back and forth, to seek a balance between centralization and decentralization. On the one hand, there was a desire to escape from the inflexibility of a large organization: on the other hand, the management of a railway business is inclined towards centralization.

Efficiency of management is necessary even for a public corporation; indeed, it is perhaps even more necessary in the case of a public corporation. To realize this, the question is how to combine the management style and ethos of small companies with the advantages of a large organization, especially one with a nationwide management. In this context, an appropriate internal control system is very important.

When JNR was exposed to radical changes, its reluctance to cope with changes, its policy of uniformity, shifting of responsibility, were major handicaps.

With regard to the reconstruction of JNR management, privatization and the break-up of the organization has been repeatedly proposed. This has been a reaction against the existing state of affairs, sometimes bordering on extreme opposition and stemming from disappointment over the current impasse. No matter what the management system, however, ways of overcoming the problems of JNR's huge organization should be examined in terms of efficient management. Not out of place would be to review some of the experience of management control attempted by JNR and to learn the lessons from them – to what extent management becomes more efficient – by decentralization, and what are the limitations of decentralization.

DECENTRALIZATION ACCORDING TO AREAS – 'SPHERE' AND 'LINE'

To manage a nationwide business like JNR, two measures have been considered: to organize it either by areas or by types of operations or functions. In addition, the former category offers two different methods of defining the area: one is the 'sphere' such as administrative districts or economic regions, while the other is the 'line' in which the railway tracks are the unit.

From the standpoint of control, the smaller the unit, the greater the efficiency obtained. However, there is a limit to how small a unit should be because there must be a sufficient scale of activities or size of area to motivate managers.

In developing decentralized control, an important consideration is how to formulate targets for the management in terms of their responsibilities. The larger the management unit, the more comprehensive the responsibilities that can be assigned to each unit, and the easier it is to view these responsibilities consistently by setting objectives and long-term targets.

The development of decentralization in JNR began with fairly large units by dividing the country into six regions, each under the jurisdiction of a Branch Office. Railway Control Offices were not considered to be appropriate management units because their scale varied widely, and it was held that the smaller offices would be unable to cope with the fluctuations in their income and expenses attributable to their normal operations. A further factor was that the Railway Control Office, given its role as a 'working group' operating daily services, was not felt to be suitable to undertake first-rate quality control. Thus, organization at a higher level and with a wider scope was settled on as the best form of management unit, and the Branch Office system was born.

Though they were part of an internal system, Branch Offices and Control Centres were given comprehensive tasks as individual and complete management units, with the view of achieving overall control that would transcend the existing vertical system. This was the main feature of the new system.

JNR had 243 railways lines. Although making each of these lines a management unit would appear to be the way to achieve separate control, the line divisions were based largely on historical factors. Thus, whereas the Tohoku Line was 759 kilometres long, there were other much shorter lines. Not each and every line was suitable as a management unit.

The Headquarters established three basic types of control organizations for branch lines – the Transportation District, Control Centre and Head Controller – as options to be selected in accordance with the circumstances of each local area. The Transportation District mainly dealt with station and conductor-related business at the district level. The Control Centre additionally handled business related to the maintenance of facilities and train operations, forming a complete working organization, a 'mini Railway Control Office.' In the Head Controller system, a head controller was stationed at a line district as its manager – although the working organizations of the line district were unaffected – and was given authority on a par with the Railway Control Office manager to govern the various business operations within the line and to promote managerial improvements.

These units of line management began to be set up in 1954, and reached their peak in 1962: 17 Transportation Districts, 30 Control Centres, and 61 Head Controllers, – a total of 108 management units responsible for 7,011 operating kilometres of track, on more than one third of the whole rail network.

By reassigning a large part of the powers of the Railway Control Office managers and by adopting the 'Economics Calculation System for Specific Lines,' these line management systems overcame the inertia of the past, and achieved remarkable results in promoting rationalization according to the circumstances of each local area. In particular, the Senseki Control Centre put in place a unique and model system of decentralized management.

CASE 1 ESTABLISHMENT OF BRANCH OFFICES

Although the local organizations of JNR had undergone repeated changes over the years, the Branch Office system (introduced in January 1957) was a notable one in that it replaced the long-established centralized system with a decentralized one.

There had been hitherto an attachment to the principle of 'nationwide control' resulting in the uniform and formal execution of JNR operations. Unnecessary time and labour had often been spent in involving Headquarters in matters which could have been dealt with at the area level. Moreover, the vertical control system affected local work sites so that the systematic integration of the functions of each department could not be properly achieved. Local organizations had to spend time communicating and nego-tiating with Headquarters and were often unable to control their own working operations while Headquarters also spent time and effort controlling local daily operations. Local management units were set up to eliminate these wasteful practices.

The Branch Office system added a new category to the existing three – Headquarters, Control Office and work site – and there were concerns that this might have the opposite effect to what was intended, by making the organization more complex and thereby reducing its overall efficiency. To deal with these con-cerns, the Branch Offices were organized as rather modest units and took over local activities which had previously involved Headquarters, while on-site Control Offices could work much more freely.

Thus, the functions of the Branch Offices related to decisions, plans, administration and inspection with respect to basic local business actitivies. At the same time, the system aimed to delegate as much authority as possible to the on-site working units; for example, authority over daily activities was left to the Control Offices.

Needless to say, a Branch Office, as an independent manage-ment unit, was charged with responsibilities commensurate with its freedom. The Headquarters gave each Branch Office a management goal, namely the 'Profit and Loss Budget' which formed the basis for its budget plan. The budgetary provision of a Branch Office was set by the amount of revenues estimated by the Branch Office itself, and the Branch Office could then implement the budget according to its own discretion.

The authority given to the chiefs of the Branch Offices was crucial to the Branch Office system. Headquarters reviewed the activities of each of its departments, and authority over more than 200 items was transferred to the Branch Offices. However, the delegation of authority was not the same for all actitivies, and in that sense was not comprehensive. For example, in the case of personnel matters – one of the major factors affecting business operations – authority over the total number and job allocation of employees was not transferred. The authority to open or close stations (other than temporarily) was also reserved for the Headquarters.

The following records indicate the climate of opinion within Headquarters at the time.

'Although some people believe that authority over maintenance operations should be transferred, this would not be a correct course of action because the different systems and methods existing among local offices in respect to signals, signs, construction, staff meetings, communication and so on, may lead to accidents.'

'Concerning the control over construction, a significant portion of such work should still be undertaken by Headquarters even after the establishment of Branch Offices, since Headquarters now control construction projects throughout the country, especially in technical fields.'

Some of the larger departments also made their views known.

'The Electricity Supply Department should transfer a major part of its daily business to local areas, so as to release time and labour for our own enterprise. In other words, an Electricity Supply Department should be established in each Branch Office while Headquarters should concentrate on tasks that have been held up by routine work, namely, getting JNR into shape in the new era.'

The Branch Office system worked well in remedying the problem of excessive centralization and improving the management of local areas. Management morale was also found to have improved, and in order to give even more freedom to local managers, a further transfer of duties was carried out in May 1959.

It was felt at that time that all authority for controlling and managing the Branch Offices should be transferred to the Branch Office chiefs, except in limited cases. This was a revolution to the concept of management in JNR.

The newly transferred items numbered more than 80, and included many substantial powers. For example, the chief of a Branch Office could now make decisions on opening and closing stations and service areas except for certain lines designated by Headquarters. Regarding the number of employees, Headquarters laid down limits for each Branch Office for the four categories of top administration, upper management, middle management, and other workers, but decisions up to these limits were left to the Branch Office. It could also allow discounts on passenger and freight fares – though only according to certain standards – and arrange some train services of its own. All of this greatly widened the responsibilities of the Branch Office as a unit of management, thus creating a framework for rational and efficient management.

In April 1959 three new Branch Offices – Niigata, Shikoku, and Chugoku – were established, making a total of nine throughout the country. These offices contributed to the success of JNR in the 1950s.

CASE 2 SENSEKI CONTROL CENTRE

The Senseki Line is a local line running along the Pacific coast between the cities of Sendai and Ishinomaki. It was built by the Miyagi Dentetsu Company in 1925 and remained privately operated for about 20 years until 1944 when it was acquired by JNR as part of the country's policy of strengthening the transportation network during the war. However, when the munitions factories along the line were closed after the war, the facilities and employees remained with JNR.

The Senseki Line had physical and operational characteristics which made it a good candidate for separate management, including the fact that it had once been operated privately. Its facilities such as the tracks were separate from those of other lines, and its train services were all along one line. Its scale operation of about 700 employees, 27 stations, and less than 50 wagons was also appropriate. Hence, this line was a suitable choice as the first Control Centre, a model for local line management.

In October 1956, a new system was introduced for the line whereby all the existing on-site organization groupings such as stations, conductors, engines, track maintenance, transformer sub-stations were discontinued and placed under a Control Centre. The document presented to the board of directors at the time – entitled 'The Establishment of Senseki Control Centre' – stated that 'General overall authority shall be vested in the head of the Control Centre who shall manage the line at his sole discretion.' The document also stated that 'exceptions may be made to traditional regulations rather than rigidly adhering to them.'

Tetsuji Endo, who was serving as head of the Sendai Railway Control Office at the time and who pushed for the creation of Senseki Control Centre, stated at its opening, 'In a very large organization like JNR – and the same tendency can be seen in private companies – the working environment for each person is not satisfactory. Although an employee may be enthusiastic about his job, the restraints he encounters everywhere make him tired and give him a feeling that he is being squeezed in the coils of a snake ... This new organization, the Senseki Control Centre, has been created to offer a relaxed and agreeable working place for you, the staff of the Senseki Line.'

The new Control Centre aimed at uncomplicated management suited to the scale of the business and its local characteristics. The aim was to overcome problems such as unsound practices of the vertical control system extending from Headquarters to the work sites, the scant regard for cost in large management structures, the lack of ideas which allowed for differences between main and branch lines.

A new sense of management emerged. At the Centre's meetings, attended by the head and six section managers, every important issue was discussed in a free and lively way. Takeo Ichikawa, the first head of the Senseki Control Centre, described the atmosphere in those days: 'When all is said and done, sectionalism depends on the way of thinking of each person ... Those in charge of tracks and electric power willingly and of their own accord joined the discussions on how to attract more passengers.[1] The system of local work sites produced good results, especially in terms of co-operation between the technical and sales divisions.

Ichikawa also described ways to raise the morale of employees, stating 'employees should be informed about the real management problems of the Senseki Line so that they can clearly understand their causes; namely, anything that hampers management.' At the same time, he noted that 'the head should make personal contact with as many employees as possible, encourage their voluntary proposals by asking, "Do you have any good ideas?" and then see if they can be put into effect. He went on to comment that as a result of these efforts to promote rationalization, all employees became so motivated that their spirits were in tune with daily management.

Every effort was made to remove unsound practices and waste. As a consequence, annual costs in the first year of the new system were reduced from 600 million yen to 530 million. Services were also improved with more trains running between Sendai and Higashi-Shiogama and at shorter intervals of 15 minutes instead of the previous 30 minutes. Services were carried out with fewer coaches – 48 in place of the previous 53. When a longer train was necessary, the procedures could be quickly put into place to deal with the matter. In the past, it took time to receive instructions from the Railway Control Office and the line often lost passengers who took to the bus services. Under the Control Centre system, the staff on duty could arrange to add coaches as soon as it was seen that there were more passengers than usual.

Prior to the new management system of the Senseki Line, its total revenue in 1953 stood at 335.3 million yen, losses were 268.8 million yen, and its operating index 180 (based on the total costs). The management goal at the outset was to reduce this index to 117. In 1959, after the new system had been in operation for three years, total revenue was 476.6 million yen, a 142 per cent increase compared with 1953; costs were down to 92 per cent on 1953, resulting in a sharp drop in losses to 78.5 million yen, and of the index to 116. During this period the number of passenger-kilometres increased by 188 per cent, and the number of employees was reduced from about 900 to 700.

Ichikawa said: 'What I would like to emphasize is not that the staff has been reduced by 200 but that we now have 700 splendid workers, and of better quality than if they numbered one thousand.'

The momentum at the Centre stemmed from the close co-operation between management and workers, thanks to a practical approach and the efforts to get agreement on labour problems in a spirit of sincerity and mutual understanding.

The Senseki Control Centre continued to function for fourteen years until it was closed down in April 1971. The Centre was most successful during its first five years when Ichikawa was the head, and it was his enthusiasm and leadership that ensured the success of the management system: the line's business results declined after reaching a peak in July 1961, when Ichikawa left. In 1970/1, the last year of the Control Centre system losses amounted to 844 million yen and the index was 169.

Later in 1981, the Senseki Line recorded 4,138 million yen in revenues, 3,393 million yen in losses, and an index of 182.

'INTERNAL BUDGET' SYSTEM PAVED THE WAY TO DECENTRALIZATION

A large-scale management structure not only has to organize activities but also have ways and means to control its activities. In JNR, each department had a scale and scope of operations comparable to those of a large company. There had to be a system getting these departments to work toward a single goal and at the same time getting them to function efficiently – a system which would also get people to work willingly.

The common language among departments with different business operations boils down to one thing: facts and figures. A budget plan based on statistics about materials and funds enables the activities of departments to be properly overseen in relation to the overall management. This is the 'internal budget' system.

In JNR, Headquarters prepared and allocated budgets with precisely specified items to its local organizations, and thus undertook budget control according to the vertical system for many years up to 1952. However, the ability to recognize whether, say, the allocation of repair expenses between locomotives and buildings is the right one, is more important than considering a nationwide figure for buildings on their own. Consequently, a change in the budget system was proposed, basically aiming toward a general overview in the place of the control of individual bits and pieces.

When the responsibilities for revenues and expenses are separate, sales activities and technical development are left without a proper sense of costs: hence the need to link revenues and expenses, as in the operating division system.

The work of formulating an objective standard for a new budget system began in 1953/54, and in 1955/56, new indices for revenues and expenses were announced as management targets.

In private businesses the management standard is quite simple: the business is either in the black or the red. In JNR, however, local management is far removed from the goal of balancing revenues and expenses. It was necessary to design an objective and rational standard of management that would endure. Four years elapsed before the introduction of the Branch Office system in 1957.

With the creation of the Branch Office system, annual targets were set in the form of an increase or decrease in the 'Profit and Loss Budget.' As long as the targets were met, the head of a Branch office was free to manage expenses except for some special items such as the total amount of salaries. The interest on capital loans before the establishment of the Branch office was borne by Headquarters but for borrowings by the Branch Office, it itself had to pay interest at 3.5 per cent.

Hence, the practice of making budget allocations according to past results – which led to a predatory ethos of 'the more money spent, the more gained,' – was discontinued. The results of efforts to improve operations such as reducing costs and promoting sales were now directly attributed to the management of the Branch Offices. The possibility of setting aside reserves for the future was opened up, further motivating local managements.

As well as its main departments concerned with actual transport services, JNR had a number of ancillary departments such as rolling-stock factories and power stations. The business conditions of these departments were not different from those of firms in the same market at large, except that their only 'customer' was JNR. Although a part of JNR from the standpoint of management, it was better to regard them as individual enterprises and to control them separately according to their individual characteristics.

To work out the results of the activities of these departments, the rule was that their costs should be 'called in' from the railway departments, an internal arrangement. As a result, attempts to balance the books became the main accounting exercise, while monitoring costs tended to be neglected. Given the manipulation of actual costs, it was impossible to discover much about the efficiency of these ancillary departments.

In July 1951, the rule was changed from using actual costs to 'standard costs.' This enabled managers to rate the efficiency of their departments and identify any operational flaws or problems in terms of 'the difference between revenue and expenses.'

LIMITATION TO AND THE END OF DECENTRALIZATION IN JNR

The Branch Offices continued developing the decentralization of management for about a decade. They were quite successful in remedying the problems of excessive centralization and the vertical system, and in granting some independence to local management.

However, the balance of revenues and expenses – the most important aspect of independent management – was affected by external factors not within the control of the Branch Offices themselves: for example, population trends, economic changes and the creation of industrial sites in Branch areas. The chief of a Branch Office had no power over fares which were the same for the whole country so that there was no way to allow for the differences in local transportation costs.

On the other hand, expenses increased on account of nation-wide practices such as the annual across-the-board pay rise for all employees. These factors put pressure on local management, and after a decade, some weak Branch Offices were severely handicapped in terms of both their revenues and expenses.

This had been expected to occur to some extent when the comprehensive 'entrustment system' was implemented, and it was inevitable that differences among Branch Offices would surface as a result of decentralized control. Some Branch Offices had difficulty even in maintaining their transportation facilities at the standard JNR level. Decentralized control seemed to have reached its limit. The 'difference between revenues and expenses' system under Branch Office control was discontinued in 1965/66, and a new budget system introduced in 1967/68.

With the introduction of computers and the rapid development of telecommunications networks, the conditions were ripe for Headquarters to control all the Railway Control Offices directly.

While still utilizing the merits of an independent local management system, Headquarters now issued a 'Standard Budget'
directly to the Control Offices, the heads of which could work to
in their own way.

The work of Branch Offices as management units was put on
hold at this time, although the organizational structure remained
in place until 1970. The end of this form of organization began in
1969 with a Cabinet decision, entitled 'Basic Policy for the Financial Reconstruction of JNR.' The policy decided on by the government called for the 'rationalization of control systems,' and in order
to do this, stipulated that 'the interim systems be simplified and
business operations centralized.' This retreat from decentralization
was considered necessary at the time as a means of reconstructing
JNR, in contrast to the calls for the break-up and privatization of
the organization as the only way to achieve the same purpose.

Branch Offices on the main island of Honshu were discontinued
in August 1970, and the direct control system between Headquarters and these Control Offices put into place. In contrast, on
the remoter islands of Hokkaido, Shikoku and Kyushu, the
Branch Offices were made into 'General Offices' with the aim of
strengthening their decentralization. For the first time the organizational uniformity of JNR was broken down. Although with the
same name, General Offices were not identical in practice, reflecting the local conditions of the three islands. This system which
was meant to achieve flexible management in response to local
requirements, gradually assumed characteristics similar to the
Railway Control Office system in Honshu, and the cherished ideal
of decentralized control for the General Offices came to exist in
name only.

With regard to the line management system, although the
Senseki Line was an exceptional case, most local lines were
impressed by its success. This led to the belief that the Control
Centre system was the best approach, and the adoption of this
system was widely advocated.

However, when the Control Centre system was introduced to a
line whose management had limited responsibilities – a line, for
example, without rolling stock, train operators, maintenance facilities exclusive to that line – its operations would be affected by
external factors. In such cases, an operational plan for the line
would have little to do with reality.

Even elsewhere, lines without sufficient resources would, in time, fail to achieve management improvements after the adoption of the Control Centre system. The outcome was that they could not bear the brunt of cost-increasing items such as uniform pay awards, and their management position worsened. The organization of the Control Centre now became too burdensome as a system of line administration.

The individual line management system was now judged to have generally served its purpose and the organizations were gradually trimmed back from 1963 and discontinued altogether in the early 1970s. The experience of JNR shows that management improvements that focus only on the railway transportation business are bound to be limited, and this can be remedied only by aiming at the development of the area itself through involvement with the many activities of the local community.

'50,000 EMPLOYEE LIMIT THEORY' AND THE LOGIC OF ORGANIZATIONS

Moral laxity in the workplace, deteriorating labour relations, low morale among managers – matters such as these in JNR pointed to a lack of control. JNR had as many as 400,000 employees, a number unmatched by any private corporation in Japan, and thus seen as abnormally large. Linking these two factors, though simplistic, gave rise to opinions such as 'The source of all problems in JNR is its colossal scale of management,' or 'The maximum size at which it is possible to control a corporation is 50,000 employees.' These views are pronounced with considerable authority as the basis of the case for the break-up and privatisation of JNR.

At first glance, it seems sensible to suppose that for any organization there is a size beyond which it becomes inefficient, and the question, 'How can a single person, the president, control hundreds of thousands of employees?' appears to be a simple and reasonable one. However, this line of thought fails to distinguish between the limits of control by a single person on the one hand and by an organization on the other. The figure of 400,000 employees undoubtedly far exceeds the limits of control by any one person, but the same applies to a figure of 50,000, or even less.

For an organization, however, this task is not an impossible one. Organizational structures for control purposes can be formed when the management of an enterprise grows to a certain scale. A management body has been described as a 'co-operative system of division of labour,' and with this in mind it is possible for an organization to exercise control down to its lowest levels. The manager controls his immediate subordinates by giving them appropriate goals or tasks and monitors their progress. In turn, each of these assigns tasks to the units under their control, and so on at each level of management, from top to bottom. Thus, decision-making is devolved to managers at various levels while the unity of the overall structure is maintained.

Such a hierarchy of tasks and responsibilities makes it possible to enlarge the number and scope of managers and to cope with increases in the scale of the business. Ikujiro Nonaka has written, 'It is difficult to define the most appropriate scale for an organization in technical terms. Due to the differences in environments, products, technological characteristics, and so on, there is no single solution.'[2]

The scale at which an organization can be controlled differs according to the methods of control. There are only a few corporations in Japan with more than 50,000 employees, but there are many in other countries, and successful at that. One of the world's largest corporations, the American Telephone and Telegraph Corporation (AT&T), employs 1,050,000 people, and General Motors 800,000.

The operational units of JNR comprise 7,400 on-site organizations, ranging in scale from just a few employees to a maximum of close to 1,500. As Nonaka points out, 'The functioning of JNR's huge hierarchy depends on how efficiently the first-line supervisors fulfill their role of controlling the smaller hierarchies, rather than on arguments about the limits of control.'[2]

CASE 3 INTRODUCTION OF 'SITE GENERAL MANAGER' SYSTEM IN SAPPORO RAILWAY CONTROL OFFICE

In 1970, in order to strengthen on-site management – especially of large-scale sites – the Sapporo Railway Control Office selected 38 managers from among the managers of its 220 work sites and appointed them as site general managers. The powers of these new general managers were dramatically increased by transferring to them a substantial part of the Railway Control Office powers and allocating budgets to support these powers.

The number of on-site staff organized into this system at that time was about 11,000 which was 63 per cent of the total on-site staff under the Sapporo Railway Control Office. Moreover, all of the selected sites were major ones. It was expected that most of the on-site business of the Control Office would now be better handled and more quickly.

The purpose of this new system was to make for the rapid identification and solution of problems at work sites, site managers being the people with day-to-day responsibility for the site and being the most familiar with its conditions. The enlarged authority of the new general managers made them an integral part of the railway's management, giving them added confidence in their work. They were thus motivated to do their very best to the benefit of the whole business.

The efficiency of on-site management improved nevertheless, including the speed at which problems were resolved. At Iwami-zawa Station, for example, it was reported that a total of 53 outstanding problems in various areas, many dating back for as long as a decade, were cleared up in a single year. With this new-found efficiency – along with a procedure for prompt rewards and penalties – the general managers soon gained the trust of their staff, and workers' morale improved dramatically.

The selection of general managers was not based on the scale or 'grade' of a particular site but on the personal characteristics of the managers themselves, their enthusiasm, leadership skills, and ability to make the best use of their new powers. Ten of the general managers of the highest calibre and judged to be most capable in the field of control, were given the largest share of the powers invested in the head of the Railway Control Office. At the same time, there was an agreement with the head of the Railway Control Office that the appointment of a general manager could be terminated if it was found that he was not carrying out his duties properly.

This system introduced a new hierarchy for on-site control under the Railway Control Office. The head of the Office had full and direct control over the ten top general managers to make sure that they excelled in carrying out their duties; this gave a boost to the administration of the major work sites. This system at the Sapporo Railway Control Office was still in force in 1987, made up of 51 station districts and 11,300 employees, 75 per cent of the total number.

CONCLUSION

Whether or not effective management control is possible cannot be judged purely on the basis of the scale of a business. No matter how big the scale, there are suitable management systems. At the same time, there are no absolute criteria for the proper form of management or organization: each has its advantages and disadvantages. In deciding on the form to adopt, the right one depends on the advantages and disadvantages of each system in the light of actual circumstances.

Unlike the case of other industries in general, the break up of operations has its drawbacks for the railway businesses. In particular, the stronger the demand for nationwide transportation services, the more difficult it is for a railway business to be broken up.

The main issue during the attempts to share out control of JNR's operations was the fact that when decentralization was proposed through the Branch Office system, the Headquarters either could not or would not transfer its full range of powers to the Branch Offices. This was true from the start of the system up to the time of its termination.

The system was also unable to allow for the disparities in management among the Branch Offices; these grew larger every year as a result of the differences in economic growth among individual areas. Compared with 1955 – when the Branch Office system was introduced – railways passenger kilometres in the Kanto region had grown by 213 per cent by 1981, but only by 7 per cent in Hokkaido and 9 per cent in Shikoku during the same period. Division into private companies will face the same problem.

Although management systems change over time and in different environments, policy must stick to the aim of creating a system that makes the best use of the actual and potential capabilities of the workforce.

It is people who make up an organization and people who use it. The experience of JNR indicates that the most important factor in determining whether or not a decentralized system functions effectively is not so much the form of the system, but the personal qualities of the managers in the system.

If an organization has a rating of say, 50, enhancing this to 100 can only be achieved by the people in that organization. Both the management organization and the behaviour of its members are important, not forgetting the need for mutual trust between the different levels of the hierarchy. Those who delegate authority must clearly understand the concept of decentralization and give it all their support.

Ichikawa's description of the workings of the Senseki Line's management shows the possibilities that exist: 'In a manner of speaking, local lines are like barren soil. The successful results achieved by one such line were the product of the broad and enthusiastic support provided by the upper echelons of the controlling organization. It was like a ray of sunshine.'

NOTES

1 Takeo Ichikawa, 'The Realities of Local Line Management – How the Senseki Line was Restructured', Kotsu-Kyoryoku-kai, 1961
2 Ikujiro Nonaka, 'How Public Corporations are Coping With the Environment', Gendai Keizai Quarterly, Autumn 1982

4

Provincial Railway Policy and the Third Sector Railways in Japan

1. INTRODUCTION

The two major sources of the losses of JNR were its freight services and the passenger service in provincial lines. From 1968 JNR had been trying to close as many as 83 provincial lines with little traffic and to replace them with bus services with much lower operating costs. There were strong protests from rural residents and politicians against these closures and JNR was able to close only 120 kilometres out of 2600 kilometres of planned closures.

After 12 years, in 1980, the central government succeeded in getting JNR Rehabilitation Act approved in the Diet with the intention of improving the finances of JNR, and then began to speed up the closure of provincial lines. The target for closure was 83 lines, the same number as 12 years previously. The government and JNR consulted with local government on each line. The management of all these lines was relinquished by JNR, and by JR after privatisation.

Many local governments were against the closures but they had to accept that JNR would no longer manage them. Where there was a strong demand for railway services to be maintained, they were transferred to the 'third sector', but local governments had to pay a share of the cost in accordance with the new policy. In other cases, private bus services replaced the rail services.

While this policy was being implemented, JNR was privatised and broken up into six companies, the JRs; this was in April, 1987. The change to the third sector railways or buses and privatisation were completely different policies, although they took place at the same time and were both part of the process of privatisation and regionalisation.

Provincial railways in Japan have been managed not only by

JNR but also by private railway companies. Now several small private companies ran a total of 2600 kilometres of local lines, although some had been closed down in 1965–75, and others rationalised to reduce costs.

The operating losses of provincial lines were due, in large, to the expansion of private car ownership. At the same time people had been moving from the countryside to big cities during the time of high economic growth. There were different reasons in individual rural lines for their decline: for example, competition with bus services, the reduction of freight traffic due to changes in the industrial structure, and changes in the route of passenger traffic as the result of newly-built railways or roads.

In November 1980, the JNR Rehabilitation Act (Nihon Koku-yuu Tetsudo Keiei Saiken Sokushin Tokubetsu Sochihou) was passed. The main point of this Act was to deal with rural lines. The proclamation of the Ordinance and the Notice of the Transport Ministry were then published to complete the policies.

2. THE RURAL-LINE POLICIES OF THE JNR REHABILITATION ACT (1980)

Up to now, the government and JNR had used different definitions such as 'rural line system' / 6,000 kilometres (1968), 'provincial lines'/ 11,200 kilometres (1970), 'rural low density lines'/ 3,400 kilometres (1972), 'provincial lines' / 9,200 kilometres (1976). In particular, JNR had distinguished between the trunk line system and the rural lines and had managed them separately in its divisional accounts. This Act of 1980 was a different affair.

The Ordinance of the Act laid down the definitions of the Trunk Line Network, Provincial Lines, and Selected Provincial Lines (see Table 1 and Figure 1). The Trunk Line Network was made up of the lines connecting large cities (population over 100,000) which had more than 30 passenger-route kilometres and a daily passenger-traffic density of more than 4000. (Lines which branched off from these were included in the Network). Also included were lines which had a freight traffic density of more than 4000 tons.

Provincial Lines had a passenger traffic density of less than 8000 of which there were 175 (10,166 kilometres). The Ordinance laid down the standard for the closure of Provincial Lines – the

separation		lines	notes
Trunk Lines	Trunk Line Network[1] (51 lines 11,687 km)	Hakodate, Chitose, Muroran, Tohoku, Joban, Ou, Uetsu, Ban-etsusai, Senseki, Senzan, Jyoetsu, Shin-etsu, Takasaki, Ryomo, Sobu, Uchibo, Tokaido, Musashino, Nanbu, Yokohama, Sagami, Gotenba, Chuo, Shinonoi, Hokuriku, San-yo, Kansai, Hanwa, Hakubi, San-in, Yosan, Kotoku, Kagoshima, Nippo, Nagasaki, Fukuchiyama, Nemuro, Mito, Kosei, Nara, Kisei, Kure, Dosan, Sasebo, Yubari, Hakushin, Yamanote, Oume, Uno, Ube, Mine	
	others (15 lines 600 km)	Akabane, Itsukaichi, Tsurumi, Negishi, Yokosuka, Kawagoe, Sotobo, Narita, Ito, Kusatsu, Osakakanjyo, Sakurajima, Katamachi, Sasaguri, Chikuhi	traffic density over 8,000
Provincial lines[2] (175 lines, 10,166.5 km)		Senmo, Rumoi, Hidaka, Ominato, Kesennuma, Aterazawa, Oga, Rikuuto, Ishinomaki, Tadami, Yahiko, Echigo, Agatsuma, Hachiko, Kururi, Togane, Nikko, Oito, Iiyama, Iida, Minobu, Taita, Taketoyo, Takayama, Jyohana, Toyamako, Himi, Nanao, Kakogawa, Ako, Bantan, Wakayama, Maizuru, Kisuki, Sanko, Kibi, Tsuyama, Tokushima, Naruto, Mugi, Yodo, Gantoku, Chikuho, Omura, Kyudai, Ibusukimakurazaki, Hohi, Sekiho, Soya, Furano, Sassyo, Esashi, Tsugaru Hachinohe, Tazawako, Ofunato, Kamaishi, Kitakami, Hanawa, Yamada, Gono, Yonesaka, Rikuusai, Aterazawa, Ban-etsuto, Suigun, Kashima, Karasuyam, Koumi, Ohama, Kishin, Sangu, Sakurai, Sakai, Inbi, Fukuen, Geibi, Uchiko, Kabe, Yamaguchi, Onoda, Karatsu, Kashii, Gotoji, Hitachikoyama, Misumi, Hisatsu, Kitto, Nichinan, Shinmei, Iwashimizu, Meisyo	175 lines have extra charges : they had traffic density less than 4000, but were exempted from closure because of 1) - 4) (p.4).
	Third Selected Lines[3] (12 lines, 338.9 km)	Ita, Tagawa, Miyata, Yunomae, Kajiya, Nagai, Okata, Noto, Miyazu, Taisya, Nakamura	
	Second Selected Lines[4] (31 lines, 2,089.2 km)	Shibetsu, Chihoku, Shihoro, Hiroo, Yumo, Nayoro, Uhoro, Tenpoku, Utashinai, Horonai, Funai, Iburi, Setana, Matsumae, Aniai, Aizu, Ashio, Mouka, Futamata, Ise, Estuminan, Etsumihoku, Gannichi, Itoda, Kamiyamada, Saga, Matsuura, Takachiho, Miyanojyo, Yamano, Osumi, Shibushi, Urushio	planned to be closed from 1983 to 1985
	First Selected Lines[5] (40 lines, 729.1 km)	Shiranui, Aioi, Syokotsu, Biko, Kohinnan, Kohinhoku, Manji, Iwanai, Ohata, Kuji, Miyako, Sakari, Kakunodate, Kuroishi, Yashima, Niccyu, Marumori, Akatani, Uonuma, Kihara, Shimizuko, Akechi, Tarumi, Kamioka, Takasago, Miki, Hojyo, Shigaraki, Kurayoshi, Wakasa, Komatsushiima, Katsuki, Soeda, Muroki, Katsuta, Amagi, Miyanoharu, Takamori, Yabe, Tsuma	planned to be closed by Summer, 1983
others (4lines, 20km)		Temiya, Shiogama, Keiyo, Shinminato	Freight Lines

Table 1:   Separation of lines and line names

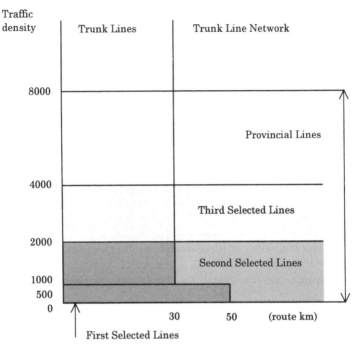

Figure 1: Outline of division of lines

Selected Provincial Lines with a passenger traffic density of less than 4000. However, there were exemptions, namely:

(1) if passenger numbers at peak times (between two stations) were more than 1000 per hour in one direction;
(2) if there was no road, on which to run an alternative bus service;
(3) if the alternative service would be closed for more than ten days a year on account of heavy snow;
(4) if average passenger kilometre per person was more than 30 and the passenger traffic density more than 1000.

The standard of 1000 passengers at peak times was used on the basis of requiring 13 buses, each seating 80 people and running at five minute intervals. There were also cases e.g. Hakkaido Development Agency, where it was not suitable to substitute bus service where the density of passenger traffic was low but where the distance of the service was long. As a result many lines were exempted from being Selected Provincial.

The standard for closure was decided at the density of 4000 persons because below this point railways would be inefficient compared with buses. The standard was proposed in the report of the Council for Transport Policy (Un-sei-shin) in January 1979.

The closure plan would be implemented gradually. For the 175 lines on the Selected Provincial group there were two further exclusions for the First Selected Lines:

(1) lines with passenger route kilometres shorter than 30 and passenger traffic density of less than 2000 persons (although linking lines and coal transport lines were not included). As a result the Ise, Itoda, Kamiyamada, Saga, Utashinai and Horonai lines were excluded.

(2) except for those in 1), lines which have passenger route kilometres less than 50 and passenger traffic density of less than 500.

As a result of this First Selection, 40 lines – 729 kilometres in length – were identified. Those were expected to be closed by the summer of 1983. In December 1979, the Cabinet agreed on 'The Rehabilitation of JNR', and it was further decided that those lines in which the passenger traffic density was less than 2000 would be closed by 1985. This was the Second Selection, involving 31 lines.

The calculation for traffic density was as follows:
Passenger kilometre in a standard time period (1977–1979) ÷ (operating days in the standard time period × passenger route kilometres). If there was some possibility of increasing traffic in the future (for example, plans for the development of residential areas or new schools), an estimated additional amount could be included. As a result the Kajiya and Urushio lines were excluded from the First Selection.

Closing rural lines went through three stages:

(1) Selection of the closures lines: JNR selected the lines and this was subject to the approval of the Ministry of Transport. The prefecture governor could comment on it.

(2) A conference would be held in the selected rural areas on how to maintain public transport after the closure of the

line. The conference would include the government's public safety commissioner, the Hokkaido Development Board (where the closure was in Hokkaido), the Ministry of Transport, the Ministry of Construction, JNR Prefectures, municipalities and prefecture police.

(3) Closure would follow with the agreement of conference. However, JNR could apply for the closure without the agreement of conference after two years. This was an important feature of the policy.

Alternative transport (by bus service or other rural lines) was decided upon after the closure of JNR lines.

3. HISTORY OF RURAL LINE POLICIES

What was the history of the rural line policies up to the Rehabilitation Act? The idea of rationalising rural lines began in 1953 when a plan was published on simplifying decision-making by management on the maintenance of rural lines and on jobs. The policy was based on the decentralized system of management centre (Kanrisho, Unyusho, Kanricho). Attempts were made to use railcars on rural lines as well. However, these policies, which were meant to keep lines open, soon reached their limits.

'What should we do about the traffic of rural lines?', a report by the JNR Consultative Committee on the policy for the closure of rural lines, was issued in September 1968 (Table 2).

Alternative bus services were proposed for 83 lines (2,600 kilometres in length) out of 145 rural lines (6,000 kilometres). Later on the term '83 lines' became a synonym for unprofitable lines. The policy set the standard for unprofitable railways compared to bus services, and examined the possibility of alternative transport for each line. Moreover, it dealt with the scope for new lines and anticipated the idea of the Rehabilitation Act. Eleven lines (121 km) out of these 83 lines were closed between December 1969 and June 1972 (see Table 3).

The closure of these eleven lines had been in preparation for a long time and at great expense, but these lines were only 4.6 per cent of JNR's total route length.

From 1971 JNR lines were separated into Trunk Lines (10,200 kilometres) and Provincial Lines (11,200 kilometres, later cor-

month / year	
Sep. / 1968	JNR Consultative Committee decided "What should we do on the traffic of rural lines?" in which they insisted on the separation of 145 lines of rural lines (6,000 km) and asked for the closure of 83 of those lines (2,600 km).
Dec. / 1969	Kobukuro line (10.1 km) was closed. 11 lines (121.2 km) had been closed by June of 1972.
Dec. / 1970	JNR Consultative Committee decided "How should we manage JNR?" and JNR Account Audit Committee answered with the separation of trunk lines (10,200 km) and provincial lines (11,200 km).
April / 1971	Separation of management of trunk and provincial lines according to these answers was begun.
Jun. / 1972	The government decided "the Outline of JNR Finance Rehabilitation " in which was proposed the closure of low density lines (3,400 km) within five years.
March / 1972	JNR bills which would have enforced "the Outline of JNR Finance Rehabilitaion were discarded in the 86th Diet.
March / 1974	The Cabinet decided "the fundamental policies on JNR Finance Rehabilitation " which promoted the closure of low density provincial lines (with the agreements of local authorities).
Dec. / 1975	The Cabinet agreed the new "Outlines of JNR Finance Rehabilitation Policies" in which the provincial lines were examined on JNR's Responsibility.
April / 1976	JNR amended the selection of lines and the total route kilometre of the provincial lines was 9,200 kilometres.
Oct. / 1976	The Committee of JNR Provincial Line Problems (CJPLP) was set up in the Deliberative Council of Traffic Policy which was a public advisory body.
Jan. / 1977	CJPLP made an interim report about the choice of provincial line policies for the local.
Jan. / 1979	CJPLP made the final report.
Dec. / 1979	The Cabinet agreed about "the JNR Rehabilitation ", and decided the outline of "the Rehabilitation Act" which was based on CJPLP's report and JNR's intention.
Feb. / 1980	The government introduced the bill of the JNR Rehabilitation Act to the Diet. The contents were an extra charge system for the provincial Lines and the closure of the Selected Provincial Lines.
May / 1980	The bill was voted down , because the Diet was dissolved.
July / 1980	The government introduced the same bill to the Diet.
Nov. / 1980	"The JNR Rehabilitation Act" was given final approval by the 93-rd Diet.
Dec. / 1980	"The JNR Rehabilitation Act" was promulgated and enforced.
March / 1981	The Ordinance of Rehabilitation Act was promulgated and enforced. The minister notified it. The definition of the Provincial Lines and the Selected Provincial Lines (the standard of closure) were cleared by it.
April / 1981	The government approved the selection of The Provincial Lines, 175 lines (10,160 km).
June / 1981	JNR applied to approve the Selected Provincial Lines.
Sep. / 1981	The Cabinet agreed the closure of rural lines which JNR applied.
Oct. / 1983	Shiranui line in Hokkaido was closed after substitution by a bus service . This was the first closed line under the Rehabilitation Act.
April / 1984	Kuji,Miyako,and Sakari lines in the Tohoku Region were changed into the third sector railway Sanriku Railway which was the first case of third sector railway in rural areas.
April / 1987	JNR was privatised and passenger traffic was left to six passenger railway companies.
April / 1990	All rural lines which were the objects of closures had been closed (substituted by buses or the third sector railways).

Table 2: History of the policy of rural lines

line	section	route km	month, year	
Kobukuro	Kotake - Futase, Kobukuro -	10.1	Dec.	1969
Konhoku	Ikisu	12.8	Dec.	1970
Karatsu	Syari - Koshikawa	4.1	Aug.	1971
Sechibaru	Yamamoto - Kishidake	6.7	Dec.	1971
Usunoura	Hizenyoshii - Sechibaru	3.8	Dec.	1971
Kajiyabara	Sasa - Usunobara	6.9	Jan.	1972
Mikuni	Itano - Kajiyabara	9.7	March	1972
Sasayama	Kanatsu - Mikuniko	17.6	March	1972
Ujina	Sasayamaguchi - Fukuzumi	2.4	April	1972
Kawamata	Hiroshima - Kamiouoka	12.2	May	1972
Sassyo	Matsukawa - Iwashirokawamata	34.9	June	1972
	Shintozugawa - Ishikarinumata			
Subtotal	11 lines (of 83 lines)	121.2		
Others	11 lines (not included in the 83)	35.1		
Total	22 lines	156.3		

* Iburi line (Kyogoku – Wakikata, 7.5Km), Agatsuma line (Naganohara – Taishi, 5.8km) etc.

Table 3: Closure of the rural lines (from Dec., 1969 to Jan., 1976)

rected to 9,200 kilometres) and they were then managed separately. The new accounting arrangement overcame the shortcomings of the old and made for greater accuracy for public use. Afterwards it was possible for JNR to publish financial results in three parts – Trunk Lines, Provincial Lines and Motorcars. As a result public understanding of rural line problems improved and it came to be accepted that the problem of rural lines was not one of managerial control. In fact, the financial loss on the rural lines was just 31 per cent of JNR's total loss during 1971–75.

In the first half of the 1970s the government proposed the closure of 3,400 kilometres of provincial low-density lines but this was voted down in the Diet. Although the proposal was made on the condition that local authorities' agreement was forthcoming, it proved to be of no avail. In the late 70s the Committee of JNR Provincial Line Problems was set up in the Council for Traffic Policy, a public advisory body. The plan for the 'JNR Rehabilitation Act' was prepared on the basis of this Committee's report.

The bill of the Rehabilitation Act was proposed to the 91st Diet in February 1980, but the Diet was dissolved and the bill was voted down in May. After the joint election of representa-

Financial year	Trunk Lines	Provincial Lines	Motorcars	Total
1971/72	-107.0	-117.2	-10.0	-234.2
1972/73	-196.7	-133.8	-11.0	-341.5
1973/74	-286.6	-154.4	-13.4	-454.4
1974/75	-451.4	-182.3	-17.1	-650.8
1975/76	-667.2	-225.5	-22.0	-914.7
Total	-1708.9	-813.2	-73.5	-2595.6
(%)	(66)	(31)	(3)	(100)

Table 4:   Change of separated accounting (profit and loss) (Y billion)
Source: JNR Audit Reports

tives of the Lower and Upper houses, the bill was again put to
the Diet in July 1980. In the 93rd Diet it was approved, in
November 1980. Then, the LDP was the majority party and was
in favour of this bill along with the New Liberal Club: the other
parties were against it. The details of the Act were left to
government Ordinances and therefore, the negotiations between
the Transport Ministry and other ministries were significant. As
a result, so it was said, the intentions of the Transport Ministry
were fulfilled, even though other ministerial views were taken
into account.

After the proposal for the closure of 83 rural lines, new rural
lines were still being built. From 1968 to 1975, 16 rural lines (267
km) were opened or extended which included the Marumori,
Sakari, Kakunodate, Tadami, Takachiho, Kuji and Sanko lines.
During that time some rural lines were closed – 156 kilometres all
told – but the length of new lines was more than the length that
was closed. The Rehabilitation Act prohibited JNR from building
new rural lines, and this problem came to an end. Table 5 gives
the names of the lines the construction of which was stopped by
JNR.

4. SUBSTITUTE POLICIES

What lay behind the JNR Rehabilitation Act for alternative
transport in place of rural railways lines that were closed? In the
case of Selected Provincial Lines for which closures were the only
option for JNR, (Figure 2) a choice was allowed between alternative bus services and other railway companies. When bus services

lines	km	lines	km	lines	km
Iwanai	44	Yagan	50	Ihara	41
Ashibetsu	31	Hokuetsuhoku	67	Sugumo	82
Kitatokachi	72	Sakuma	35	Asa	113
Meiu	56	Nakatsugawa	37	Imafuku	54
Biko	58	Himi	25	Ganjitsuhoku	41
Kohin	51	Gero	48	Yusubaru	8
Shiranuka	43	Tarumi	12	Yobuko	60
Konpoku	44	Kojuru	57	Okuni	44
Kuji	32	Miyafuku	31	Hokusyo	13
Sakari	15	Sakamoto	23	Takachiho	23
Omoto	10	Chiju	54	Etsumi	24
Yokaku	35	Nansyo	43		
				Total 35 lines 1,471km	

Table 5:   Constructing rural lines

were selected, those were to be managed by private bus companies. Government grants were on offer for the change to buses, and subsidising the operation costs for five years in the event of financial loss.

When a railway was chosen to continue as a Selected Provincial railway, it was possible to give it or lease it free to a private railway company, and then the subsidy was equal to half the actual loss for five years. It was possible to give or lease provincial lines other than Selected Provincial Lines (Figure 2.1) but in that case the lease would not be free, although no such case arose. In building provincial lines which had to do with Selected Provincial Lines, new services could be given or leased to these on their completion (Figure 2.3). In practice, however, there were many other more promising markets for bus services and in places where it would be difficult to continue with a railway service. The Rehabilitation Act was clearly intended to keep public transport by running bus services, a characteristic feature of the Act.

If after the first five years, there were still operating losses, then subsidising rural bus companies was possible under the 'Outline of preservation of rural bus routes'. This subsidy was available for lines with an average passenger traffic density of not less than five.

The Provincial Lines would still be managed by JNR but with

① In the case of the Provincial Lines except Selected Provincial Lines

	1 JNR	2 Others
I Railway	I -1	II -2
II Bus		

② In the case of the Selected Provincial Lines

	1 JNR	2 Others
I Railway		I -2'
II Bus	II -1	II -2

③ In the case of line construction
(equivalent to the Selected Provincial Lines)

	1 JNR	2 Others
I Railway		I -2"
II Bus		

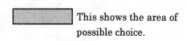 This shows the area of possible choice.

Figure 2: Choice and outlines of subsidisation

higher fares. When JNR lines were replaced by bus services or private railways, people would still have to pay a different fare, and one that was more expensive than on trunk-line networks or city lines.

Removing unprofitable rural lines from the main part of transport companies and leaving them to the third sector, local government or other companies had already taken place other than through JNR. For instance, there were subsidised municipal bus services (based on 4,24–2, 101 Articles of Road Traffic Law) and Nippon Short Distance Airlines (the third sector of three main airline companies and local governments). Unprofitable parts would be hired off if they became non-viable even with cross subsidies.

The JNR Rehabilitation Act set out to choose the mode and the management style for local government transport services (Figure 2), although if the central government were to ask local government to run these services, some budget apportionment had to be arranged. In decentralizing from central to local government, there had to be a rational basis for local fiscal responsibility.

5. 'SELECTION' BY LOCAL GOVERNMENTS

Local government was brought in for rural lines whose density of traffic was less than 2000. After selecting which lines should be

	JNR	others	total
Railway	0	38 lines	38 lines
Bus	(1 line) *	45 lines	45 lines
Total	(1 line) *	83 lines	83 lines

* Half of the Osumi line was substituted by the JR Kyushu Bus service

Table 6: Selections for 83 lines

closed, conferences of JNR and local councils were held for each one of them. There were conflicting interests. JNR (or the government) would try to persuade local governments to agree to the closures, explaining the structural nature of the losses of the local lines and the financial problems of JNR. The Rehabilitation Act was the basis of JNR's proposals, especially the 'Give up' Article whereby JNR was allowed to close rural lines without local agreement. Not that JNR liked to use this power, even though use was made of it.

The outcome of local conferences was never in doubt. Every local authority insisted upon the importance of the line to its local residents even when there were local bus services. The only pro-railway policy suggested by local governments was the 'Ride-the-Railway' campaign, but it was a poor attempt to get residents to use railways. Not that they could take a strong policy stance without financial resources. In effect, local public opinion was not enough to hold up central government policies. Petitions for local traffic services never did have any effect.

The Rehabilitation Act gave local governments a choice of transport service: they had three to choose from, JNR service being ruled out.

There was no real choice in favour of JNR bus services because the policy was about replacing JNR with other enterprises, not just a change of mode from railway to bus services.

The Government had decided to give up the management of rural rail transport and to leave it to local governments. In principle, local government could choose the modes of traffic, but local governments had little if any financial resources to spare so that, in practice, their options were severely limited.

When rail management was changed to the local authority, the government paid several types of grant – a subsidy for the season ticket holders, a subsidy for the initial capital investment, and a

subsidy for the implementation of the change. From the management point of view the subsidy for the initial investment was the
most valuable one, the money usually being spent on buying
rolling stock or buses. The grant for the change itself was equal to
30 million yen per 1 kilometre of track.

Moreover, for the first five years a subsidy to cover the operating deficit was available. For bus services the government met the
whole deficit, and for railway services half the deficit. On this
score it was more advantageous to take on bus than railway
services.

After the change, how would local payments be financed?
First, the fares would be raised in spite of the subsidies for
season ticket holders. After five years any deficit would be paid
mainly by local government given the established government
subsidies. Capital construction cost would be paid mainly by the
central government.

From the point of view of costs, bus services have considerable
advantages over railway services in sparse markets. The system of
subsidy gave an advantage to bus services so that more local
governments would choose bus services. There were a few bus
services which were managed by local governments, one being the
Shiranui line (the 101st Article Bus), but most of them were
managed by local private companies. The 101st Article Bus was
included in the Road Traffic Law (1951) and prohibited the use
of private cars for passenger traffic (except in emergencies). If
private companies do not provide bus services local governments
can do so as if there had been an 'emergency' resulting from the
closure of JNR lines.

For bus companies the alternative bus services were not particularly attractive but at least they were not unprofitable.

6. THE ESSENCE OF 'THE THIRD SECTOR'

If local groups insist on keeping railway services, the JNR line is
replaced by a private railway company but if no company is
forthcoming, a new private company has to be set up. Typically,
these new companies do not make enough profit and tend to need
public money to support them. The Regulation Authority accepts
this and allows the creation of a Third Sector company.

In other words, the Third Sector can be both a public and

Kinds of enterprises	Lines	Substitution for selected Provincial lines		Line Construction	
		company	JNR line name	company	planned name
The Third Sector	Semi- public Corporation	Sanriku	Kuji, Sakari	Sanriku	Kuji, Sakari
		Miki	Miki		
		Hojyo	Hojyo		
		Akita -Nairiku- Jyukan	Kakunodate, Aniai	Akita-Nairiku- Jyukan	Yokaku
		Yurikogen	Yajima		
		Minamiaso	Takamori		
		Akechi	Akechi		
		Amagi	Amagi		
				Yagan	Yagan
				Miyafuku	Miyafuku
				Hokuetsu- Express	Hokuetsuhoku
				Kashima- Rinkai,	Kashima
				Aichi-Kanjo	Okata Seto
	Semi- private company	Tarumi	Tarumi	Abukuma- Express	Marumori
		Kamioka	Kamioka		
		Abukuma- Express	Marumori		
private company		Konan Railway	Kuroishi		
		Shimokita- Kotsu	Ohata		

note; From the name of the railway companies the word "Railway" has been omitted. Aniai line is a Second Selected Line.

Table 7: Lines which became the selected railway mode from the first selected lines

private 'joint' company. Thus, the enterprises are of three types – private, public and joint public-private. Usually the profit-making companies are private; JNR and TITP (Eidan) are the public; the joint public-private are Rinkai Railways, Senboku Railway and Hokuso Railway. Despite differences in ownership, they are all joint stock companies and are legally similar.

Table 7 shows the lines which were managed as railway companies at the start. There are lines which have substituted private companies, and the others are all Third Sectors joint companies. These are in conjunction with local governments such as prefectures, cities, towns, villages and private companies.

For investment purposes we must identify the main or major

company shareholder. Kamioka Railway, Tarumi Railway and Abukuma Express each had a main shareholder. Kamioka Railway's main shareholder was Mitsui Kinzoku Kogyo (Mitsui Materials) which had 51 per cent of all shares, while the local authorities – two prefectures and four towns and villages – had 49 per cent. Seino Railways had 51 per cent of the shares of Tarumi Railways, and Sumitomo Cement Company (the main user) and local authorities (one prefecture and nine towns and villages) each had 24 per cent. Fukushima Kotsu had 51 per cent of the shares of Abukuma Express and local authorities – two prefectures and 22 cities, towns and villages – 49 per cent.

These three companies were Third Sector semi-private companies. Some established private companies such as Konan Railway, Shimokita Kotsu, Seino Railway and Fukushima Kotsu were keen to manage those railways. Konan Railway wanted to take on the Kuroishi and Yajima lines but this plan came unstuck. It was said that Shimokita Kotsu decided upon the Ohata line because another company, Nanbu-Jyukan Railway, was after it, and Shimokita Kotsu wanted to save its bus network. Fukushima Kotsu stressed the importance of railway over bus services.

Sanriku, Miki, Hozyo, Yuri-Kogen, Akita-Nairiku-Jyukan Railways are Third sector railways in which local governments held more than half of the shares. Sanriku Railways was set up by Iwate prefecture (48 per cent of shares), and 28 other cities, towns and villages (totalling 27 per cent): these local authorities therefore had 75 per cent of all shares. For Akita-Nairiku-Jyukan Railways 77 per cent of its shares were held by local authorities: for Yurikogen, 75 per cent, for Miki and Hojyo, 51 per cent. They were therefore all a brand of public enterprises. Public and private joint-owned enterprises are often public enterprises as they have only a small amount of shares owned by the private sector. Akechi, Takamori and Amagi lines were also similar Third sector railways. In the case of the Takamori and Amagi lines the prefectures had no shares; only cities, towns and villages did.

There are thus two sorts of Third sector railways – semi-public and semi-private ones. They are not likely to make much of their 'jointness'. Whatever the formal arrangements, enterprise is either public or private.

The capital of each of the Third sector railway companies was 100 million yen except for Sanriku Railway with 300 million and

Kamioka Railway with 200 million. The capital of the private companies was 50 million yen on average, the largest being 100 million for Mitsui Kinzoku Kogyo. These were not large sums since capital construction costs were financed by the national treasury, and each company 'borrowed' all its infrastructure free of charge. In one sense, therefore, a split between infra-structure and operation has taken place. Depreciation amounts would be charged to each company in order to maintain its real assets, and hence its services.

The Third sector is one made up of 50–50 partnership of local government and the private sector; in some cases railway users can become shareholders. Neither government nor JNR were part of the capital funding – if funds were insufficient from the private sector then the local government's share had to be increased.

JNR supported the arrangement of giving all the railway facilities to the Third sector companies or leasing them free of charge. Rolling stock was purchased using government subsidies.

Any trading losses in the first five years of operation of a Third sector company was borne equally by the government and the local authorities; thereafter the local authorities had to bear all losses. The responsibility for any financial deficits in public transport services was thereby shifted from central government to the local area where it occurred.

Staff expenses of Third sector companies were kept to a minimum by having one-man operation on the trains and by eliminating restrictive practices. Additional staff were hired according to need, using local retired JNR staff.

Fares would be increased every two years, and although initially cheaper than the private companies, they will fall into line in time.

To increase business (and income), Third sector companies started to provide more trains, improve station facilities and some even considered faster trains. Despite an initial increase in business, the longer term view was not optimistic, since the private car would continue to be a threat to rail travel.

Each new Third sector company bought 'rail buses' and small rail cars to replace the heavy JNR rolling stock. These new items used half the power of the old ones and their repair costs were estimated to be a third less. This was also an opportunity to redesign facilities so as to attract tourists and sightseers.

This work illustrated the enthusiasm of the local communities

Million Person

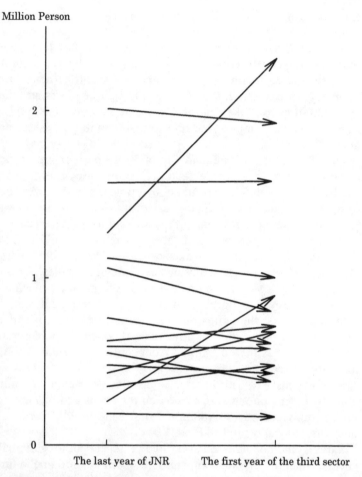

The last year of JNR   The first year of the third sector

Figure 3:   Change of Passenger Volume – 14 lines of the first stage
Source: Mitsuhide Imashiro, Public and Private Commuter Railways in Japan,
Erich Staisch, Suburban Railways – a chance for our cities, UITP. Nov. 1989.

who did not want to lose their rail link. Decisions on the future of
each line was the responsibility of the local authority and its
residents. It was they who had to decide about bus services if costs
become too great, or bear the losses. Since passenger volume on
these lines was more suited for buses than trains, the likelihood of
financial viability was small. Even so, of the 28 companies which

JNR Provincial Lines / 1985   15 Third Sector Companies / 1986

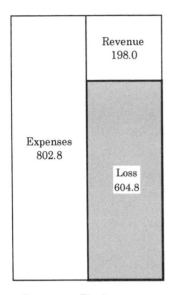

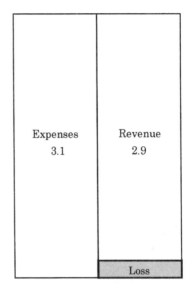

Source : see Fig. 3

(Billion yen)

Figure 4:   Revenue and Expenditure

had been trading long enough to publish annual accounts in 1989, eight of them had made a profit.

Compared with the JNR era, overall revenue for these lines increased considerably. Sanriku Railway, the first of the Third sector companies, started in 1984 and made profits in all its first five years. It had 107 kilometres of line, linking places on a north/south route along the eastern coast of the Tohoku Region. Transport was not well developed here and the local residents had been campaigning for 50 years to get their own rail link.

The success here was surprising since the construction of the line had been slow and the partially completed section, taken over by Sanriku Railways in 1984, was in a sparsely populated area. Despite this inauspicious start, after the central government had completed the unfinished sections of the line, Sanriku began providing a service. Despite the fact that a good road network

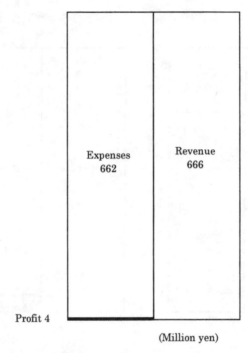

Figure 5: Revenue and Expenditure of the Sanriku Railway 1986
Source: see Figure 3

had changed travel potential in the area since campaigning for a rail link had started, the local residents welcomed this new facility with open arms. The first year's usage was much better than estimated, a large amount of this being students who liked the rail link between their homes and their schools. The second year of trading was not so good, with passenger usage falling off due to severe competition from private cars. To combat this, Sanriku Railway introduced several innovative measures to attract people back to the trains. These included special services for daytime shoppers, services for those needing hospital treatment and a 'Ride-the-Railways' campaign aimed at those people who lived near the line.

Although not providing an answer to all the problems of rural rail networks, this model does show that it is possible to revive and return interest in a local service facing closure. This is also of

	Share of infrastructure	Operating Loss Subsidy
Central Government	Subsidy for rolling stock and engine sheds	Half of the operating loss during the first five years by subsidy
Local Government	In principle, investment of 50% of the capital	Funds put aside to cover future operating losses
JNR	Free transfer of tracks, stations, signaling etc.	
Private Enterprise	In principle, investment of 50% of the capital	

Table 8: Third Sector Railways

a benefit to JR in dealing with its deficits by giving up local lines that are losing money.

Third sector railways can thus be made profitable by an arrangement whereby central government bears the infrastructure costs and the local authority made responsible for the day-to-day management.

7. 'EXPECTATION' OF LINE CONSTRUCTION

The rural lines of JNR were built in accordance with the Railway Construction Act (1922). The budget for constructing lines which came under the Selected Provincial Lines was frozen when the Rehabilitation Act was decided. Some of them were frozen just before construction was completed. However, the Rehabilitation Act allowed construction to continue where the local residents agreed to manage the line as the Third sector, and on completion, the line would be leased free of charge. Some sections of Kuji and Sakari lines (which were transferred to the Sanriku Railway) came under this dispensation.

There were also some lines constructed so as to be opened as Third sector railways; for example, Yagan, Miyafuku Railways and Hokuetsu Express. Abukuma Express and Akita-Nairiku-Jyukan Railways have part of their lines as formerly unfinished sections.

Yagan, Miyafuku and Hokuetsu are Third sector railways which have large local governments imputs. Local government shares accounted for 85 per cent of Yagan's total shares and 84 per cent of Miyafuku's. Yagan railways were electrified, since it was linked

with Tobu Railways, and Miyafuku Railway also had electrification plans.

Abukuma Express planned to complete the Marumori line and
to open it after its electrification. It used the same line from
Fukushima to Sendai as JNR-JR. Akita-Nairiku-Jyukan Railways
was linked to three lines – Kakunodate (a First Selected line),
Aniai (a Second Selected line) and Yokaku (under construction)
– but its traffic density was very low. For the Sanriku railway the
government paid a grant for the new line to be in the Third
sector, the amount being one-third of that of the Selected Provincial Lines (10 million yen per kilometre). There was no good
reason to pay this grant, since there was only a plan to build a
line (for which the budget had been frozen) – and after it was
built it did not become a JNR line.

The Kashima line was opened by Kashima-Rinkai Railway.
This line had been expected to be in greater use than as a Selected
Provincial line, and JNR did not stop its construction. Although
conforming with the Emergency Proposals of the JNR Restructuring Supervisory Committee, JNR refused to take on this line, and
its management was left to the Kashima-Rinkai Railways. This is
a Third sector company which was helped with JNR, local government and consignor company money. JNR's capital share was 36
per cent. JNR also refused to take on the Okata-Seto line on the
same grounds and the line was left to local management.

There were many attempts to transfer lines to be constructed to
the Third sector, but not all have been successful. Some lines have
been left unfinished and the central government should be made
responsible for this state of affairs.

8. CONCLUSION

The closure policies for the Selected Provincial Lines of JNR-JR
were carried out according to the original plans. The 'substitution'
grants succeeded in securing local government agreements for
closure and the subsidies for operating costs have influenced
decisions on managing bus services and Third sector railways.
There was a time limit for the system of subsidies and management problems are bound to arise in the future when subsidies
come to an end.

At the beginning of the Third sector railways traffic volume increased on many lines, due to the greater frequency of railway services. The fares of the Third sector railways were higher than JNR's but still cheaper than private bus services. Thus there were some benefits to users in spite of the higher charges. The volume of traffic did reach a peak and has fallen off somewhat.

In rural railways the fall in the number of passengers due to the increase in fares has been large, and this is causing difficulties in fixing fares. The cost of managing Third sector railways for local governments is bound to increase. The rise in passenger numbers when JNR lines were replaced by Third sector railways did not last long, and did not reverse the long-term trend of falling traffic volume. At the time when the Third sector railways were opened, the problems of rural public transport were thought to have been solved, or that the problems stemmed from the JNR management system.

New problems of the Third sector railway managements began to emerge. In May, 1991, a JR train – using the track of the Third sector railway, Shigaraki-Kogen Railway – crashed into the Shigaraki-Kogen Railcars; 42 people were killed, and 614 injured. There had been few such serious accidents as this in Japan in recent times.

Ignoring a traffic signal by the Shigaraki railcars was the direct cause of the accident, but there were also at least two other factors. The first was that the Shigaraki-Kogen Railways was carrying an unusually large number of passengers as local government was holding a world exhibition, and one purpose of the exhibition was to increase the revenue of the Shigaraki-Kogen Railway. There were pressures on the company in having to carry so many passengers since it had a low traffic capacity. The second related to a new automatic signal system. Not that the system itself was faulty but it was a new system and therefore an unfamiliar one at the time.

How to retain staff has been a hard problem for the Third Sector railways. In many cases they have had to depend upon retired JNR staff, older and not always able to learn new skills. The number of this type of worker is bound to fall. Staffing problems are also caused by the low level of Third sector railway wages.

The decrease or the stagnation of traffic on rural railways has also been brought about by the growth in two-car ownerships.

Housewives have come to use a 'second' car for shopping, for taking children to and from school and the elderly to and from hospitals, and so on. All this has been helped along by the provision of good roads.

Rural residents had been opposed to railways closures and had called for rail services to be continued by the Third sector railways. However, after the initial boom, they have not maintained their use of these rail services. Nor have the alternative bus services been much used. No public transport is as convenient as cars whatever the improvements to the service. If public transport has a 'social' value, it should be provided not by train but by bus services (which have lower costs). Rules must also be put in place for meeting the cost of the 'social' value.

Some local governments were against the closure of railways because the names of towns would disappear from the JNR timetable and thereby hasten their decline. This was rather fanciful and it is the railways that have been forgotten, not the places they used to serve.

What can be done about alternative bus services after the closure of the Third sector railways when traffic falls off? Local governments may try to prevent the closing of Third sector railways in the first place, perhaps on electoral grounds. Subsidies for the Third sector railways may have to go up, since fares cannot be raised any more nor costs cut, rationalisation having reached its limits.

The policy for provincial railways was to transfer responsibilities from the central to local government. This is what is meant by the 'regionalisation' of railways and is a sound policy. The same policy is widely practised in EC countries – although in Japan local governments do not have the financial resources to adopt the policy on a large scale.

The policy has had a cost-saving effect on JNR-JR. However, the lines that were closed were less than half of all provincial lines so that the effect has not been all that great. In addition, while the overall traffic volume has been falling, the policy did lead to new lines with a traffic density of less than 4000, lines for which there are no grounds for their closure. The JNR Rehabilitation Act set the standard for closure at the time, and was a short-term policy. How to maintain unprofitable lines in the future or how to close these lines within the legal framework is a new problem.

Principles should be established as to how to meet the cost of lines with low traffic density for which there are certain social reasons for their continuance as a JNR-JR line.

NOTES

1 Mitsuhide Imashiro, Public and Private Commuter Railways in Japan, Erich Staisch, Suburban Railways – a chance for our cities, UITP. Nov. International Conference in Berlin, 1989.

APPENDIX 1 PASSENGER DENSITY OF JNR PROVINCIAL LINES/ THIRD SECTOR LINES

	1965	1975	Std.	1983	1984	1985	1986	1987	1988	1989	1990
Chihoku /											
Hokkaido Chihoku Kogen	1799	1107	943	...	...	726	677	...	...	516	476
Ohata / Shimokita	2490	1667	1524	1081	1090	1162	811	717	...	553	513
Kuroishi / Konan	1999	2176	1904	1297	1165	711	685	648	...	565	592
Aniai /											
ANJ North Line	2562	1587	1524	1039	982	927	845	728	693	-	-
Kakunodate /											
ANJ South line	-	372	284	182	176	170	193	199	227	-	-
Akita Nairiku Jyukan	-	-	-	-	-	-	-	-	-	567	515
Yashima /											
Yuri Kogen	3958	2201	1876	1310	1151	1153	982	901	884	886	869
Nagai /											
Yamagata	3935	2395	2151	1589	1555	1445	1377	...	1466	1286	1298
Kuji /											
Sanriku North line	-	530	762	684	1224	1123	1009	944	936	957	981
Mikako /											
(Sanriku North)	-	692	605	831	-	-	-	-	-	-	-
Sakari /											
Sanriku south line	-	928	971	865	1158	1075	991	892	858	846	866
Sanriku (Total)	-	-	-	-	1202	1107	1003	926	910	920	942
Marumori /											
Abukuma Kyuko	-	1270	1082	906	926	870	1207	1391	1753	1804	2049
Aizu /											
Aizu	2195	1562	1333	1101	1016	960	971	1390	1317	1248	1258
Ashio /											
Watarase Keikoku	2491	1732	1315	858	884	886	851	626	1271	828	892
Mouka /											
Mouka	3205	1820	1620	1427	2024	2066	1943	...	1406	1398	1443
Kihara /											
Isumi	3286	1680	1815	2256	2248	2307	1930	2015	1339	1267	1266
Akechi /											
Akechi	2124	1525	1623	1119	1132	1354	1221	1178	1171	1161	1134
Futumata /											
Tenryu Hamanako	3320	1904	1518	1077	1022	959	1466	955	1057	1090	1163
Okata /											
Aichi Kanjyu	-	-	2757	...	...	2951	2930	3049	3298	3756	4162
Ise /											
Ise	-	2007	1508	...	...	1354	2634	1268	1332	1480	1876

	1965	1975	Std.	1983	1984	1985	1986	1987	1988	1989	1990
Etsuminan /											
Nagaragawa	2498	1620	1392	1058	993	976	907	896	798	745	812
Tarumi /											
Tarumi	2049	1192	951	652	864	798	869	876	1110	1026	1088
Shigaraki /											
Shigaraki Kogen	2452	1667	1574	2079	2079	2078	1529	1372	1328	1318	1413
Miki /											
Miki	2268	1496	1384	1088	1027	822	631	514	548	545	519
Noto /											
Noto	2139	2542	2045	1581	1500	1454	1392	2197	1267	1193	1194
Kamioka /											
Kamioka	–	477	445	255	394	265	239	194	161	138	167
Miyazu /											
Kitahinki Tango	5600	3659	3120	...	...	2365	2164	...	...	1060	1467
Hojo /											
Hojo	3599	1957	1609	973	883	667	637	643	616	647	690
Wakasa /											
Wakasa	3268	1781	1555	2058	2028	2023	1768	1138	1099	1009	1009
Gannichi /											
Nishikigawa	2201	1389	1420	11231	1155	981	874	1030	997	971	971
Nakamura /											
Tosa Kuroshio	1801	2583	2289	...	...	1689	1629	...	1543	1509	1623
Ita /	7959	3399	2872	...	...	1959	1883	...	...	–	–
Itoda /	1805	1561	1489	...	...	1049	907	...	...	–	–
Tagawa /	4621	2594	2132	...	...	1362	1230	...	...	–	–
Heisei Chikuho	–	–	–	–	–	–	–	–	–	1543	1601
Amagi /											
Amagi	2002	868	653	389	397	397	1238	1498	1392	1917	1993
Matsuura /											
Matsuura	3383	2235	1741	1303	1266	1288	1170	...	1166	1145	1181
Yunomae /											
Kumagawa	3998	3475	3292	...	...	2310	2129	...	...	2190	2196
Takachiho /											
Takachiho	1958	1593	1350	934	1042	939	846	727	...	785	750
Takamori /											
Minami Aso	1687	1280	1093	748	692	715	780	694	700	699	682

JNR / Third sector railways — No data

Std. Standard Time Period, 1977–79 ... Unknown

Sources: Unyusho (MOT), Chiho Kotu Sen Jittai Chosa, Unyu Chosa Kyoku (ITE),
Mintetsu Tokei Nenpo 1984–86 (MOT), Tetsudo Tokei Nonpo 1987–90 (MOT)

APPENDIX 2 DETAILS OF 83 PROVINCIAL LINES

JNR - JRs Lines	Route kms	Closing date as a JNR - JRs line	Section, Prefectures / Substitution
Tenpoku	148.9	1989. 5. 1	Otoineppu - Minami Wakkanai, Hokkaido / Bus
Kohin Hoku	30.4	1985. 7. 1	Hama Tonbetsu - Kitami Esashi, Hokkaido /Bus
Biko	21.2	1985. 9.17	Bifuka - Niupu, Hokkaido / Bus
Kohin Nan	19.9	1985. 7.15	Okkope - Omu, Hokkaido / Bus
Nayoro	143.0	1989. 5. 1	Nayoro - Engaru, Naka Yubetsu, Hokkaido / Bus
Shokotsu	34.3	1985. 4. 1	Shokotsu - Kitami, Hokkaido / Bus
Yumo	89.8	1987. 3.20	Naka Yubetsu - Abashiri, Hokkaido / Bus
Aioi	36.8	1985. 4. 1	Bihoro - Kitami Aioi, Hokkaido / Bus
Shibetsu	116.9	1989. 4.30	Shibecha - Nemuro Shibetsu, Naka Shibetsu - Attoku, Hokkaido / Bus
Shiranuka	33.1	1983.10.23	Shiranuka - Hokushin, Hokkaido / Bus
Chihoku	140.0	1989. 6. 4	Ikeda - Kitami, Hokkaido / Third sector railway
Hiroo	84.0	1987. 2. 2	Obihiro - Hiroo, Hokkaido / Bus
Tomiuchi	82.5	1986.11. 1	Mukaya - Hidakacho, Hokkaido / Bus
Manji	23.8	1985. 4. 1	Shibun - Manji Tanzen, Hokkaido / Bus
Iburi	83.0	1986.11. 1	Date Monbetsu - Kuchan, Hokkaido /Bus
Matsumae	50.8	1988. 2. 1	Kikonai - Matsumae, Hokkaido / Bus
Setana	48.4	1987. 3.16	Kunnui - Setana, Hokkaido / Bus
Iwanai	14.9	1985. 7. 1	Kozawa - Iwanai, Hokkaido / Bus
Horonai	20.8	1987. 7.13	Iwamizawa - Ikusunbetsu, Mikasa - Horonai, Hokkaido / Bus
Utashinai	14.5	1988. 4.25	Sunagawa - Utashinai, Hokkaido / Bus
Haboro	141.1	1987. 3.30	Rumoi - Horonobe, Hokkaido / Bus
Ohata	18.0	1985. 7. 1	Shimokita - Ohata, Aomori / Private railway company
Kuroishi	6.6	1984.11. 1	Kawabe - Kuroishi, Aomori / Private railway company
Aniai	46.1	1984. 6.22	Takanosu - Hitachinai, Akita / Third sector railway
Kakunodate	19.2	1986.11. 1	Kakunodate - Matsuda, Akita / Third sector railway
Yashima	23.0	1985.10. 1	Ugo Honjyo - Ugo Yashima, Akita / Third sector railway
Nagai	30.5	1988.10.25	Akayu - Arato, Yamagata / Third sector railway
Akatani	18.9	1984. 4. 1	Shibata - Higashi Akatani, Niigata / Bus
Uonuma	12.6	1984. 4. 1	Raikoji - Nishi Ojiya Niigata / Bus

Kuji	26.0	1984. 4. 1	Kuji - Fudai, Iwate / Third sector railway
Miyako	12.8	1984. 4. 1	Miyako - Taro, Iwate / Third sector railway
Sakari	21.5	1984. 4. 1	Sakari - Yoshihama, Iwate / Third sector railway
Marumori	17.4	1986. 7. 1	Tsukinoki - Marumori, Fukushima, Miyagi / Third sector railway
Nicchu	11.6	1984. 4. 1	Kitakata - Atsushio, Fukushima / Third sector railway
Aizu	57.4	1987. 7.16	Nishi Wakamatsu - Aizu Kogen, Fukushima / Third sector railway
Ashio	46.0	1989. 3.29	Kiryu - Ashio Honzan, Gunma, Tochigi / Third sector railway
Mouka	42.0	1988. 4.11	Shimodate - Motegi, Tochigi / Third sector railway
Kihara	26.9	1988. 3.24	Ohara - Kazusa Nakano, Chiba / Third sector railway
Shimizuko	8.3	1984. 4. 1	Shimizu - Miho, Shizuoka / Bus
Akechi	25.2	1985.11.16	Ena - Akechi, Gifu / Third sector railway
Futamata	67.7	1987. 3.15	Kakegawa - Shinjohara, Shizuoka / Third sector railway
Okata	19.5	1988. 1.31	Okazaki - Shin Toyota, Aichi / Third sector railway
Ise	26.0	1987. 3.27	Minami Yokkaichi - Tsu, Mie / Third sector railway
Etsuminan	72.2	1986.12.11	Miho Ota - Hokuno, Gifu / Third sector railway
Tarumi	24.0	1984.10. 6	Ogaki - Miho Komi, Gifu / Third sector railway
Shigaraki	14.8	1987. 7.13	Kibukawa - Shigaraki, Shiga / Third sector railway
Miki	6.8	1985. 4. 1	Yakujin - Miki, Hyogo / Third sector railway
Takasago	6.3	1984.12. 1	Kakogawa - Takasago, Hyogo / Bus
Noto	61.1	1988. 3.25	Anamizu - Takojima, Ishikawa / Third sector railway
Kamioka	20.3	1984.10. 1	Inotani - Kamioka, Gifu / Third sector railway
Miyazu	84.0	1990. 4. 1	Nishi Maizuru - Toyooka, Kyoto / Third sector railway
Kajiya	13.2	1990. 4. 1	Nomura - Kajiya, Hyogo / Bus
Hojo	13.8	1985. 4. 1	Ao - hojocho, Hyogo / Third sector railway
Wakasa	19.2	1987.10.14	Koge - Wakasa, Tottori / Third sector railway
Kurayoshi	20.0	1985. 4. 1	Kurayoshi - Yamamori, Tottri / Bus
Taisha	7.5	1990. 4. 1	Izumoshi - Taisha, Shimane / Bus
Gannichi	32.7	1987. 7.25	Kawanishi - Nishikicho, Yamaguchi / Third sector railway
Komatsushim	1.9	1985. 3.14	Chuden - Komatsushima, Tokushima / Bus

Nakamura	43.4	1988. 4. 1	Kubokawa - Nakamura, Kohchi / Third sector railway
Katsuki	3.5	1985. 4. 1	Nakama - Katsuki, Fukuoka / Bus
Muroki	11.2	1985. 4. 1	Ongagawa - Muroki, Fukuoka / Bus
Miyada	5.3	1989.12.23	Katsuno - Chikuzen Miyada, Fukuoka / Bus
Ita	16.2	1989.10. 1	Nogata - Tagawa Ita, Fukuoka / Third sector railway
Itoda	6.9	1989.10. 1	Kanada - Tagawa Gotoji, Fukuoka / Third sector railway
Tagawa	26.3	1989.10. 1	Yukuhashi - Tagawa Ita, Fukuoka / Third sector railway
Soeda	12.1	1985. 4. 1	Kawara - Soeda, Fukuoka / Bus
Urushio	7.9	1986. 4. 1	Shimokamoo - Shimoyamada, Fukuoka / Bus
Kamiyamada	25.9	1988. 9. 1	Iizuka - Buzen Kawasaki, Fukuoka / Bus
Katsuta	13.8	1985. 4. 1	Yoshizuka - Chikuzen Katsuta, Fukuoka / Bus
Amagi	14.0	1986. 4. 1	Kiyama - Amagi, Fukuoka / Third sector railway
Matsuura	93.9	1988. 4. 1	Arita - Sasebo, Nagasaki, Saga / Third sector railway
Saga	24.1	1987. 3.28	Saga - Setaka, Saga, Fukuoka / Bus
Yabe	19.7	1985. 4. 1	Hainuzuka - Kuroki, Fukuoka / Bus
Yunomae	24.9	1989.10.1	Hitoyoshi - Yunomae, Kumamoto / Third sector railway
Yamano	55.7	1988. 2. 1	Minamata - Kurino, Kumamoto, Kagoshima / Bus
Miyanojo	66.1	1987. 1.10	Sendai - Satsuma Okuchi, Kagoshima / Bus
Osumi	98.3	1987. 3.14	Shibushi - Kokubu, Kagoshima / Bus
Shibushi	38.6	1987. 3.28	Nishi Miyakonojo - Shibushi, Kagoshima, Miyazaki / Bus
Tsuma	19.3	1984.12. 1	Sadowara - Sugiyasu, Miyazaki / Bus
Takachiho	50.1	1989. 4.28	Nobeoka - Takachiho, Miyazaki / Third sector railway
Takamori	17.7	1986. 4. 1	Tateno - Takamori, Kumamoto / Third sector railway
Miyanoharu	26.6	1984.12. 1	Era - Higo Oguni, Oita, Kumamoto / Third sector railway

Sources ; Unyusho (MoT), Kotsu Tokei Kenkyujyo (ITS)

APPENDIX 3   SELECTED PROVINCIAL LINE MAP

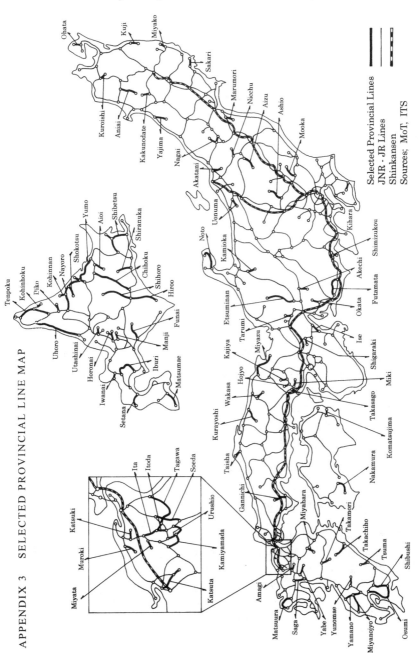

Selected Provincial Lines
JNR - JR Lines
Shinkansen
Sources; MoT, ITS

5

Issues After JNR Reform

The six JR passenger railway companies and the Japan Freight Railway Company ended their first year with their accounts showing excellent results. All seven companies exceeded their first targets and made profits, the combined total of which was 151.6 billion yen, four times the level projected in the initial plans.

The mass media and the public welcomed these reports. Together with examples of improved services and a more dynamic development of rail business, the results were seen as evidence of the new spirit within JR companies resulting from the privatization of JNR.

On the other hand, a close examination of these reports reveals aspects which cannot be viewed with much optimism. JR Hokkaido, Shikoku and Kyushu made large operating losses of almost 100 billion yen, reflecting the fact that the structure of railway operations in these areas has not changed. Moreover, while the Freight Railway Company is reported to have achieved a notable swing into profit, its revenues were 9 billion yen less than the year before. True, freight revenues have been falling every year since 1980, and the latest drop of 9 billion yen shows that this long-term trend remains unchanged (although the rate of fall was slightly smaller than in the past).

The first annual results of each JR company should be seen in the context of the various measures and systems that were adopted in breaking up and privatising the former JNR. One purpose of these measures was to even out profit differentials due largely to the differences in the economic prosperity of each area. The results show that these measures and systems have worked as well as expected. Of course, great operating efforts are assumed, but the results do mean that only 'artificial balance' has been achieved.

In the set of accounts of JNR in 1986/87 – its last year in business – the ordinary loss – the balance after deducting the abnormal expenses incurred by retirement allowances and pension fund contributions as well as capital expenses for the Tohoku and Joetsu Shinkansen lines – stood at 56.1 billion yen, a loss on top of the existing 19.7 trillion yen of long-term liabilities.

With the conversion of JNR to the JR companies, the debt was taken over by the three companies operating in the Honshu region and the freight company, and the total amount was reduced to 4.4 trillion yen. (The remainder was apportioned as a debt of the JNR Settlement Corporation.)

To deal with the huge operating losses of Hokkaido, Shikoku and Kyushu, a Management Stability Fund (Keiei Antei Kikin) of approximately one trillion yen was created. In 1987/88, these three JR companies received from the JNR Settlement Corporation an amount equal to the operating income of this fund to be counted as non-operating revenues. They thereby realized not only a balance of income and expeditures but also some profit.

The Freight Railway company conducted its business operations – and made profits – by using 10,000 kilometres of tracks belonging to the passenger railway companies. However, the charge paid by the freight company were only for the so-called 'avoidable costs' thereby allowing the company to use the facilities of other companies at a relatively low cost. Moreover, at the time of conversion, the assets allocated to the freight company were entered at their lowest possible value to minimise the depreciation costs and the interest that was payable.

As for the three companies in Honshu – JR East, JR Tokai, and JR West – a balance of income and expenditure was achieved by pooling a part of the revenues from the Shinkansen operations of the Shinkansen Holding Corporation. Each of the JR companies was a separate private business, but they were still as one at the basic management level, held together by an internal subsidising system for the group, a system inherited from JNR and designed to cope with differences in terms of business areas and lines.

If the term 'private company' means 'controlled by market forces', the actual operating conditions of the new JR companies were remote from the concept. Some financial aspects of these companies were quite peculiar in not following what would be considered normal in railway operations.

In JR Tokai, for example, the revenue from the Shinkansen operations accounted for as much as 86 per cent of the company's total operating revenues. However, the source of these revenues, namely, the Shinkansen facilities, was not owned by the company except for the rolling stock. As a result, the cost of leasing the remaining facilities accounted for 52 per cent of the total expenses of the company. Such a large amount of fixed costs reduces the company's freedom to adapt to changing business conditions and consequently restricts its independence. The lease charges were reviewed every other year, but if the number of passenger kilometres were to increase, the charges would be raised correspondingly: clearly this is no incentive for a private company.

Because the company does not own some of its facilities, it cannot claim depreciation costs on them. Thus, JR Tokai was paying a large amount of rent on the one hand while on the other, it could not run an internal fund to maintain or renew the facilities some of which had been in service for 25 years.

The Management Stability Fund worked well in the initial year and helped the companies in the three islands to avoid making losses, but it was a double-edged sword. JR Hokkaido depended on the fund for one-third of its revenue. There was no problem in 1987 because the company received an amount equal to its operating income from the JNR Settlement Corporation, and calculated at an interest rate of 7.3 per cent. From 1989/90, however, a gradual shift would be made towards operating the fund independently. This would mean variations in interest rates; with a 1 per cent drop, for example, operating revenue would have to be increased by nearly 10 per cent to cover the shortfall. A company with a structure in which its business results are influenced by the financial markets cannot be seen as an 'ordinary' company.

The JR companies would 'float' their shares in due course. The question then was what role, if any, would be played by the internal system of subsidies once the companies became completely independent.

Though all the JR companies made profits during their first year of operation, conditions will change as time passes; inflexible standards would be a handicap and prevent them from functioning in ways typical of private companies. Hence, measures were required to ensure that these companies could adapt and keep abreast of new developments.

In analysing the cause which led to the collapse of JNR management, the JNR Restructuring Supervisory Committee found that 'it could not cope properly with the changes of the times ... in spite of changes in the environment of the railway business.' The importance of this issue remains the same for JR as it was for JNR.

As the systems with JR companies evolve, the right direction of management suited to the characteristics of each company will become apparent. In a sense, the game has just begun.

'Overcoming a colossal organization' was always a major problem for the JNR management to solve. During the decade from 1955, repeated attempts were made toward decentralized operation. The 'branch' system for wide-area management, and the 'control centre' and 'head controller' systems of line management, were among the efforts to promote the independence of local management and to remedy the drawbacks of extreme centralization and a vertical control structure. These measures achieved good results in their own way by motivating local management and helping to ensure the prosperity of JNR during that time.

However, decentralization under the structure of JNR was limited by such factors as nationally uniform fares and wages: it was not possible to set fares and wages which took account of local operating conditions. These were the kinds of obstacles which JNR could not surmount.

The JNR Restructuring Supervisory Committee in its Urgent Report pointed out that 'there is a possibility that uniform fares may weaken the business foundations in fields where railways should be able to allow for their special characteristics, and also cause unfair conditions for competition.' The report went on to note that 'fares should be differentiated after careful consideration of costs.'

Although the division of management has been achieved, the JR companies have not yet cleared this hurdle. JR fares were a legacy from JNR and were applied uniformly everywhere and set purely from the viewpoint of balancing income and expenses for the country as a whole.

This cannot be appropriate in view of differences in local conditions. The process by which each company sets its own fares in the future is one which will put to the test the real meaning of dividing up JNR in the first place.

Income and expenses of such and such a line? Losses incurred in freight transportation? These are unnecessary points for discussion. We see JNR as a single organization. Nothing else need be said. Rigid ideas like these have hampered a proper understanding of the problems and the measures to cope with them. Relying only on balance sheets will not clarify the real problems with the result that the opportunity to solve such problems will be lost.

'In order to realize the dynamic operation of the railway business, it is necessasry to grasp the circumstances of operation in every area and business sector ... and to manage the business with a clear sense of costs and of the goal of profits,' asserts the JNR Restructuring Supervisory Committee.

The business of JR and the assets held by the JNR Settlement Corporation and Shinkansen Holding Corporation were public assets, built up as a result of customers using the services of JNR for more than a century. To cope with the structural problems, the understanding and support of the public were as indispensable in the future as they have been in the past.

The financial reports of the JR companies acknowledged that they had been helped by a fair wind in their first year. It is hoped JR will have the strength to achieve good results as circumstances change, even when ill winds blow.

The financial results of the new JR companies for their first fiscal year were much better than was expected. The main factors for these favourable results were: (1) the settling of liabilities, (2) the reduction in staff, and (3) upturn in the market due to general economic recovery. Although off to a good start, there are several issues still to be resolved in considering the course of events in the future.

REDEMPTION OF LIABILITIES AND RAISING OF FUNDS

As regards long-term liabilities, 25.0 trillion yen was determined as the original liabilities of JNR. Capital costs of the railway facilities of the Japan Railway Construction Public Corporation and the Honshu-Shikoku Construction Corporation, pension costs, and payments to the Management Stability Fund were added in to give a total of 37.2 trillion yen. Of this amount, 11.6 trillion yen (31 per cent of the total) was apportioned to the new companies, and 25.6 trillion yen (69 per cent) to the JNR Settlement Corporation. The lighter burden of long-term liabilities for the JR companies was good news to their management. However, 11.6 trillion yen was 46 per cent of the debt if we relate it to the original liabilities of JNR; (if pension costs were added, it would come to 38 per cent).

Paying off liabilities by the new companies was done in two ways: (1) by direct repayment, and (2) by a lease charge to the Shinkansen Holding Corporation. The amount to be repaid directly by the JR companies was 5.9 trillion yen and payment through the Shinkansen Holding Corporation 5.7 trillion. If the figures are kept down to JNR's original debt, the amount to be paid directly would be 4.8 trillion yen, and the amount to be paid through Shinkansen 3.9 trillion. Thus, the new JR companies would only have to pay 8.7 trillion yen, or 34 per cent of the 25.0 trillion of JNR's debt. Public discussion of this issue often did not distinguish clearly between the total burden of 11.6 trillion yen, the burden of JNR's original debt of 8.7 trillion and the inerhited liabilities of 4.8 trillion.

Of the 4.8 trillion yen debt inherited from JNR, 3.3 trillion was allocated to the East Japan Railway Company (JR East) while the JR companies in the three islands of Hokkaido, Shikoku and Kyushu, inherited absolutely nothing. JR East had the profitable Tokyo metropolitan market, and is thus capable of repaying debts; its amount of inherited liabilities was amongst the heaviest. The new companies have all put much effort into repaying their debts, and have also been able to reduce interest payments.

Even companies that have not enjoyed a large increase in revenue have got on with repaying their debts: their capital investment has been financed in such a way as to reduce the total debt and this (combined with the change in the depreciation system) to a fixed per cent method. The repayment of long-term liabilities led to a shrinkage in fixed assets which was in line with the expectation that efficiency calls for as little operating assets as possible. Assets made available by funding from local government were settled as advanced depreciation.

During the JNR era, methods for financing capital spending were extremely limited, and made for the rigid financial condition of JNR. Reform has opened the door to a variety of funding methods, the primary aim being the successful floating of shares.

Meantime, bonds had to be issued. The new companies have another goal, namely, to raise their net-worth ratio.

Repayment of liabilities through lease charges had some beneficial impact on the JR companies, especially Central Japan Railway Company (JR Tokai) which operated Tokaido Shinkansen. There is less freedom to the company if debt payments are made through lease charges compared with the direct repayment of debts, and are counted as a fixed cost. Moreover, the charges and any revision of the charges, are enforced by an outside body, a matter of concern to the management. Another disadvantage of the leasing system is that the operating company cannot allow for the depreciation of assets owned by the Shinkansen Holding Corporation. This is an important issue where there has been no experience of leasing systems and also, where the accounting system of the lessor company is in its infancy. A new approach would also be necessary when deciding on passenger fares using the 'rate base' method.

DIVERSIFICATION OF OPERATION AND REGULATION ON FARES

The operation of private railway companies served as a model for JNR reform especially in respect to the regulation on fares and the development of their non-rail operations. The main private railway companies in Japan were based in metropolitan areas running city transportation services as well as other types of business. Before the Second World War, diversification projects were directed towards creating demand, to increase revenue from their main operation in the form of fares. In the post-war era, however, since fares had to be kept quite low as part of government policy, other related operations were expanded in order to boost profits.

The restraint on fares of private railways was strongest during the period right after the end of the Second World War but also later on during a time of high economic growth and inflation. The diversification of private rail business centered on the provision of services in areas such as real estate, hotels and the retail trade. After the oil crisis, some companies began to revert to their main business, and other operations were seen as a way to shift older employees to other services as well as to facilitate job rotation.

Since the fare increase in October 1962, the total cost has been the basis of which the fares of private railways have been fixed. The calculation is as follows: the operating expenses + non-operating expenses (excluding interest payment) + operational assets (excluding accumulated depreciation) × appropriate rate of return. This was traditional formula regulating public corporations where a fair return was determined by multiplying the 'rate base' by the appropriate rate of return. Both operating and non-operating expenses are costs in the operation of railways but interest payments which are difficult to apportion between the amount used for railway operation and for other businesses, have been treated in terms of a 'fair' return. The rate of return is decided by the regulator from outside the industry while for the electric power industry, for example, it is fixed at a certain rate; for private railway companies, it is determined every time there is a rise in fares.

The division between the main operation and other rail businesses was determined by looking at the rate base, or the net worth of assets used for the main operation. This method was introduced by the amendment to the regulations regarding accounting systems of regional railways, and implemented in March 1975. Monopolistic public utility companies, which provide services in other sectors, constitute something of a problem for anti-trust policies. The electric power and gas industries in Japan were subject to strict regulation concerning the operation of their other businesses. As competition is likely to increase, regulation in this field is likely to be strengthened.

When classifying the main operation and others business by reference to the assets used, there is some room to alter this division so as to benefit the operators. Diversification is undertaken either by the railway company itself or by subordinates, and this depends on factors such as labour management, business size, the market, and the potential for expansion: in real estate, for instance, it is generally shared between the railway operator and its subordinate. JR companies may co-operate with other private companies in this field.

A periodical fare increase may motivate operators to streamline their main business, but it also affects profits from one year to the next. A difference in profit in this way has an adverse impact on outside bodies, such as the stock markets. Private railways have made use of their real estate business to even out the amount of profit from one year to the next: for example, by varying the amount of land lots put up for sale. In doing this, however, business opportunities may be missed, and to avoid this the real estate business may be hired off to another company.

Many of the JR companies' subsidiary businesses have been troubled by labour problems. They have a potential surplus of labour but rationalising policies cannot be called off and a labour surplus does make job rotation easier. Deregulation of land use will make for more diversification into real estate business.

Private railway operations can offer a model for the new JR companies though there are differences between the two, especially in the volume and type of their rail service. Private railways operate mainly in monopolistic markets around metropolitan areas whereas JR companies face more competition and price-sensitive markets. More deregulation is called for especially on fares. The three rail companies in mainland Honshu make profits which cannot be matched by private operators, so that any attempt to aim for comparable profit would be inappropriate. In any case, the new companies must move ahead of the private railways and develop their own style of business.

JR East, JR West and JR Freight – all large operting companies – are keen to decentralize their management. The three JR companies in the smaller islands (Hokkaido, Kyushu and Shikoku) inherited unprofitable lines, and the relationship between the passenger companies and the freight company is not without its problems.

6

The Problems of JNR as a
Public Corporation

JNR RECONSTRUCTION REGARDING ITS FUNCTIONS AND
FINANCE MOVING BEYOND PRECONCEIVED IDEAS

In the 1970s 'second thoughts' about macro-economic theory began to appear: it was reported that in the United States very few professors of economics were teaching the same theory as five years earlier. These changes accompanied actual economic events; a theory becomes useless if it ignores reality, no matter how attractive it may seem on paper. If we are unable to accept reality on account of preconceived ideas, how can we develop new policies to deal with any problems facing us?

Looking back at the 70s, 'concepts' about the problems of JNR management and their causes were studied closely and extensively; at the same time various preconceived ideas were in circulation which led to no changes in the actual situation.

It is perhaps inappropriate to examine the problems of JNR – how local lines operating at a loss should be treated, for example – purely from the viewpoint of JNR management, and we should not insist upon a balance of revenues and expenditures. At the same time, JNR's characteristics as a public service provider cannot be ignored. But these and other principles can only be relevant when the national finances are in good shape and adequate funds are allocated to JNR from tax revenues. Financial policies which enable JNR not be solely concerned about the balance of revenues and expenditures are necessary.

National financial and economic forecasts in the 1980s indicated that sufficient financial support would not be forthcoming. The rapid growth of the economy was abating and national revenues had become highly dependent on borrowing. The national budgetary deficit for the fiscal year 1979 was predicted to be 60 trillion yen. However strongly it may be argued that JNR management should base its decisions on national policy concerns, much fiercer competiton for financial resources could now be expected from other fields. Even if JNR management were to feel little concern about balancing its own budget, it could never function independently of national finances. However, if management does not attend to balancing revenues and expenditures, it would be inclined to overlook costs. Even if only some of the management were to act in this way, the consequences could be serious.

As a general rule, the public welfare should not be seen in terms of financial considerations, but this does not mean that financial concerns should be ignored. The critical question is how to provide the proper financial framework for the provision of these services. If any costs are to be passed on to the public, through taxation for example, it is even more important to be aware of the costs so that they can be minimized.

It is difficult to deal with the problems of JNR management and JNR's reconstruction in terms of JNR as a single entity or in the context of the entire organization. The geographical scope of JNR's activities is very wide – and likewise its contacts with society – so that problems and conditions can vary greatly from one place to another. Apart from its legal attribute, JNR as a single entity is not realistic. Although the general statement, the 'reconstruction of JNR' is used, what needs to be reconstructed is not JNR as a whole, but each of its separate functions. If they can be carried out successfully, financial reconstruction will be easier to undertake. Reconstructing JNR functions must be based on the merits of the railway as a transportation system being properly recognised and developed in terms of actual conditions, varied as they are. This is how private organizations survive and prosper. This points to the one path that reconstruction can take.

THE ESSENCE OF STREAMLINING MANAGEMENT

In 1965 Sanyo Special Steel Co., Ltd., the second largest company in the special steel industry, made use of the Stock Company Reorganization and Rehabilitation Act. The company was on the brink of bankruptcy with a total debt of 4.6 billion yen, the largest since the end of the Second World War. Just twelve years later, in

November 1977, Sanyo had repaid its debt and completed its reorganization – and this in five years less than projected.

This was not an easy task. Many thought that reorganization would be impossible even though the company enjoyed high productivity and well-developed technology as well as having a large share of the ball-bearing market.

In the course of reorganization the company changed its product lines drastically, focusing on the areas where it was strongest and investing as much as 9 billion yen to increase its capacity to manufacture steel pipes. Annual sales increased sharply from 18.7 billion yen to 100 billion by 1980.

The company was fortunate to have favourable external factors but it was the management who took advantage of the conditions facing them.

Reconstructing a company brings to mind the concept of streamlining management, and this in turn implies a reduction in the number of employees. Whether reconstruction succeeds, however, depends less on whether the number of employees is reduced than on whether the company is then able to redevelop its business, and continue to do so.

In November 1979, the *Nihon Keizai Shimbun* (a Japanese business daily) carried the following report:

> Sasebo Heavy Industries Co., Ltd. held its first orientation on the 19th to recruit staff currently employed by the *Nagasaki Shipyard* of *Rinken Shipbuilding Co., Ltd.* but who wish to retire from that company. The meeting was held in vain, however, because no applicants showed up.

By that time, as many as 3,000 employees had left Saseboy Heavy Industries, reducing to half the number of persons employed in its heyday. The shortgage of workers had begun to cause problems at the dockyard. If reconstruction meant only a reduction in the number of employees, Sasebo Heavy Industries would have already completed reconstruction at the time it started to recruit more workers. Its subsequent development indicated that this was not the case.

The essence of streamlining management lies in eliminating activities that have become unnecessary, and integrating management functions. Streamlining is otherwise merely shrinking in size.

A Cabinet decision on the reconstruction of the Japanese National Railways in December 1979 declared the objective as the reduction in the number of personnel from 420,000 to 350,000 by 1985. According to the *Basic Reconstruction Plan* for JNR, this would reduce personnel costs to the same level as at the time the revenues and costs were in balance and a basis for sound management would thereby be established. The question is, however, whether or not the *ratio* between revenues and expenses is improved. Operating revenue in 1979 was 2.6 trillion yen with 420,000 personnel. The reconstruction plan will have been effective only if revenue is much the same or more when the workforce has been reduced to 350,000. Will the smaller workforce be accompanied by the same or greater revenue (apart from other factors)? A strict policy is called for to identify priorities in the streamlining process. If the reduction in personnel is simply carried out uniformly in each area and in each department of management, the result is bound to be a poorly structured organization – some departments which should have been reduced and others which should not have been reduced or should even have been increased. The overall target may be achieved but the basic structure no better and the reconstruction plan unfulfilled.

Although streamlining management seems to move things backward at first glance, it contains the potential to energise the business, and if this materialises, then reconstruction will succeed.

BLIND SPOTS IN ACCOUNTING SYSTEMS

Conclusions based on statistical analysis can differ – even if the data are consistent and accurate – depending on the way in which the raw data has been treated. Even completely different conclusions can be drawn from the same data. Great care should therefore be taken in reading and interpreting information, especially numbers.

The US Navy is said to have once launched a recruitment campaign publicizing the fact that the death rate was lower in the navy than among New York citizens. The mortality rate of New York citizens at the time was sixteen per thousand; that of the navy during the Spanish-American War nine per thousand. The data on which the recruiting figures were based were accurate, but the New York citizens included infants and the elderly, which made its death rate higher. Though the data are about the same subject – death rates – they were used in a crude and misleading way. Manipulating data to obtain an acceptable result is a form of statistical sophistry. There is too the simple misreading of information and quite unintentionally.

In management accounting, for example, both the purpose and the method of calculation are important. To draw conclusions by analyzing and evaluating only the results while neglecting to consider the relationship of those results to the purpose of the exercise, is pointless and sometimes harmful. Some would question JNR's cost accounting system. The system is designed to present the actual amounts of total revenue and costs as they relate to overall transportation activities, a system with a limited purpose and usage. Nevertheless, not a few people draw hasty conclusions from the figures. Repeated alarms have been made that something is wrong with the system. Thus, the ratio of revenues and expenses used by the system results in misleading figures that show a rise in the deficit as the number of passengers increases. Similarly, complaints are made that the current method for calculating costs of individual lines is rather odd because even if a line is closed, the cost of the line is not eliminated because the costs of stations, yards, administration and so on would still be relevant. Figures based on past results cannot be directly applied to this situation, as is true when making estimates for special situations. It is wrong to conclude the system is worthless for it depends on the use to which the system can be properly put. To arrive at the pros and cons of closing a line or not, we should take into account avoidable costs and work out the marginal costs of this or that service.

No single system is ever suited to answer all types of questions. If any one of them was used to deal with every problem many situations would simply not be properly addressed. The question is not about the best accounting system but what is the purpose of any one system and to what uses can it be properly put.

In discussions about the reconstruction of JNR, its annual balance sheets are used to suggest that management has deteriorated, leading to the conclusion that reconstruction is not possible and should be abandoned. This conclusion stems from a misunderstanding of the data for management purposes. A balance sheet is a summary of management activity over the past twelve months. Reconstruction, however, is about the future. However we study the current JNR balance sheets, the case for or against reconstruction will never be adequately made from these alone.

The amount of information about JNR and its activities is vast, and this includes not only data about the past but forecasts about the future. It is not an easy task to get all this into the right perspective so that it can be properly analyzed and evaluated.

THE GESTATION PERIOD OF RAILWAY INVESTMENT

'Sailing up the Kushiro River, we reached Shibecha at last, then on to Naka-Shibetsu making our way through the tall, thick bush cover . . .' Thus a farming report described the Nemuro wilderness in about 1919. In the next few years up to the mid-1920s, 8,400 farming families settled on this wild plain – 3,000 square kilometres in area or 1.3 times the size of Kanagawa Prefecture – located in eastern Hokkaido and facing the Sea of Okhotsk.

Between 1933 and 1937, a railway 117 kilometres in length was constructed along the Nemuro Plain. The standard of living in the area was so bereft of modern conveniences in those days that a candidate for the Hokkaido Assembly made a promise to 'bring electricity to the wilderness of Nemuro.' For a long time, however, only the railway had been provided.

Although the role of a railway as a pioneer in regional development is often noted, a case of regional development being preceded by a railway in this way is rare in Japan. No other case is so good an example of the value of the railway – its benefit to society and its limitations.

Many years have passed since then. The former wilderness is now dotted with farms, and a two-lane paved road stretches through herds of cattle. In Nemuro, the total length of paved roads is 450 kilometres, a length per person which is nearly three times the national average and even far greater than that of former West Germany – and much of this can be attributed to the impact of investment in Hokkaido's development. These roads are used by about 20,000 private vehicles, and more and more women drivers are to be seen. Although pedestrian-crossings are not all that common, there are many 'cow-crossing's, a rarity elsewhere in Japan. Compared with a total population of 45,000 for Bekkai, Naka-Shibetsu and Shibetsu towns, the Nemuro district has 100,000 head of cattle, not an irrelevant figure for transportation purposes. The vast expanse of land and low population density have resulted in an American style of transport which is motorized to an extent that is exceptional in Japan. And this has occurred in the very place where a lot of investment in railway services was made ahead of general development. This is relevant to transportation theory and demonstrates how the choice of transportation modes has changed over time.

Railway investment has a long gestation period, but this concept often causes confusion in recognizing and solving transportation problems.

The minimum unit of railway construction, even for demand that is very small, is a single line, providing about 80 operations a day. Hence, following the completion of construction, there is usually a gap which could be quite long between the capacity of the railway and the amount of demand, and this takes time to bridge. The notion of a gestation period in railway development refers to this feature of railway services on the provider's side, and not to the specific conditions of demand. There is no basis for claiming that the demand for rail services is somehow different from that of other modes of transportation such as automobiles. While it is true that demand sufficient to make a line feasible as a means of transportation takes time to grow, this does not occur simply with the passage of time. Indeed, changes in the social and economic environment of the area where a railway is located may be such that the railway may never flourish as a mode of transportation.

Merely constructing a line and waiting will not necessarily mean that the number of railway users will rise and rise; on the contrary, the number may diminish. This is what happened in the case of the Shibetsu Line which was closed down in 1980.

MISUNDERSTANDING RESULTING FROM THE UNIFORM
RATE SYSTEM

The rate system of JNR has for long been based upon a system whereby any losses incurred by some lines were compensated for by profits from other lines, mainly trunk lines. However, a recent paper on the subject has again argued that such a standpoint is based on a misconception, and that losses incurred by lines running at a loss should, in fact, be compensated for by profits derived from overall services through the establishment of a rational rate system for JNR as a whole, though it is unclear what type of system would conform to this description. JNR had a uniform national rate which aimed to balance costs and revenues for the system as a whole.

This was convenient for management divisions where losses were a normal state of affairs. In spite of its appearance as a user-orientated system it resulted in odd situations; for example, at the western entrance of Shinjuku Station a ticket for Hachioji cost 440 yen at one ticket office while at another next to it a ticket for the same destination cost 220 yen. The former ticket was issued by JNR and the latter by the Keio Line, a private operator whose track ran almost parallel to JNR's. What was the reason for this difference in rates? Costs did not differ to the extent of being twice in one service over another. The reason was not that costs differed but that one of the parallel tracks belonged to JNR which also operated the nationwide network. The higher fare was merely a reflection of the policy that JNR users should share the cost of nationwide management equally in the section between Shinjuku and Hachioji. The focus here was not on how to run the two lines efficiently as parts of the metropolitan transportation network but that all JNR customers should pay equally on a pro rata basis, whether travelling on the Chuo Line in Tokyo or on the Ibusuki Line in southern Kyushu.

A manager of a private company told the following story:

> Because a traffic jam was reported on the highway, I bought a ticket for the Hankyu Line, a private railway line from Sannomiya in Kobe to Kyoto, for 350 yen. When I returned by JNR, however, I was surprised to find that the fare was 860 yen, two and a half times higher than the Hankyu Line. As is well known, the level of service provided by JNR is not consistent with the higher rate and illustrates the difference between private and national management.

It was the inflexible uniform rate system that generated this type of criticism of JNR, and it was easy to conclude that the difference in rates reflected a difference in management efficiency. The impression that JNR was insufficient was widely held. While JNR made efforts to improve its image, spending a lot of money and using the media as the publicity vehicle, to allow negative impression to continue was ill judged since its impact was by no means insignificant.

It would have been difficult to abandon the long-standing

attachment to the uniform rate system overnight. Some contended that in such a huge enterprise as JNR, discussions were in order with respect to reducing costs as a whole, but that the apportionment of costs made no sense since there was no reliable accounting system to do this.

In a railway business, costs can not be attributed exclusively or accurately to individual lines or types of transportation service. However, the degree of inaccuracy need not be serious and certainly does not excuse or warrant the situation where fares are sometimes so different from those charged by private railways for comparable services, and for reasons that are unclear and difficult to understand. What may be seen as social capital is an important element of metropolitan transportation, and the capacity of a double-track railway should be used to the full. This is not something that should simply be left to the choice of the individual user.

RATIONALIZATION AND UNPROFITABLE SERVICES

The most common points of criticism made against JNR management, especially concerning its rationalization, can be summarized as follows: JNR should make more effort to reduce its deficit by improving its style of management, the organisation of its workforce and work methods, and so on; it was odd that the prime cause of JNR's deficit was the local lines; and JNR should make a greater effort to streamline its operations before considering closing down any of its lines.

These criticisms were based on two sets of perceptions and judgements. The first was the view that JNR's moves toward rationalization were always inadequate as long as a deficit was not eliminated. The concurrent judgement was that the deficit could be reduced simply by making the right efforts in the future. The second view was that rationalization should not result in any change or decline in the current level of services provided by JNR. Thus it was thought both possible and desirable for JNR to carry out a radical rationalization without altering the scale of its operations or range of services. Was this a realistic option? True, rationalization could be undertaken on a small scale but not in this case.

Since 1975/76, JNR has suffered 900 billion yen in losses

annually which meant that about one-third of its operating costs were not met out of revenues. This situation could not be remedied by rationalization limited to changing current methods of operation and on a small scale. Opinions that fail to take into account the seriousness of the situation could not provide a proper perspective on the prospects and future turning points of JNR, except as an expression of hopes and desires or to provide a framework for discussions of principles among those who are merely observers.

The number of personnel employed by British Rail (BR) is reported to have fallen to 240,000, less than half the figure of 500,000 in 1963 when BR was reorganized as a public corporation. The view that JNR's rationalization is as yet half-hearted compared with BR and that JNR should follow BR's example cannot be dismissed out of hand. It is true that the number of personnel in the *railway division* alone decreased from 476,000 in 1963 to 182,000 at the end of 1989, a reduction of about 300,000 in seventeen years. Even excluding the 37,000 personnel within the *railway factories* which were separated from the *railway division* as a subsidiary, and the 26,000 personnel of the *small-lot freight division* which was absorbed into the *British Freight Corporation* in the process of reorganizing the country's nationalised transportation network under the 1968 *Transportation Act*, the net decrease in the number of personnel in the *railway division* was nevertheless as large as 230,000, a cutback of 56 per cent. JNR should seek to emulate this performance.

The question remains, however, whether such a drastic reduction in the number of personnel was promoted without regard to other policies including assessing the organization's scope of business activities. Could such achievement be realized without lowering the level of operating services, as called for by those in Japan who consider JNR's rationalization inadequate? Over the years mentioned above, the length of BR's operating lines decreased from 27,000 to 18,000 kilometres, the number of stations fell from 6,400 to 2,800, and freight stations were reorganized so drastically that their number declined from 4,600 to about 470. These data suggest that BR made a thorough re-examination of the scope of its activities, aiming at reorganizing its functions and system for the years ahead. Ordinary citizens always expect that current transport services will be improved indefinitely, and that any reduction in services is unacceptable for any number of reasons. The reality is usually far more severe.

Does some ideal form of rationalization exist where a financial reconstruction of JNR is undertaken while the current level of services is maintained? The result would perhaps not be similar to the fate that befalls someone who tries to chase two hares at once. It is more likely that to indulge in wishful thinking over the long term results in greater delays in dealing with the fundamentals of the existing situation on a day-to-day basis. The day is surely not far off when a choice will have to be made between the two.

A BIRD'S-EYE VIEW OF JNR'S SETTLEMENT OF ACCOUNTS

A meandering river sometimes heads north and sometimes south, even as the river itself flows to the west. To decide from some point along the bank where the water happens to be flowing north that the river itself follows the same direction to its end, is too hasty a conclusion and can result in inaccurate judgements. The same can be said in identifying and evaluating trends in business management.

From the published financial accounts for JNR for 1979/80, the results of some of JNR's management efforts are evident even in the summarized data: for example, that the annual general net loss amounted to 81.7 billion yen less than in the previous year; that container freight traffic showed an increase of 111 per cent over the same period, the highest rate of increase in recent years; and that among operating costs, personnel costs increased only 104 per cent in spite of the implementation of an arbitration award and an increase in retirement allowances.

Although a single year's results can be described in this way, the fluctuations in any one year are not as important as knowing the direction in which the management is heading as a whole. Especially when attempting to discern the trend of an organization as big as JNR, an overall view is necessary. Without a bird's-eye view of management over a relatively long period of time, an accurate picture of trends cannot be made and some aspects will be impossible to evaluate. Thus, by taking a bird's-eye view and extending the time period from one to five years, minor or temporary phenomena disappear and only the essential changes are revealed. Five years is considered the minimum time period to monitor the business activities of an entity as large as JNR. What then are the issues revealed by the recent five-year history of JNR?

First is the change in passenger traffic. The extension of the Shinkansen ('Bullet Train') Line to Hakata was completed in March 1975, and although operating kilometres increased sharply by 70 per cent with the newly-constructed 465 kilometres between Okayama and Hakata, passenger taffic rose only slightly from 40.7 billion passenger kilometres in 1974/75 to 41 billion in 1979/80. On the other hand, ordinary passenger traffic on the regular lines decreased from 101.1 billion to 77.2 billion passenger kilometres. This decrease was a direct consequence of the shift of express passengers to the extended Shinkansen, but at the same time it was a reflection of the continuing decline in demand for JNR's services even among intercity passengers using local trunk lines. Moreover, the situation is even more serious than it first appears because in the case of the Shinkansen – to which the passenger traffic has shifted – the extension beyond Okayama has not produced any significant increase in total traffic.

The second issue is the increase in the value of fixed assets. The year-end book value of these assets now exceeds 11.2 trillion yen, an increase of 4.2 trillion over the past five years. Of course, long-term liabilities have also increased. These liabilities (including loans corresponding to the amount of accumulated losses each year) have increased by as much as 7.2 trillion yen in the same period. Included in JNR's liabilities are investments in facilities that will represent an increase in both the quality and quantity of business activities. In particular, investments newly made in the process of reconstruction will have been decided upon by management with a clear goal in mind, and not simply entered upon by reference to past circumstances.

The third issue is that though there is an overall increase in losses, the number of profitable lines has increased. Five years ago, only three lines were profitable – the Shinkansen, the Yamanote Line, and the Takasaki Line (totalling 1,299 kilometres in length); that profit came to about 166 billion yen. Last year, however, eight lines totalling 1,950 kilometres in length made as much as 361.6 billion yen in profit. At a time when almost everything else seemed to be going against JNR's management, this increase was the only bright spot. The fact that some of the lines improved their profitability in spite of worsening overall losses clearly shows that the railway is still an effective mode of transportation – especially in areas where mass transportation is the case. It also shows that for certain levels of traffic demand, a railway can be financially viable as a provider of transportation services. Roughly speaking, a profit of 361.6 billion yen is sufficient to cover the losses of unprofitable lines, which represent about 80 per cent of passenger transportation and 70 per cent of freight transportation services. In other words, the tax money paid to JNR every year is used for the remaining 20 per cent of passengers and 30 per cent of freight. The question is one of balancing tax allocations between various uses within the framework of the national finances.

Losses in areas other than in mass transportation will continue to grow. The division between the two areas have become more pronounced, not just in principle but as a reality for management.

WHAT LIES AT THE CORE OF JNR'S PROBLEMS?

Acknowledging exactly what the real problem for JNR is and where its core lies is not easy. Many different opinions are held by various people on everything from the current conditions of JNR to the possibility of its reconstruction, but some cannot be the basis for effective proposals.

Some of these viewpoints on the reconstruction of JNR are based on the following reasoning:

> Because JNR, in the form of a public corporation, incurs huge losses every year, the only way to solve its problems is to change the form of management. To accomplish this, only two means can be considered: privatisation and nationalisation (a form in which JNR was operated before World War II). To divide and privatise JNR is not realistic; thus the only option is nationalisation. It is wiser to concede this than to continue with an illusion – the idea of reconstruction.

In this approach, the fact that losses are incurred by a public corporation is confused with the notion that it is the public form of the corporation which is creating the losses. The causes of JNR's losses are not so simple, nor can they be assumed to disappear if JNR's management were nationalised. Common sense suggests that the operation of a national organization is not as efficient as that of a corporation. Although it is easier for a national corporation to utilize tax revenues, nationalising JNR simply because it is a more convenient way to pay for losses would not lessen the burden on taxpayers. Furthermore, in the light of the national finances, it is difficult to imagine that JNR's management would be allowed to disregard losses simply because it has become a nationalised organization. Thus, there seems no reason to conclude that a nationally-owned railway would be inadequately provided for as a public service organization unless its management were also nationalised. In any case, the means for resolving this problem will not be discovered while we ignore the question: how can adequate transportation services be provided at least cost to the people?

Another example of this kind of thinking which is evident in discussions of local line problems, relates to the significance these lines have in the local areas. A withering peach tree cannot be saved by dwelling on the value of the fruit – what is necessary is to water the tree. With respect to local lines, there is a similar distinction to be made between what lies at the core of their problems and the value of their existence. The point is not to judge their importance to local areas but to clarify who should bear the costs of local lines since vast sums of money are required to maintain these services to the benefit of local areas. Some people contend that the nation as a whole should bear these costs and others that JNR should do so. The money paid by the nation to support local lines comes from the taxpayers and the general public; JNR has no source of revenue of its own other than fares paid by users – in this case, users in other areas. Although the trend has been to shift as much responsibility as possible on to government or the corporate world, this does by-pass direct discussion with those who are really paying the costs and thereby delays finding a solution to the problems. How should the costs of maintaining local lines be borne? The answer may generate new forms of social unfairness and tensions. To establish a national consensus in response to this question is important.

Marcus Aurelius, the philosopher and emperor of Rome in the second century A.D., made the following observation in his *Meditations*:

> The healthy eye ought to see all visible things and not to say, 'I wish for green things'; for this is the condition of a diseased eye.[1]

If one insists on seeing only what one likes, the current situation will not be changed. The railways should be seen as they actually are and not through rose-coloured spectacles.

ALIGNING ACCOUNTING PRACTICES WITH THOSE OF THE
PRIVATE SECTOR

While operating losses sustained by JNR in 1979/80 (according to the published income statement) amounted to 842.5 billion yen, the trial audit report showed operating losses at 362 billion. What is the reason for this difference? The audit report explains that the trial balance was obtained by reallocating the subsidies and interest to non-operating revenues and losses. In effect, this applies the accounting method of the private sector to JNR. It is said that this enables the operating results of JNR to be analyzed in a way similar to those of private companies – that is to say, in the absence of the advantages and disadvantages to which JNR is subject as a public corporation. In other words, the purpose is to evaluate the management of JNR by putting its accounts into a form that makes it comparable to that of private companies. However, the form of a set of accounts is meant to embody management practices. To bring JNR's accounting method into line with that of private companies does not change the nature or quality of the contents of the accounts. The critical question is whether each accounting item is given a meaning comparable to that of the private sector.

On the trial balance sheet, for example, all categories of expenditure were counted as non-operating costs. It is true that some types of interest, such as those incurred as a result of loans taken out to cover losses, should not be treated as operating costs. However, there are other interest payments which are related to investments in equipment – employing outside capital for operational purposes to promote modernization and rationalization – that lead to a reduction in personnel costs, service costs, repair costs, and so on. The interest expenditures of such activities could be considered as part of personnel and material costs and are costs necesssary for production. As Katsunosuke Moroi explains:

> To an enterprise which employs outside capital, the financial costs incurred in the course of its main business activities are the same as

material and labour costs. Thus, financial costs are related to operating revenues, not to non-operating revenues.

Some types of interest are similar to costs in this way, and the efficiency of a company which relies heavily on fixed assets cannot be clearly evaluated without considering this particular character-istic of interest expenditures.

The trial balance sheet also shifted government subsidies from operating to non-operating revenues. The subsidies that JNR receives from the government, however, are not all of the same kind. Although some are intended to cover losses, some should be regarded as compensation for the costs of activities that JNR has undertaken on behalf of the government. For this type of subsidy, corresponding costs exist. While the costs of 'proxy' activities are included in operating costs, removing all the corre-sponding revenues from operating revenues would be unjustified in terms of the principle that costs and revenues should be about the same activity. In fact, this undermines the purpose of the trial analysis which is to restructure the shape of JNR's management on the same basis as private companies.

In JNR's current accounting system – where the burden stem-ming from its role as a public corporation is reflected in all types of expenditures – moving an amount from one column to another alone would fail to portray the actual circumstances of the organ-ization's management. Although it appears that operating losses are reduced from 842.5 billion to 362 billion yen, both amounts are still strongly influenced by many factors outside the control of management. Hence, either approach is equally unclear in making an accurate assessment of which costs should be regarded as the direct responsibility of management. The key to JNR's reconstruc-tion lies in determining how to curtail the inefficiency and unprof-itability inherent in its management. JNR's inefficiency, however, does not stem only from internal factors; there are external influences. In this sense, JNR's management results should be analyzed using a method that is similar to that of private com-panies in the future. But this is not easy to achieve: simply following the private sector's form of accounting will not immedi-ately result in a statement of accounts corresponding to that of the private companies. The only way to isolate the external factors that influence JNR's accounts is to make precise analyses based on actual circumstances. It is not merely the form of the accounting system that matters but its actual content in respect to the responsibilities of management. Nor should we ignore in the case of private companies their single-minded pursuit of successful results and their recognition of the realities of management.

THE SPIRIT OF SELF-HELP

Many people had their way of life greatly disrupted by heavy snow in the winter of 1981. The *'Tensei Jingo'* column in a major Japanese daily, *Asahi Shimbun*, (on 25 January, 1981) told of a letter from a person who had been stranded in his car on the Hokuriku Expressway. Various questions and ideas had occurred to the driver as he sat stranded in his car and these the columnist passed on to the Japan Highway Public Corporation. The following is an excerpt from the driver's questions and the answers received from the corporation:

> Q: The time at which the highway would reopen should have been estimated and we should have been informed of this by a loud-speaker vehicle. The lack of information was annoying.
> A: How could a loud-speaker vehicle have been driven in such conditions?
> Q: Because they were afraid of running out of fuel, many drivers turned off their heaters and shivered in the cold night. Parents fed their babies orange juice because their thermos were emptied. Isn't it possible at least to provide fuel and hot water to stranded drivers in such an emergency?
> A: It is the drivers who should be prepared with sufficient fuel and hot water before going out to drive in the snow.

The drivers expect the Highway Corporation to look after them and the Corporation expects the drivers to be prepared and to fend for themselves. This is an example of the trend toward shifting responsibilities for unfortunate circumstances onto others. Rather than attributing their difficulties to the forces of nature, people are now pointing their fingers at each other. In fact, the attitude reflected in these questions and answers is rather strange.

At about the same time, a contribution to the readers' column of a newspaper read as follows:

> The other day, an accident occured in which a driver who had been stranded in his car because of deep snow and had kept the engine on,

died of carbon monoxide poisoning. It reminded me of something my Canadian friend told me – that drivers in Canada always carry a sleeping bag and a red flag in their cars in winter. If they get stuck in snow, they never leave the engine on, but instead hoist the red flag and wait to be rescued while sitting in the sleeping bag to keep warm. I thought your readers would find this information useful.

Last fall, a book called *A New Standpoint for the Development of Hokkaido and the Challenge of an Independent Economy* was published by the Hokkaido Future Research Institute. This is the result of a study led by a noted researcher, Shuzo Inaba, which was commissioned by the *Nihon Keizai Shimbun* (a Japanese business-oriented daily) to commemorate the tenth anniversary of its publication in Hokkaido. The development of Hokkaido began 110 years ago and there is no other area in Japan where national subsidies have continued to be provided for such a long time, and the amount of national expenditure spent in Hokkaido is very high indeed. Moreover, the economy of Hokkaido has not broken free from its deficit of expenditure over income. The sense that this is the normal state of affairs and that Hokkaido must there-fore always be supported by the nation has become deeply rooted. The book is of much interest because it dares to offer the 'challenge of an independent economy' as the standard for future development. The book observes:

> If the standard for public investment is efficiency, is there any basis for spending such a large amount of money in Hokkaido? The answer is no ... What if the standard is fairness in the sense of improving differences among various regions, rather than efficiency? In that case, the regions to which precedence should be given are southern Kyushu, northern Tohoku and San'in, not Hokkaido since the income level in Hokkaido, while relatively low, is nevertheless higher than those in these other regions.

The book makes a bold and vigorous analysis of current con-ditions and rigorously examines and criticizes the reasoning on which the development of Hokkaido is based.

Since local development is intended to attract population and industries, a change in population can be taken as an indicator in evaluating the effectiveness of that development. In Hokkaido, there has been hardly any growth in population since the mid-1950s. Regional income and expenditures showed a deficit of 1.3

trillion yen in 1975, 3.4 times the deficit of five years earlier. This shortfall is covered – the economy of Hokkaido saved from collapsing – by national subsidies which are not limited to the amount included in the national development budget. JNR, for example, has as many as 51,000 personnel in Hokkaido, as well as providing railway services throughout the region's vast expanse of mountains and plains. As the population of Hokkaido was about 5.3 million at that time, the figure of 51,000 personnel meant that one out of every hundred people in Hokkaido was a JNR employee. The history of JNR in Hokkaido is one of an ongoing mission in the face of this enormous burden. Times have changed over the years and any rise in expenditures from the national finances is constrained by the slowdown in national economic growth. The report emphasizes the importance of facing the fact that it is increasingly unrealistic to expect special treatment for Hokkaido in the future; private economic activity is also not encouraging. On the other hand, the book views these circumstances as an opportunity to consider new prospects, and from this viewpoint, it proposes the following:

> We would like to ask the people of Hokkaido to reconsider their tendency to rely on the nation based on a sense that the region suffers from an excessive number of handicaps, such as its remote location, heavy snow, and cold climate ... To establish a steady course toward greater independence, which Hokkaido will inevitably be forced into at some stage, it is necessary that the true frontier spirit of its people, and their determination to build a future entirely on their own, be fostered and strongly encouraged.

INSISTING ON JUST THE SENSE OF DIRECTION

Road maps usually indicate not only major expressways but also ordinary national roads, local main roads, prefectural roads, city, town and village roads, and even walking paths – and this by varying the width and colour of the lines that represent them, even showing whether or not they are paved. On railway maps, in contrast, all the trunk and branch lines, except for the Shinkansen ('Bullet Train'), are drawn with lines of the same width. Thus, railway maps show only how areas or places are connected; they do not show anything else about the lines such as their capacity or function.

During the heavy snowfall of 1963, trunk line services along the coast of the Sea of Japan were seriously disrupted in many areas, resulting in a lengthy suspension of railway services: only services on the Oito Line, located in a snowy mountainous area, were uninterrupted. This gave rise to a demand by local factories that JNR operate freight services on the Oito Line to the Kanto district. From a railway map alone, people would have no idea of the bad state of the Oito Line. For example, there was no way of knowing that it ran along the banks of the Hime River, or that its track was ill-suited to operate heavy trunk-line locomotives. What would happen if road maps were made in the same way, showing all roads in one and the same way. Drivers would have information only about direction from the maps and would choose what appeared to be the shortest route. Differences in actual road conditions, such as the width of the various roads, would create bottlenecks everywhere resulting in traffic jams and widespread confusion.

Opinions are often expressed that are based solely on ideas which – like a railway map – suggest no more than a direction, and even if the direction is right, proposals that fail to take account other important factors will also fail to deal with problems that actually exist.

A recent proposal – welcomed by the public – was that JNR could be reconstructed without raising fares. Indeed it was proposed that fares and charges should be reduced to attract more users and thereby increase revenues. Like a railway map, however, this proposal offers no more than a sign-post. Of course, some demand for JNR's services would be greater following a reduction in rates, and making its services more competitive. However, to conclude that the reconstruction of JNR is possible without raising fares is not all that relevant: the question as to whether or not reconstruction is possible is linked to the scale of the problem. However sound a proposal may be in itself, reconstruction would not be under consideration if the benefit of the proposal is not all that great.

Reducing fares will undoubtedly increase the number of users, but unless the increase is large enough to increase total additional revenue then even a fare increase should be considered. If fares are reduced by 40 per cent, a 67 per cent increase in the number of users would be required to compensate for the reduction in fares and ensure no fall in total revenue. Moreover, to provide more revenue, a growth in traffic of more than 80 per cent would be necessary. Even in metropolitan areas where there is a problem with overcrowding and in areas where the population is sparse, an 80 per cent increase in traffic would be required. Although a fare increase is no longer regarded as being vital to JNR's reconstruction, to applaud a fare reduction for its own sake is both naive and idealistic.

In a nationwide business like JNR, the local conditions of management and traffic flow vary greatly from area to area. Raising fares would be effective in some areas and reducing fares effective in others. If the individual characteristics of each area are disregarded simply because JNR is a nationwide organization and problems must therefore be uniformly dealt with throughout the country, neither raising nor reducing fares across the board can be a sensible measure in showing the direction that should be taken towards reconstruction.

CHANGING VIEWPOINTS

Around Lake Biwa are many tasteful old temples which, although not well known, are repositories for many images of Buddha which are considered first-class works of religious art. Among them is a wonderful image of *Jyuichimen Kannon* – the goddess of compassion with eleven heads – in Doganji Temple, located in a small forest surrounded by the rice fields of Takatsuki-cho on the northern shore of the lake. Unlike the forceful and domineering splendour – which Tetsuro Watsuji expressed as 'divine dignity' – of her image in Shorinji Temple in sakurai-city, Yamato district, this image has a friendly countenance in spite of its massive and dignified appearance. Both of these statues have been designated national treasures. The village people are said to have protected the image in Doganji Temple throughout the Warring States period (1467–1568), and although most of the gold leaf has peeled away from the black lacquered surface, it gives the impression of a buddha image surviving along with the ordinary people.

Crowned with its eleven *Kebutsu* (aspects of Buddha), its expression varies depending on the angle from which it is seen. When viewed from the front, the facial features are that of a

Bodhisattava – mercy itself – but from behind, the *boake-daisho-men* (face to evil laughter) smiles grimly; the three faces on its right side, the *shin-men* (faces of anger with eyes wide open), stare with a furious gaze. *Jyuichimen Kannon* symbolizes the various aspect of society in its human expressions, while at the same time unifying and embracing them. Therein lies her appeal.

We tend to focus on what appears immediately before our eyes, without reflecting on the relative position of that view; in other words, whether the direction from which something is viewed affects its appearance. When JNR's fares were raised, a user commented:

> Not long ago, I moved to an apartment far from the school I attend because the accommodation nearby was so expensive. After the recent fare rise, the cost of commuting now offsets any gain I expected for my willingness to put up with the inconvenient location of the new apartment.

It is not only students but commuters in large cities who may rely on low fares to compensate for other difficulties in their living arrangements. But is this not putting the cart before the horse? Looked at from another standpoint, this is surely a problem of housing policy. The cost of living close to one's place of work is extremely high in large cities.

Those responsible for providing housing did not face up to this problem, the result being the creation of an enormous number of long-distance commuters. To cope with this, rather costly investments have had to be made. Along with the social costs of people living in metropolitan areas, one wonders how a balance sheet of the national economy would look.

The problems of local lines are usually discussed from the perspective of the benefits arising from local needs, but this is not the only side to the problem. The reason that local lines are sustainable in spite of the losses they incur is that others are paying for these losses. Who are these people and who should be responsible? The maintenance of local lines cannot be relied on without taking a view as to who should bear the burden of their operation based on considerations of social fairness. In the current situation, where most of the profitable lines are concentrated in metropolitan areas, the real supporters of the internal subsidy – appropriating revenues from profitable lines for the benefit of local lines – are metropolitan residents. Within the same group of JNR users, some bear the strain of the housing policies and pay fares which exceed the cost of the services provided, while others do not even bear the direct cost of the services they use. If this is regarded as an equitable way of distrbuting the burden, all being members of the same society, then no problems exist: but is it equitable?

With respect to the losses incurred by local lines, one frequently comes upon opinions that express the following:

> The amount of losses incurred by local lines accounts for only about one-third of the total losses of JNR. Even if the lines that might be closed in favour of bus services were all removed from JNR, the resulting decrease in losses would only be in the tens of billions of yen, an amount that falls far short of JNR's total deficit.

According to this logic, every proposed form of rationalization must be ruled out because no one proposal can completely get rid of the overall losses. Life takes on a different quality depending on whether one considers a hundred yen as only one-tenth of a thousand yen or as ten times ten yen. The approach described above represents a narrow view akin to looking at a hundred yen as a tenth of a thousand yen. By looking at that hundred yen as ten times ten yen, however, a decrease in losses of tens of bllions of yen becomes a major achievement. The essential element of rationalization lies in the accumulated effect of many small-scale efforts.

The human world is full of biases and attachments that result from seeing just one aspect of various phenomena. Under the skies of the northern shore of Lake Biwa, *Jyuichimen Kannon* in Doganji Temple must be watching the struggles of so many people with great sufferance.

Jyuichimen Kannon is a goddess of compassion with eleven heads, each head symbolising an aspect of the Kannon. The Jyuichimen Kannon in Doganji Temple has an image of Bodhi-sattva, or a Buddhist saint at the crowning Buddha aspect. The figure is said to have been made about 1,230 years ago, by a priest named Taicho, after receiving an Imperial edict from Emperor Shomu to pray for the end of an infectious disease. It is made of wood and has a height of 1.95 metres. It was designated as a national treasure in 1987, and again in 1953.

WAYS OF PERCEIVING THE TRILLION YEN DEFICIT

In reacting to the JNR accounts for 1980/81 the main theme of the mass media was that the deficit exceeded one trillion yen. To accept operating losses of this amount as a normal condition of management would be lamentable, and many people have expressed feelings of anxiety and distrust regarding the future of JNR. On the other hand, it also seems to be understood that because JNR is a national railway, the standards applied in the private sector – where a deficit is held to be a consequence of inefficient or inept managment – cannot be directly applied to the management of JNR.

It is accepted for JNR to incur some losses in view of the reasons for its existence and its social role as a national railway. However, this fails to establish whether the general public is prepared to accept a deficit of one trillion yen. People have reacted to what is a serious situation by bewailing its existence or warning of its seriousness, or becoming so pessimistic over the size of the deficit that they fall back on extreme options. A deficit of this size is undoubtedly attributable in part to factors outside the scope of ordinary business management, and simply to announce the total amount of the deficit without explanation will only deepen the suspicions of the general public that JNR's management is inept.

The subsidy paid by the German government to the country's national railway, the Deutsche Bundesbahn (DB), reached a high point of 14.5 billion Deutsche Marks, or roughly 2 trillion yen, in 1979. Out of fears that people would regard this amount purely as a deficit and that the image of DB as a giant loss-making organiz-ation would lead to distrust among the public and undermine employee morale, DB distinguished between the components of the subsidy according to their characteristics based on its purpose and function; namely, compensation for obligations imposed on the railway such as maintaining and operating local lines and charging fares based on social objectives; measures to help finance joint commitments such as excessive pension payments; a subsidy for the construction of infrastructure for which the government as the owner of DB was responsible; and only lastly, a subsidy to cover losses.

DB was thus able to claim that the portion of the subsidy used to finance the 'net' deficit, as defined in normal management practice, was only nine per cent of the total subsidy, the equivalent of slightly less than 190 billion yen. DB made this information available to the public so that people would come to recognize that the actual deficit was not all that large. What DB tried to do was to account for the subsidy by revealing its various components before making proposals about reducing its size. These efforts to remove the public's distrust of management should be noted by JNR.

JNR is facing similar problems. Because of its colossal scale, the numerical data do not clearly show its actual conditions of management. It was back in 1971 when, as a measure to stem difficulties such as this, a system of accounting for each type of line was introduced. Thus, the balance sheets that have been published since then show the operating results for the trunk line system separately from those for local lines. As regards the 1980/81 audit report, some issues still call for further consideration such as determining the appropriate accounting classifications and defining revenue and expenses items more clearly. Even so, the fact that the report divided the trunk lines into three categories – Tokyo and Osaka, Shinkansen, and other trunk lines – and clarified operating conditions for each of them, should be regarded as a significant step towards a realistic evaluation of management.

Anyone commenting and suggesting measures simply from seeing the final figure of a one trillion yen deficit would have to be exceptionally gifted at reading between the lines. Ordinary members of the public cannot have any idea about the cause of the deficit or how to resolve it, not to mention the prospects for the future. An examination of the one trillion yen deficit is not aimed at simply explaining it or making excuses, but is motivated by fears that the functions provided by JNR maybe lost – functions that could well continue to benefit society for many years to come – since they may be abandoned if no measures are taken to reduce the deficit.

The designation of 'other trunk lines' as a separate category has revealed unexpected aspects in the field of intercity passenger transportation and regular bulk freight transportation, prompting a re-evaluation of the belief that these services would support JNR in the future. A close examination of the many examples of such changes, which are among the constituents of the one trillion yen deficit, will ultimately point the way towards reconstruction.

For the effective evaluation of management to become a reality, it is necessary to address two fundamental issues. One is the way in which management systems should be subdivided to best reflect the actual situation. Whether or not this works effectively depends on what managerial categories or units are distinguished. The other issue is the worth of the accounting method used. The problem here is to what extent detailed accuracy should be sought, taking into account both the benefits and the costs in time and labour of doing so.

A REMOTE VILLAGE RISES TO A CHALLENGE

Sawauchi Village in Waga County, Iwate Prefecture, is located at the edge of the Ou Mountains and is surrounded by mountains on all sides. The weather there is variable and in winter the snowfall is usually two or three metres deep, and sometimes even more. A magazine article written by Soden Ota, the village headman, describes the following situation:

> The local people have long suffered from extensive cold-weather damage, and their income level is among the lowest in the prefecture. The entire village is designated as a rural area, with the district's two main centres, Morioka City and Kitakami City, some 55 kilometres away with mountains in between. The village nestles quietly in the valleys of the Ou Mountains.[2]

According to the article, the village took action in 1957 to tackle the problem of heavy snowfalls. Although the villagers were not all of the same mind, they decided to break with tradition and began a large and well-organized programme to clear the snow from the roads. They set up an Association for the Security of Winter Transportation Services, and hired a bulldozer for snow-clearing, the cost being met with funds donated by the residents. The changes that resulted from these efforts were noted in the article:

> At the very least, it was now possible to outwit a snowstorm. Giving in to snow turned to hope of overcoming it, and a new-found confidence grew among the population that transportation services could be secured throughout the winter months.

In the following year, the village council approved the purchase of a bulldozer at a cost of 5.3 million yen, even though the village's annual tax revenues amounted to only 12 million. The residents opened up new rice fields and reshaped arable land with the bulldozer in the summer, using the income from this work to repay the loan and to build up funds for snow clearance. By increasing the number of bulldozers every year in this way, they eventually reached the point where they were able to keep all the main roads in the village clear of snow, relying entirely on their own resources. The article continues:

> During the heavy snowfall of 1974, when the snowdrifts were up to 4 metres deep, all the railways as well as the national, prefectural, and town roads were blocked, but in Sawauchi Village, vehicles could get to even the smallest communities.

Conditions of location and weather are part of the natural environment and can be quite difficult to manage. The way in which the people of Sawauchi coped with these difficulties by themselves is impressive.

The public believe too readily that rail services cannot be held up by snow, and that it is a good transportation system in areas of heavy snowfall. However, that impression may have shifted to the opposite extreme as reflected in the newspaper headlines such as 'Shinkansen Easily Stopped by Snow'.

When the Hokuriku region suffered heavy damage in the big snowfall of 1963, neither the roads nor the railway were able to provide a proper service. From that experience, both the road and railway authorities made great efforts to improve their snow-clearing capabilities. Then, in the big snowfall of 1981, JNR's Hokuriku Honsen Line was forced to suspend operations three times, while National Route 8 and the Hokuriku Expressway were seldom blocked at one at the same time. Although short, intermittent, or partial closings or lane limitations occurred on both of these highways, they proved to be reliable for the Hokuriku region's economy.

Snow-clearing by machine is not as easy for railways as for roads. Furthermore, rail services are held up as the snow is being cleared since snow-ploughs use the same tracks as the trains; on the roads, parts of them can be used by regular traffic while the work is under way. Moreover, even when the snow has been cleared from the main tracks, freight services cannot be provided unless the yard lines used for sorting wagons are cleared.

Thus, railway systems are not without risk during the winter months.

Railways were thought of as not being vulnerable to snow for a long time because in the past rail workers worked hard to clear the snow, while next to nothing was done about clearing snow from the roads. The account of the way in which the Sawauchi villagers tackled the problem, breaking their traditional practice, testifies to this point. Even though a pedestrian can overtake a parked vehicle, the pedestrian is not thereby faster than the vehicle. The idea that railways are not troubled by snow must have stemmed from this kind of comparison; that is, from comparing two phenomena which cannot or should not be compared with one other. This is illustrated by the growing criticism of JNR as unduly vulnerable to snowfall as improvements continue to be made in mechanized snow-clearance on the roads.

There are many cases where JNR is urged to adopt certain measures based on firmly-held beliefs – but beliefs based upon an inability to distinguish between reality and mere appearances such that can obscure the actual situation. Appearances are just that and will fade away in the light of reality. Hence, the position of JNR relative to other modes of transportation will, in time, be seen in the context of a proper social perspective.

The inspiring report of the Sawauchi Village headman continues:

> A great sense of self-reliance has grown among us, and we are convinced that even the poorest village in a remote area can succeed if everyone unites and co-operates. We now have ten snow-ploughs, and there is not the slightest fear that roads will be blocked no matter how heavy a snowfall we may have.

THE TWO SIDES OF RECONSTRUCTION

We are seldom able to foresee at the beginning of a year what will actually happen in the year to come but many current problems which have been neglected for too long will have to be tackled, regardless of what it may take to do so. Even though people may recognize that a problem exists, there is a tendency to avoid having to 'pay the piper' until finally no choice is left but to face up to the issue in hand.

Many of JNR's problems have reached this stage just when

management difficulties have resulted in a volatile and unpredictable situation. The current focus of JNR management centres on reconstruction, but the word *reconstruction* gets interpreted only in terms of the organization's deficit problem. The reconstruction plan appears to be founded on the notion of cutbacks; that is to say, reconstruction can succeed only through removing the burden which JNR has shouldered as a result of implementing social policies on behalf of the government. Although this is an important factor, whether or not reconstruction can be successfully achieved also depends on another fundamental aspect.

Among those fields listed in the JNR reconstruction plan as important to the national economy and people's way of life, are inter-city passenger transportation, metropolitan passenger transportation, and the regular bulk transportation of goods. The key to predicting the success of reconstruction should be whether the organization that remains after the cutbacks can sustain and develop its potential after five or ten years. If not, merely reducing the scale of management will only result in making the goal of JNR's reconstruction plan disappear into the future. Setting a criterion based on the traffic data of each line – less than 4,000 passengers a day, for example – and making cutbacks according to that criterion would focus attention on the heart of JNR. This may be an effective way of looking at current conditions but only the most optimistic could expect this to be enough to meet future requirements and expectations. If these expectations were at all realistic, JNR would never have fallen so out favour with the public in the first place.

At the beginning of the Meiji era (1867–1912), it was natural that the railway – the first modern trnasportation mode to be adopted in Japan – would be expected to meet all types of demand for transport. It was also natural that as other modes of transportation such as motor vehicles and airplanes appeared, the government would spend large sums of money on roads and airports, and the range of rail transportation would be reduced to an extent better suited to its own special characteristics; and this cannot be seen as a decline in the usual sense. If JNR were to lose its competitive edge in those fields best suited to it and its responsibilities were to dwindle a great deal, the situation would be much more serious. If, too, JNR's unpopularity continued to grow while its management concentrated only on promoting streamlined operations, conditions may become irreversible.

If there is good reason for JNR's reconstruction, it is that there are certain social functions which can be performed only by JNR on a long-term and nationwide basis. These should not, however, be simply identified as an accidental remainder after the unreasonable burden on management has been trimmed, but should be accepted with a clear and positive intention. It is for JNR to take the initiative to select and reorganize inter-regional lines and systems which can most effectively serve these social functions. In this task, there is no room for blind optimism.

Not that nothing is already being done in this matter. Elaborate measures to attract passengers and freight, including fare discounts, have been introduced, but to the extent that these measures have been carried out on a small-scale or in a intermittent way, they have failed to make much of an impact. Measures such as these call for a more positive and aggressive approach as well as for more fundamental policies. Conditions must be created that will permit JNR to maintain its predominance for a long time in carefully chosen fields, and this includes the standard and layout of the lines, the schedule of train operations, the system of fares and charges, service at ticket booths and costs, so that all will add up to produce something more than the effect of each separate item on its own.

To promote the streamlining of management on the one hand and to estabish a nucleus system on the other is not 'chasing two hares simultaneously'; rather do they constitute two sides of reconstruction that go hand in hand.

THE BASIC DISCUSSIONS ON THE FORMS OF MANAGEMENT

> Ceaselessly the rivers flows, and yet the water is never the same, while in the still pools the shifting foam gathers and is gone, never staying for a moment.[3]

In thinking of the debate, past and future, concerning JNR, this passage by Kamo no Chomei (1155–1216) describing the vicissitudes of life comes to mind. In a decade of discussion about JNR, the tone of the debate has changed many times, and currently its focus is on the form of management.

In a recent newspaper interview a question as to how JNR's reconstruction should be carried out was answered as follows:

> First, the accumulated deficit should be written off. Then, fares should be set so as to avoid further deficits, although some public subsidy may be assumed. In addition, JNR should be divided into individual, specialized corporations on a regional basis.

This opinion represents one of the current trends in the thinking about the form of management. However, while JNR's history so far has proved that neither doing away with past liabilities nor changing public subsidies or fares alone can be the answer to the problem of its reconstruction, no rationale has yet claimed that changing the form of management has any particular virtue. After all, a form of management is merely the cloak of an administrative system. The problem is not so straightforward that all problems will simply fade away just by a change of costumes.

There is another viewpoint that changing the current form of management is not required for reconstruction. What JNR needs is not to become a private company but simply to enhance its efficiency, and this requires JNR to adopt the methods of the private sector and not to be privatized. It is not clear, however, what kinds of private company methods are actually being thought of for a non-private organization. Similarly, if it is intended that reconstruction is possible with the current organization, there is a simple question: why, in that case, could reconstruction not have been achieved earlier?

The challenge of decentralizing control has been a part of the history of JNR's internal management since its beginning as a public corporation. JNR has tried various kind of decentralized control, and this peaked in the branch office system of the mid-1950s. Under this system, internal management units were established on the basis of area, line and division, each unit being responsible for revenues and expenses, for quotas and sometimes even for interests on loan for investments in equipment. Only the nationwide uniformity of fares and salaries was sacrosanct. Now that the more radical methods are to be introduced, can one expect to move toward differentiated fares and salaries in different areas?

Some point out that the electric power industry is a good example of the effects of privatization and the division of management, but there is a large difference between the circumstances in that industry and JNR. For example, when the division of management takes place on the basis of area, differences in the management base of individual areas are reflected in revenues and expenses, and consequently in the burden placed upon customers. When the national electric power company was split into nine regional companies, the main difference between the service areas was in the mix of thermal and hydro-electric power plants, but this was easy to deal with because each business was more or less a monopoly in each area. Within JNR's network, however, cost differences among different areas are much more complex and differences in economic conditions between areas have a greater impact on revenues from fares. Moreover, fares have to be matched with those of other transportation systems within each area, so that adjustments are required not only between individual areas but within areas as well.

At the root of the situation that has called for the reconstruction of JNR, there are factors that stand in the way of efficient management. Some of these are conventions that grew up in the course of a century of management, and some the result of a gap that has developed between the characteristics of the railway as a transportation mode and the changing transportation environment. The reconstruction of JNR must incorporate a plan to show how these factors would be dealt with.

In the background of discussions concerning various forms of management lies the fact that the public – impatient with JNR as it 'reconstructs its reconstruction plans' – becomes attracted to the alternative of privatization and division. Both JNR's labour and management should take note of this.

The key to resolving the problem lies in identifying measures with the greatest net advantage or the least net disadvantage. This exercise should be conducted from a realistic business perspective so that actual situations that arise will be properly handled.

It is said that when the great samurai leader Minamoto no Yoshitsune (1159–89) made his way down from the mountains for the decisive battle of Ichinotani, he said:

> Although snow has covered the fields, my old horse knows the way to go . . .

THE LIMITS OF CONTROL

When the cause and effect of something have been determined, it can be a mistake to link the two just because they happen to exist side by side. Darrell Huff, a psychologist and statistician, warns of errors such as this in the following example:

> The people of the New Hebrides [believe] that body lice produce good health. Observations over the centuries had taught them that people in good health usually had lice and sick people often did not ... The conclusion these primitive people arrived at came from their evidence: Lice make man healthy ... [The reality was], however, [when] anyone had a fever (possibly carried to him by those same lice) the body became too hot and the lice left.[4]

This is an example of an observation that correctly established a fact but an error is made in drawing a conclusion from it. Reasoning on less accurate grounds may also often be seen.

Revelations concerning the state of affairs in the workplace within JNR give the appearance of a lack of control. As a result, it may be thought that the scale of JNR's management must be beyond its powers of proper control. JNR has as many as 420,000 employees, a figure unmatched by any private corporation in Japan, and much of the criticism made of JNR attributed the cause of its problem to this fact. Some former managers of private organizations claim that the maximum scale at which it is possible to control a corporation is 50,000 employees. No single person can control a business with as many as 420,000 people and it is this colossal scale which is at the heart of JNR's problems. However, is there not some confusion or misunderstanding in this analysis?

A situation where the management does not know properly what is going on in the workplace will not be rectified simply by reducing the number of employees from 420,000 to 50,000 and this is because the problem lies not in the scale of the business, but in the way its work is organised within the business; that is, the internal management is at fault. During the ten years from the mid-1950s when JNR operated at a profit and was in many respects in much better order than it is today, it had 450,000 to 460,000 employees. How can it be said to be beyond control when the number of employees has since been reduced to 420,000?

A management body is nothing more than a co-operative

system for sharing and exercising control. Each manager is responsible for, say, a division, and the hierarchy of these divisions creates a management body. It should not be thought that management cannot fulfill its role unless it can monitor and supervise the details of each employee's work directly. If the limits of control are discussed with this type of direct control in mind, even a scale of 50,000 employees is much too large.

Of course, the fewer employees there are, the better they can be controlled but whether or not a management body is in control does not depend just on the number of employees. Not all small-scale management bodies are necessarily in control. The critical issue is whether information and the management's goals are effectively communicated between all the levels of the organization. In this event, it is possible to enlarge the scale of management by creating a hierarchical structure of control without damaging overall efficiency.

Alfred P. Sloan Jr. built General Motors (GM) into the world's largest private company with 600,000 employees and made it an excellent model of a modern management body, and he said:

> I do not regard [corporate] size as a barrier ... I am glad to face up to the issue of size, for to my mind the size of a competitive enterprise is the outcome of its competitive performance ... Growth, or striving for it, is, I believe, essential to the good health of an enterprise.[5]

He established a unique, decentralized control system which was responsive along with a system to stimulate productivity, and this was the basis of GM's long-lasting prosperity. No matter how good an organization's control system, however, if there are blockages in the routes along which internal information and the goals of the management are meant to flow, even a scale of 10,000 employees would not succeed, not to mention 50,000. Sloan also said:

> No organization is sounder than the men who run it and delegate others to run it.... *The role of the individual has great importance as regards the issues faced by an organization.*

REVITALIZING JNR – A QUESTION OF RESTRUCTURING
FUNCTIONS

Never before has there been so much discussion about JNR along with proposals about the direction its management should take, with the form of management and morale in the workplace attracting particular attention. However, while these are factors in the problems underlying the state of JNR, they should not be regarded as essential issues in the sense that reconstruction can be achieved just by tackling these problems.

The problem of JNR's reconstruction dates back to the decade after the mid-1960s, but JNR became a public corporation more than ten years before that time, and workplace morale started to deteriorate only after reconstruction began. These matters, therefore, cannot be regarded as major causes of the conditions necessitating JNR's reconstruction today, although they did contribute to the problem to some extent. It would thus be optimistic to expect the current situation to be improved simply be creating an organization to improve management efficiency – primarily by privatising and dividing up JNR – since the crux of the management crisis facing JNR is not a result of internal factors alone.

The origin of the problem stemmed from the fundamental changes in JNR's long-held position in Japanese society and the Japanese economy. These changes are still continuing, and it is this which is at the heart of its management crisis. In other words, the present situation is a result of social changes which JNR faced because it happened to be the transportation system that preceded all other forms of transportation.

The essential characteristic of the railway is that it can meet the needs of mass rapid transportation using a minimal amount of land – although with limited flexibility because the tracks are physically fixed. For a time, the railways served almost all types of transportation needs from long-distance to local services. Now that alternatives have appeared – and the government has promoted the use of small-unit transportation modes, and spent a lot of money on improving roads and airports – a shift of roles between JNR and other forms of transportation is only to be expected. Hence, the situation may not be remedied simply by measures such as revising operating systems, promoting sales actitivies and setting train schedules more meticulously.

Assuming that external changes in transport demand continue, if the conditions on the supply side are adapted to the changes on the demand side, no problem with management will occur. The unique characteristics of the railway business, however, make it difficult to adapt its existing capacities and facilities at short notice in response to changes in demand. Unless rail traffic demand falls to zero, a decrease in demand cannot be met with an equivalent reduction in capacity. There are also restrictions of a social nature. These factors contribute to management difficulties which will exist even if JNR is privatised – unless lines are closed and JNR's range of activities is greatly altered once privatisation takes place, but the social conditions of Japan do not presuppose any of this.

Umeo Oyama's definition of reconstruction as 'efforts to remove the causes of potential collapse' suggests that the basic theme of JNR's reconstruction should be to define its social functions while simultaneously developing conditions to permit JNR to carry out these functions. Unless this point is taken on board, JNR's problems cannot be resolved no matter what form of management is adopted, even though the need to break away from established patterns and create a new starting point is understandable.

The future scope of JNR's activities should not be decided solely by JNR's internal management. A general consensus on the part of the country as a whole is required, and it is therefore a political matter. JNR must take the national viewpoint into account. For example, the number of employees – a major issue within the framework of reconstruction – is dependent upon the range of activities undertaken by JNR. Unless the basic stance is clear, the appropriate scale of operations cannot be determined, and numbers can only then be discussed in theory.

Within JNR's range of activities, however, provisions could be made for it to exercise its own initiative in particular areas. Such areas are those where it is feasible for JNR to compete with other modes of transportation, and where it can insist on its own decision-making procedures.

THE DEPTH OF FOCUS – RESERVE SYSTEM FOR RETIREMENT ALLOWANCE

A photograph does not capture every aspect of a subject or scene with equal distinctness. This is because a camera lens has a certain range – its depth of focus – within which it operates.

When I first took up photography, I had the opportunity to take a picture of an alpine flower which had been cultivated with great care at a hot-spring inn in the mountains. I took a close-up of the flower, adjusting the focus. Later, I was surprised to find that the photograph which showed the white bloom clearly against a dimmer background, had an unexpectedly beautiful quality. Quite unintentionally, I had brought the main subject of the photograph into focus and left the surroundings out of focus. Although it is harmless and rewarding to create an artistic picture such as this in photography, it is unwise to adapt a similar technique in respect to social phenomena.

Every social phenomenon has depth. People often discuss a subject and arrive at a conclusion about it by simply observing its surface nature and failing to look at the subject in depth. This habit is common in the discussions of JNR's problems, and conclusions should not be drawn based on facts at 'surface' level.

Recently, the annual number of employees retiring from JNR exceeded 20,000 and paying retirement allowances has become a serious burden on JNR's management. Moreover, JNR's accounting system provides no reserve fund for these retirement allowances. Some people cannot imagine a situation such as this occurring in the private sector, and therefore attribute it to JNR's form of management, criticizing the organization for disregarding the problem and not taking appropriate measures. But is this criticism sound? By changing the focus a little, various other issues can be brought into the picture.

In its early years, JNR's management was aware of the fact that there was an unusual age structure among its 400,000 employees – in part a result of World War II – and that the time would come when about 20,000 employees would retire every year. JNR's management at the time, realized that the accounting method then employed would require huge amounts of money in the future. They understood the need for a reserve fund for retirement purposes to avoid not only difficulty in meeting retirement cost but also the periodic distortions in the profit and loss statements. In 1964, when the number retiring had not reached even the 10,000 level JNR submitted an application to the Minister of Transport to set up a reserve fund for retirement allowances. (Ministerial approval was required to make any basic changes to JNR's accounting rules.) Thus, the criticism that JNR did not foresee the need for a retirement fund because its management had a 'governmental' approach to accounting, is clearly not justified.

The proposal, however, was never approved. After leaving the matter for almost six years, the application was rejected by the Ministry of Transport and the issue laid to rest in 1970. This was not necessarily because the authorities failed to understand the need for a reserve fund; we must alter the focus of our analyses in order to grasp the fundamentals of the problem.

Although it is not difficult to set up a reserve fund in an accounting system, a major-problem is how such a fund should be financed. If this was not resolved, the introduction of the new system would be pointless. The critical question was whether the fund should be or could be covered by the fares that were charged. JNR's fares had always been kept low as part of government policy, and there was no room for a new cost item to be included in fares. This was the truth that lay at the heart of the issue. JNR's retirement fund was disallowed on account of the government's policy on fares. The time has now arrived when large numbers of employees are retiring without any opportunity for JNR to establish a reserve fund – either to be financed out of fares or as an independent system. By relying on a shallow and simplistic understanding of JNR as a public-sector system of management neither the circumstances of the problem nor its nature are 'in focus'.

Magazines often feature photographs in which shapes and distances are exaggerated by means of a 'fish-eye' lens. This is a useful technique if one wants to make a subject look larger, and some of the critics of JNR are using a similar technique. Attracting attention by intentionally distorting the subject is not appropriate when dealing with social phenomena – although it may be in order in the case of photography. This makes it more difficult to deal with a situation and to arrive at an accurate understanding of it. Advice and proposals concerning the difficult future facing JNR should not rely on exaggerated or distorted descriptions of its activities and problems.

THE FUNDAMENTALS OF THE PROBLEM

Many views and proposals have been expressed with respect to JNR's reconstruction, all with a common theme in calling for changes in JNR's current situation. However, the extent to which an accurate analysis has been made regarding the real nature of the problem varies a great deal. To decide upon the direction of reconstruction, it is necessary to assess whether various views and proposals can really contribute to JNR's recovery.

Measures dealing with JNR's deficit, for example, are usually discussed with an emphasis on how to deal with its cumulative debts. But simply to pump out overflowing water will not solve the problem: the first step is to turn off the tap at the source of the problem. To evaluate measures to control the deficit, one should identify what measures are proposed to deal with the sources of JNR's deficit, and to what extent they can halt any further losses. If the policy is not clear on this point, the problem of the deficit will not be solved even if the cumulative liabilities are written off at some stage. At the heart of problem are the internal factors that result in the deficit being incurred in the first place. Hence proposals that do not include plans to alter these factors cannot be adequate.

With regard to the rationalization of management, merely working out the effect of rationalization measures does not guarantee that management will recover based on those measures alone. If the goals of rationalization – a reduction in personnel, for example – are achieved after several years and operating revenues at that point correspond to the initial estimates, only then can it be said that the proposal has contributed to JNR's reconstruction. There is no guarantee, however, that JNR will not become even more unpopular as it itself promotes a rationalization plan, resulting perhaps in a defensive management. A situation could arise where the goal of rationalization has been achieved while management conditions have worsened.

JNR's reconstruction depends on how efficiently JNR's functions can be implemented in the future and how much future profit can be expected from providing for these functions. Public opinion sheds little light on these aspects. At the heart of this, no doubt, lies an assumption that reconstruction can be achieved without unduly interfering with the current state of affairs and without drastically changing the range of JNR's activities as a transportation system. If JNR's reconstruction could be achieved while maintaining the current situation – the product of its history for more than a century – the problem of reconstruction would not be all that complex. Ultimately a basis must be established which demonstrates that the decline in JNR's role in society will be halted and that these roles will be sustained in the future.

Otherwise, proposals would be no more than an expression of optimism.

Another feature of the current debate concerns JNR's image as the product of the attitudes of its managers and employees. These attitudes are an important aspect of reconstruction, especially in terms of nurturing a set of values in support of the workforce. But it would be too hasty to conclude that everything would change for the better and every problem solved merely by improving attitudes: this could never, by itself, answer the question of how the railway should function as a mode of transportation.

There is also a broad range of opinions with regard to the characteristic of the railway as a public service. One reason for this is that this characteristic is not clearly defined and is given different meanings by different people. Some opinions emphasize JNR's role as a public service provider, blaming management for not having developed this role, and overlooking the question of costs. A public service provider entails expenditures, and the question is who should cover the costs of developing and maintaining the public service with due regard of being fair to society. To place the responsibility on the government or to rely on tax revenues – as has been done up to now – cannot be the solution, and especially when government finances are in a poor state. If we insist that JNR fulfill the role of a public service provider, the problem of cost will not be resolved unless it is examined at some depth.

Merely dealing with the minor details of a problem, no matter how assiduously, is no substitute for a review of its fundamental nature and substance.

WORSENING OF THE SITUATION VS. THE RATE OF RECONSTRUCTION

The balance of revenues and expenditures of JNR continues to deteriorate. In 1981/82, the deficit was 1.86 trillion yen, the worst figure in JNR's history. The total deficit carried forward as at the end of 1981/82 was about 7.58 trillion yen, while long-term liabilities amounted to about 16.15 trillion.

Editorials in virtually every newspaper in Japan have focused on the above results with comments such as the following:

> JNR's management and labour should confront these results directly ... The serious and urgent situation which JNR is facing should be recognized appropriately ... Earnest and sincere efforts are required for JNR's reconstruction ...

These comments are certainly in order but it is already eighteen years since JNR's accounts first went into the red, and an entire decade since newspapers in 1971 announced JNR's 'bankruptcy' with its 800 billion yen in cumulative deficit and 3.4 trillion in liabilities. However, simply to admonish JNR for its negative attitude cannot be a meaningful way of finding a solution.

While the situation has been going from bad to worse, discussions continue to reiterate familiar principles instead of delving deeply into the issues at hand. One is left with a feeling of great emptiness after more than a decade of these discussions, and little if anything has been achieved. Any improvement in JNR's situation is held back by barriers which cannot be broken down through its own efforts alone, but will require some kind of social reform. To this end, positive guideposts to lead public opinion are needed. Great efforts are called for when JNR is seen to be stuck in a deep quagmire.

Delay or slow-acting measures have a disincentive and demoralising effect on management and can result in harmful consequences. This reality is difficult to grasp as an aspect of JNR's operations. In spite of its problems, the fact that trains continue to operate reduces the overall level of concern and slows down the rate at which these problems are addressed.

With regard to the problems of designated local lines, which are in difficult straits in many areas, there are those who advocate greater efforts to obtain the understanding and co-operation of the people affected by possible service changes in the area, as well as a more aggressive promotion of what needs to be done. But can it be believed that these problems would be solved simply by getting the understanding and co-operation of local people? As the burden on areas that have railway services is not all that heavy, it is obviously more convenient for the residents to have a wider choice of transportation modes available, regardless of how often they are actually used. Moreover, these areas get financial benefits based on a system which provides for annual payments by JNR to cities, towns and villages where its tracks run. Many of these local bodies refuse to take part in official negotiations to discuss changes to the services in their area – and they have no reason for concern because the local trains continue to operate even when negotiations come to a standstill. As long as local lines are supported and continue to operate, it is unrealistic to believe that local co-operation can be achieved by words rather than deeds.

The urgency with which this problem must be solved will not disappear while it is left as it is; rather, the problem will simply edge more and more into JNR's management and the situation will steadily worsen.

Losses inccurred by local lines – which account for 5 per cent of JNR's overall services – amounted to 347.3 billion yen in 1981/82 – even after the special grant from the national government. There is no way to make up for this deficit other than by more borrowing. What could be the effect on JNR's management if no progress was made with the problem of local lines during the coming decade? Assuming that the scale of these local lines and the deficit incurred by them continue at current levels – actually, the deficit is increasing every year and an increase in the national grant cannot be expected under the current circumstances – and assume too that the deficit is covered by borrowing at 8 per cent per annum then the interest alone would amount to 347 billion yen in the next decade. Thus, in order to maintain the local lines, an amount almost equal to the current deficit would be required to pay the interest, and the accumulated deficit would exceed 5 trillion yen in ten years. This would surely put considerable pressure on JNR's management in the near future. The question is whether the public would accept, on social grounds, a deficit of this size for a service which accounts for just 5 per cent of the overall transportation services provided by JNR.

The safety of railway lines can be ensured if maintenance and repair work at least match the amount of wear and tear of these lines. The same principle applies to the reconstruction of management. Reconstruction is possible only if the rate of implementing improvements exceeds the rate at which management conditions are worsening. Consideration must be given as to how much will be lost as a result of further delays in improving the situation.

THE DECADE SINCE THE CENTENNIAL OF THE RAILWAY

October 14, 1982 was the 110th anniversary of the railway in Japan. JNR greeted the occasion in an unusual manner when the government issued a declaration concerning the JNR's management, the 'Declaration of Emergency', at around the same time. Ten years previously, the centennial was celebrated with a ceremony organized by JNR and attended by the Emperor and Empress. What are the changes in JNR's management since that day? What did this decade mean for both JNR and the public?

If a transformation of the current situation, namely, JNR's reconstruction, is to be realized in the next ten years, it is useful to recognize the limits of what can be achieved by examining what was accomplished or not accomplished during the last decade, and to find the reasons for the events.

To what extent was JNR's current situation predicted in 1972? To what degree was the problem recognized and what measures were planned? Several newspaper editorials that appeared in 1972 are quoted below.

One editorial entitled 'A Century of JNR' which appeared in the October 14, 1972 edition of the *Asahi Shimbun* (a major Japanese daily) said:

> With a stack of difficult problems on its plate, JNR find itself at a point of crisis on its centenary ... JNR's situation must be seen as catastrophic in terms of both material assets and spirit ... It cannot be allowed to celebrate the centenary of the railway in a festive mood. Now is the time for JNR to think about the cause of this crisis and to contemplate its future. To that end, JNR should be required to review its composition and reassess its role.

In its astute assessment of the problem, this editorial seems to have bridged the intervening decade. In fact, it would still be relevant even if it had appeared in the papers on *Railway Memorial Day* ten years later. Although the relevance of this statement made ten years ago is remarkable, it is also regrettable since it means that the situation has not changed very much and that there has been almost no progress over the past decade.

A previous editorial in the August 27, 1972 edition of the same daily assessed JNR's policies and management attitudes:

A new implication can be discerned in the audit report ... which suggests that the closure of local lines operating in the red should not be considered only from the management standpoint of balancing revenues and expenditures. This is a major change from the 1970/71 audit report issued the year before, which suggested that an application be made to the Minister of Transport to close lines even if there is opposition in the areas where they are located ... On receiving this report, JNR President Isozaki declared that it is desirable for JNR to play a role in rebuilding Japan – currently facing serious problems due to the growing disparities in population density – and that JNR should become something more than a business enterprise. These words do not sound like those from the same organization which was burdened with a tremendous deficit a while ago ... [But] notwithstanding the president's advocacy of a role in rebuilding the country, JNR's enormous deficit will remain unchanged. In fact, it will almost certainly grow like a snowball rolling downhill. Who will then balance the budget?

In the decade since this editorial was written, the serious issues it raises have come to a head, affecting JNR's management approach and making the crisis all the more serious.

The editorial also indicated that JNR was vacillating in its reconstruction policy:

Trying to increase the number of lines under the banner of this slogan, when they were once targeted for closure from the standpoint of the national economy, will only cause much confusion.

JNR's hesitant approach toward adopting a firm policy was nothing but a waste of time. To make matters worse, what was forfeited was not only time itself but also the opportunity for implementing the necesssary measures, an irretrievable loss. Management characterized by a passive approach, sensitive to outside pressures, achieves nothing and is ultimately a futile exercise. Management should rely on its own resources and should do what it can by its own efforts. This is the best foundation for reconstruction.

The editorial continued:

JNR even seems undecided with respect to what kind of roles it should fulfill and in what manner it should accomplish them. What is most urgently required now is to establish a clear management concept.

In order to accomplish the important task of reconstructing JNR, it is necessary to pursue consistent policies and to continue to make every effort to solve the problems which stand in the way of achieving its goals. The editorial written in 1972 ended with the following observation:

> A company which has lost its concept of management must die, and JNR is possibly no exception to this rule.

SHOULDERING RESPONSIBILITY FOR A NATIONAL PROJECT

The Joetsu Shinkansen Line, connecting the Pacific and the coasts of Honshu by the Sea of Japan in only two hours, was opened in 1982 after eleven years and an enormous outlay of 1.7 trillion yen. Expectations and enthusiasm for this new line were high in the areas along its route, as shown by such comments as 'this marks the opening of a new era for the regions along the Sea of Japan,' and 'this is the world's first super-express train which runs through areas with heavy snowfall.'

The traffic on this new line, however, is considerably less than that on the existing Shinkansen lines, but this was to be expected. The Tokaido Shinkansen passes through a region with a population of over 30 million – an unusually high density – while along the Tohoku Shinkansen the population is about a quarter of that figure. Compared to these lines, the Joetsu Shinkansen, which has a track length of 270 kilometres, is shorter and its service area smaller than that of the Tohoku Shinkansen. Any difference in population density is reflected in a difference in the level of traffic, and this undoubtedly has had a crucial effect on efficiency and Shinkansen's investment fund.

Unlike the existing Shinkansen lines which were built and operated by JNR itself, the Joetsu Shinkansen was built by the Japan Railway Construction Corporation under the direction of the national government, and leased to JNR. JNR initially anticipated about 50 billion yen annually in fare revenues from the line while the rent paid to the corporation was 100 billion yen. The costs of running the line and maintaining it – coupled with the decrease in revenues from ordinary services due to passengers shifting to the new line – were factors to be taken into account by JNR's management. Some believe that even if the line operates in the red initially, revenues will cover expenses in the long term, and that the line will be profitable in about twenty years. But how credible can a forecast of profitability twenty years hence be in a changeable and uncertain world? Such a forecast has a hollow ring to JNR being already in great financial difficulty. If all of JNR's deficits are covered by loans until that time, interest on its debt will mount up and JNR will find itself in a hopeless situation.

The government and the Diet seem to want to apply a different standard to JNR than to the other public corporations in respect to the wages of its employees; in view of the deficit they are thinking of lowering the wage component in JNR's budget. On the other hand, JNR are renting facilities and being charged double the amount that JNR earns operating them. What explanation could the government and the Diet possibly have for this arrangement governing the operations of the Joestu Shinkansen? Even if the only way to deal with the relationship between the Japan Railway Construction Corporation and JNR is by means of a rental arrangement, it is strange that the responsibility of the government as the promoter of this project disappears upon the completion and opening of the facility. The government – particularly after taking such a strict stance with respect to JNR's responsibility for its deficit – should acknowledge its own responsibility in creating such a large and long-term contribution to JNR's deficit at this time.

External factors that were the result of similar arrangements have contributed to JNR's losses in the past as well. Although it is very difficult now to identify the sources of past burdens stemming from national policies, it is clear that if JNR is burdened with new long-term additions to its deficit, reconstruction will be postponed indefinitely.

Renting a building for 100 billion yen when sales are estimated at only 50 billion would clearly not be a sensible way to start a new business, and it goes without saying that those in control of a business should not adopt any policies that would put its management at risk even if it is in favour of a national project. While it is considered that the pay of JNR's employees should be treated differently from other governmental organizations in view of its deficit and measures that are being taken in connection with its reconstruction, JNR puts up with an enormous prospective addition to its deficit without clarifying the conditions on which it is based. Instead, all that is heard are wishes and hopes that things will be better in twenty years, or that the situation can be handled through the efforts of JNR's own management. One cannot help but wonder just where the responsibility for managing JNR lies.

Events have taken place in this case without a clear statement of policy even by those who were so concerned with JNR's deficit, including the authors of *Second Special Government Inspection*. This is another example of JNR's helplessness in the face its own problems.

A green and white bullet-train runs under the gentle sunshine from the Kanto Plain to the Echigo Plain in early winter, passing en route through the tunnels under the snow-capped mountains dividing the two regions. If this Shinkansen Line was built as a symbol of the nation's wealth, this should be reflected in the way the line is managed. JNR should not be left to bear all the cost on its own.

CONCERNS ABOUT INDISCRIMINATE REDUCTION OF MANAGEMENT

In the draft of JNR's 1983/84 budget submitted to the Diet, one aspect that draws our attention is those items for which estimates are lower than the year before. These items vary widely and include rail traffic income, labour costs, material costs, construction costs, and subsidies. JNR's management calls for comprehensive rationalization and reconstruction cannot be achieved without streamlining management. A reduced budget, therefore, should be welcomed if it means progress in dealing with JNR's management. If, however, the smaller expenditures in the budget are simply a response to smaller revenues and the only purpose of the exercise is to make ends meet, then the future for reconstruction is bleak.

Although JNR's budget is a part of the government's budget, JNR's expenditures are working costs, not costs of government: they are the costs of running over 20,000 trains a day, transporting as many as 19 million passengers and a lot of freight day in and day out. Two decades have passed since JNR's expenditures first exceeded its revenues; in other words, JNR is not in the early stages of making a loss. As JNR has already made some attempts to deal with this, it cannot be expected that tens of millions of yen worth of further cuts will be easily found or that expenditures can be reduced indefinitely simply through the enthusiasm of its staff whatever the encouragement offered to it.

There has surely never been a case where a company has succeeded in reconstruction by reducing its overall expenditures without reassessing the scale of its business and reorganizing its place of work. The operating kilometres of JNR's lines which represent the extent of its business activities, stood at 20,600 kilometres in 1963. By 1973, a decade after JNR first went into the red, the figure had actually increased slightly to 21,000 kilometres, then rose again to 21,400 kilometres by March 1981. 800 kilometres have newly come into service on the completion of the Tohoku and Joetsu Shinkansen lines. Thus the business scale of JNR has been enlarged, not reduced. Though in need of reconstruction, JNR has been placed in a difficult situation which it cannot be expected to deal with by itself.

According to the draft of the 1983/84 budget, the capital costs of the Tohoku and Joetsu Shinkansen lines alone have increased expenditures by 135.5 billion yen; at the same time the subsidy from the government has been reduced by 28.9 billion compared to the previous year. Moreover, personnel and material costs (which include the operating cost of Tohoku and Joetsu Shinkansens) have been cut by 26.5 billion yen compared to the year before. It is impossible to make out how the government intends to share the responsibility for these new Shinkansens which were, after all, national projects until they became operational.

It is clear that the general reduction of management expenditures – including the operating costs of the Shinkansens – will affect the overall railway system and the services it provides. If a general reduction is not made based on a definite prospect of an improvement in business activities and made merely as an aimless response to the existing circumstances, even those parts of the railway business which are doing well could suffer from 'anoxia,' or a chronic lack of life-sustaining oxygen. Even the grounds on which JNR can claim to have 'social' value would be undermined.

Judging from experience, it is expected that JNR's attempts to improve its range of activities will proceed rather slower, and that the gap between its services on offer and actual traffic will continue to grow. Together with the unfavourable trend in fare revenues, a budget based only on the need to make ends meet will surely mean that JNR's management will continue to be reduced. Those responsible for JNR's business affairs will thus be forced to decide whether future reductions in expenditures will result in real cuts in rail services and whether JNR will gradually lose some important aspects of its work.

The situation is certainly urgent and it is this very urgency that makes it all the more important to avoid measures that are merely temporary in nature. Rather than simply being swayed by imme-diate circumstances, it is necessary to get to the root of the problem. Since there is no realistic prospect that JNR will ever recover the ground it has lost or that fare revenues will rapidly increase, it is a matter of course that every effort should be made to streamline management. Merely balancing revenues and expen-ditures will not solve the problem.

Above all, any cuts in rail services and activities that play an important role or are expected to do so in the future, must be avoided. This is the issue that will determine whether or not reconstruction will be successful.

COMPARING JNR REFORM WITH THE REORGANIZATION IN THE ELECTRIC POWER INDUSTRY

Comparative analysis is never easy especially if one is responsible for its conclusions and these should not be hastily drawn on the basis of superficial similarities.

Those who support the division and privatisation of JNR often make a comparison with the reorganization of the country's electric power industry. This took place in 1951, when the state-owned Japan Electric Generation and Transmission Co. (JEGTCO), the nation's sole electricity supplier during World War II, was split up into nine regional companies. People who are regarded as well informed have observed that:

> The electric power industry was split up and privatised thirty years ago. This sets an excellent model for JNR.

Is this true? JEGTCO used to suffer from an on-going deficit, the development of energy resources did not progress as efficiently as expected, and the public was often troubled by power failures due to strikes by *Densan*, the powerful *Electrical Workers' Union*. Shortly after JEGTCO was split up, profits started to be made and no more strikes took place. Given these marvellous changes, the policy seemed to offer the perfect model for JNR's reconstruction – and this would be the case if these changes could be brought about simply by altering the form of management, regardless of the individual characteristics and structure of the business. However, although division led to the revitalization of the electric power industry, the main reason for this success stemmed from the structure of its production and supply system.

In the hundred-year history of the electric power industry in Japan, it was in the hands of a single company for only twelve years. Moreover, that system was limited to generating and transmitting electricity, and local power-distributing companies existed even during those twelve years. JEGTCO's existence was an abnormal state of affairs during the war years, and its break-up can be viewed as a return to normal conditions. Things are quite different with the JNR.

In the opinion of the well-informed people referred to above:

> One aspect that the electric power and railway industries have in common is that both transmission lines and railways connect various parts of the country. Since separate management has been a success in the electric power industry – even though power can be instantaneously transmitted from Kyushu to Hokkaido and would appear better suited to unified management – it should be all the more successful with respect to JNR.

In contrast, Kunie Sakuragi of the Federation of Electric Power Companies points out:

> The characteristic of the electric power industry – the instantaneous transmission of electricity from Kyushu to Hokkaido and the quantity supplied can be easily measured – facilitates business transactions between the different parts created by division.[6]

Clearly comparisons differ depending on the standpoint from which they are made. How does the division of management change things? In Hokkaido, where management is largely affected by low population density and the fact that it has a low level of demand, JNR incurred a 257.9 billion yen deficit in 1981/82, while the Hokkaido Electric Power Co. made 25.3 billion in profits. The level of its charges for electricity was not all that higher than those in other areas; indeed, they were lower than those of Tokyo Electric Power Co. The reason why such profits were made notwithstanding these low charges was due to the nature of the industry – apart from it being a local monopoly, there is almost no difference between individual areas in terms of producing, supplying and selling electricity.

The efficiency of power-generating facilities, for example, is the same in Tokyo as it is in Hokkaido. Because units of power generation can be supplied and matched to the amount of actual demand, production per unit can never be inefficient even in an area with a small demand. The smallest scale at which a railway can operate, however, is a single-track line with a capacity of 80 trains per day. Inefficiency is thus inevitable in an area where rail traffic falls short of this capacity. This is an inescapable aspect of the railway business.

Efficiency in supplying electric power also shows little variation among different areas. Long transmission lines may be required to reach customers in areas with a low population density, giving rise to higher costs than in urban areas where one line can serve several customers. In urban areas, on the other hand, higher costs are incurred by the more extensive use of underground cables. These factors offset one an other so that overall expenditures show little variation between regions. In the case of the railway, however, differences in natural and social factors among individual areas such as geographical features, snowfall, cold weather and low population directly impinge on its activities and create a variety of problems which can be difficult for the local management to handle.

Even if the division and privatisation of JNR were the best option, it should not be based on the experience of the electric power industry, however attractive the prospect may seem. An even stranger and more lamentable notion is that JNR should be divided into nine organizations because the electric power industry has succeeded with nine regional companies. The electric power industry has its own set of circumstances, as does JNR. Conclusions should be drawn only after a thorough study of the history, characteristics and actual management conditions of the railway industry independently of other industries.

A DELAY IN FREIGHT OPERATION REFORM

Many years have passed since H. G. Wells wrote *The Time Machine* in 1895. It is interesting that science fiction with the theme of time travel – perhaps the most unscientific of themes since it is unlikely ever to be realized – should continue to attract readers even in this highly scientific era. To wish that the time barrier could be broken down is a dream since people can only live in the present not in the past or the future. Only a few people have no regrets about their past. Others may well view the present with regret and wish they could live life over again. The great appeal of science fiction is that the reader can dream of unlimited possibilities in a fantasy world.

The book *Sengoku Jieitai* ('The Self-Defense Force in the War Period') by Ryo Hanmura has as its theme a time warp where a group of soldiers accidentally find themselves transported back to another era, more than four centuries ago. In *Rengo Kantai Tsuini Katsu* ('The Combined Fleet Wins at Last') by Akimitsu Takagi, the hero goes back in time to a battle field where he teaches the combatants new tactics based on lessons from actual history. These writings are a source of enjoyment and fantasy. But even in the real world, there are instances highly suggestive of a time warp.

In March 1983, a proposal entitled '*What is Needed to Revitalize JNR's Freight Service*' was issued by the Study Group on Management Systems of Freight Services. So-called industry tracks are described in this proposal to provide bulk door-to-door service, regularly and efficiently, offering substantial benefits to both customers and JNR. In order to increase the demand for industry tracks to make services fully efficient – primarily by providing direct point-to-point service – improvements should be made in several areas to reduce track maintenance costs and make the service more and more convenient.

Here is another statement:

> An industry track is the most typical type of door-to-door service provided by railway transportation. It is of great benefit to both JNR and customers in various respects ... It is necessary to continue to cultivate the demand for industry tracks by taking further advantage of this characteristic. In order to utilize the characteristic of railway freight transportation, a method of locating industry tracks should be considered so as to enable bulk and regular point-to-point services.

This excerpt is quoted from the report by *the Committee for Improvement of Freight Service Management*. This appeared in

February 1972, a decade or so before the proposals of the 1983 Study Group.

JNR's freight traffic was reported to have fallen below 100 million tons in 1982/83, less than half the volume of the amount carried in its most prosperous years. The proposals in 1972 were made to try and revitalize freight services. The recognition of the importance of industry tracks and container services, however, is almost the same as ten years ago. There was nothing wrong with the original ideas. At the same time, when faced with proposals dating back ten years, then either they were of the kind that take a long time for results to be obtained or they have been disregarded. It is unlikely that measures proposed to revitalize JNR's freight services would be so slow in producing results – hence the proposals were not implemented in the first place.

Freight traffic industry tracks declined from 108.5 million tons in 1970 to 63.9 million tons in 1981/82. Why were proposals disregarded for such a long time? This is an important question to ask in order to avoid the same mistakes in connection with other services: nothing will damage reconstruction more than wasting time not doing what clearly needs to be done.

> The coming decade, when environmental changes and a revolution in distribution modes are expected to take place, will be the most favourable period in which to reconstruct JNR's freight services. It is necessary to take note of these conditions, and in every aspect of the freight service industry, to break away from the old structure so as to create a new railway fit for the distribution revolution that will take place.

This statement was made in 1970. At that time, JNR could still record peak amounts of traffic. Not a few people must have read the recent proposals with feelings of regret that it is not possible to travel back in time to implement the measures which are now again being contemplated.

A COMMONSENSE APPROACH TO DIFFERENCES AMONG PUBLIC CORPORATIONS

For public corporations operating at a loss, including JNR, the bonus paid this summer was 1.82 times the monthly pay, a lower level than that of other public corporations. This is a reflection of the view that a difference in pay should be allowed as between profitable public corporations and those operating at a deficit.

This view is based on the notion that wage and salary payments should reflect the financial state of the business. In a private company, this would be a straightforward matter. In business activities managed or owned by the government, however, it is doubtful whether the same rule can be applied. Thus, it seems unreasonable to call for pay to be linked to any deficits in so far as the deficits are not the outcome of business. Some activities of public corporations are placed on them as a result of governmental policy, and these incur costs. These public corporations are not always compensated for such costs by the government, and are counted as part of their operating expenses.

The increased costs borne by JNR for operating the new Tohoku and Joetsu Shinkansens have worsened JNR's deficit. Although the initial operating conditions of the Tohoku Shinkansen are reported to be better than first expected, 'better' does not mean a level high enough to cover the shift in passenger traffic from the traditional main lines to the Shinkansen and the capital costs of construction. The reality is that these will place a long and heavy burden on JNR's management. The Tohoku Shinkansen will undoubtedly remain the country's most valuable transportation system in the future, and this makes it more reasonable that the losses incurred at the beginning of its services should be shared by those will will enjoy the benefits in the future. The pay of employees who happen to work for JNR in 1983 should not be reduced for that reason. If the Japan Railway Construction Corporation built the Joetsu Shinkansen as a national 'government' project, its operation on completion must also be a national 'government' matter. It is unacceptable that those who operate the Shinkansen should be solely responsible for any deficits by a reduction in their pay (while a reduction in the summer bonus is not even suggested for employees of the corporation that constructed the line). JNR's deficit includes other losses with similar characteristics. If JNR's deficit is a matter for its employees, then the salaries of government officials should perhaps be reassessed in the light of the national debt which stands at over 100 trillion yen.

If the profits of public corporations are the result of their monopoly position, then the profits cannot be said to reflect differences in management efforts between profitable and unprofitable corporations. Business results are affected by the efforts of management and the quality of employees' work even in government-run businesses, and it is necessary to make clear about what or who is responsible for the results. The standard for determining this, however, should not simply be profitability; in other words, profits do not necessarily mean good work just as deficits do not necessarily mean bad work.

Looking at the content of their work, it is hard to justify the fact that the operators of a super-rapid transportation system such as the Shinkansen get paid less than general government officials (although airline staff are an exception). Even granting these operators equal pay would still be insufficient. Indeed, if profitability is the yardstick, there is no reason why the pay of JNR employees who work for passenger services in the Tokyo metropolitan area – which have long been profitable – should not be only lower than the pay of employees of private railways operating in the same areas but also lower than the pay of their counterparts in government service.

If it is insisted that the pay of employees in public corporations should follow the practices in the private sector and reflect differences in management efforts, it is necessary to be able to have an influence on management beforehand and to establish a mechanism good enough to measure the contribution of management to the business. But in the case of an organization like JNR in particular, where business conditions vary widely among local areas, analyses that focus on the overall balance of profit and loss have obscured the real problems of management and led to the exclusion of what is needed in the way of appropriate policy measures. A practice which has lasted so long cannot be easily changed. If management continues to be inhibited by the overall deficit, even business activities that are currently doing well will be harmed in the future. The division of management would become the only option.

JNR's reconstruction is ultimately in the hands of its personnel; reconstruction is impossible without their enthusiasm and co-operation. This is one of the reasons why JNR's workforce should be well treated.

BRIGHT AND DARK SPOTS IN JNR'S MANAGEMENT REVEALED
BY NUMERICAL DATA

Two sources of data providing a bird's-eye view of the status of
JNR's management were the set of accounts for 1982/83 and the
1984/85 budget request. The accounts were based on the operating
results and thus portray the state of JNR's management. The
budget, on the other hand, was a set of estimates about the
immediate future incorporating a number of uncertain factors,
although the data still said something useful about the general
trend of management. Comparing these two will reveal the past,
present and future shape of JNR's management.

The 1982/83 accounts revealed that the deficit increased by 290
billion yen to 1,378 billion. Newspapers reported that this was 'the
largest deficit in history,' and 'evidence of a disastrous state of
affairs.' A glance at the figures on their own confirms these
reports, but JNR's problems cannot be properly understood nor
resolved if the deficit continues to be discussed only in terms of
whether JNR's business is generally declining or whether labour
and management are making the right efforts.

Compared to the previous year, traffic and other income
increased significantly by more than 120 billion yen. Among
expenditures, on the other hand, ordinary personnel costs
excluding retirement allowances and pension fund contributions
decreased by 25 billion yen. Ordinary material costs, excluding
lease charges paid to the Japan Railway Construction Corporation and payments to cities, towns and villages, increased
by only 50 billion yen; this includes the rise in operating costs
due to the new rail services of the Tohoku and Joetsu Shinkansens. In spite of operating services with results like these –
which can hardly be called 'a disastrous state of affairs' – the
overall results were the worst in JNR's history. What, then, has
led to the increased deficit and the worsening condition of
management?

The problem lies in expenditures other than ordinary operating
costs. For example, the increase in expenditures such as interest,
lease charges for newly constructed lines, and payment to cities,
towns and villages, amounted to an increase of 350 billion yen. In
addition, increases in retirement allowances and pension fund
contributions exceeded 75 billion yen. These expenditures are the

result of circumstances that JNR was once placed in, and which it currently has no way of managing.

In particular, the interest payments included in the profit-and-loss account alone were 476.4 billion yen in 1980/81, 789.9 billion in 1982/83, and are estimated at 1.1 trillion for 1984/85. Investments in equipment, on the other hand, have shown the opposite trend, declining from one trillion yen in 1980/81 to 880 billion in 1982/83 and an estimated 600 billion for 1984/85. The increases in interest payable in spite of the slowdown in equipment investment show that the deficit itself is creating a greater deficit; annual losses are covered by loans, the interest on which causes still larger losses.

The estimated traffic income in 1984/85 is about 3 trillion yen, including the additional income due to a fare raise; the total amount of interest, debt repayments, lease charges paid to the Japan Railway Construction Corporation, and payments to cities, towns and villages is put at 2.26 trillion yen, equal to about 75 per cent of the traffic income. An organization with this financial structure cannot escape from the vicious circle of a deficit by reducing and rationalizing ordinary costs alone – especially in circumstances that will not easily permit even a part of its activities to be phased out.

JNR's own efforts to help itself are necessary as a preliminary step, but these efforts are becoming less effective as the deficit grows. It is now a race against time. As the deficit grows, the later that remedial measures are put in place, the harder it will be to keep the situation from worsening. This calls for emergency measures.

A salient aspect of the 1982/83 results involves the Tohoku and Joetsu Shinkansens which started up in that year. Apart from the operating results themselves – the operating indices were 254 for the Tohoku Shinkansen and 263 for the Joetsu Shinkansen – the revenues of existing lines running parallel to them were reduced by 39.4 billion yen between Omiya and Morioka, and by 8.5 billion between Omiya and Niigata. Considering the fact that the new Shinkansen lines were opened during the course of the year, then, the decrease would be about 30 per cent in a full year. Although this was anticipated, the shift of traffic to the Shinkansen lines and the decrease in the revenues of the existing lines will have a long-term influence on JNR's management and finances;

the more sparsely populated an area, the more difficult it is to identify and create alternative demand.

There were some bright spots in JNR's accounts. The number of profitable lines increased from eight to ten, and the fact that the Sobu line had one of the best results (after the Yamanote Line and the Tokaido and Sanyo Shinkansens) points to the strategy the management should take. In the mid-1960s, although JNR had already begun to go in the red, it began its investment in the 39-kilometre section of the Sobu line between Tokyo and Chiba, allocating 160 billion yen to improve commuter services. As a result, the line suffered a deficit in 1972 when the service was introduced but recovered its profitability in just five years and eliminated the accumulated deficit two years later. Since then it has contributed revenues of more than 60 billion yen to JNR during the four years up to 1982. The fact that this type of investment brought about such a fast improvement both in terms of benefits to the area along the line and to JNR's management as a whole, is evidence of the advantages of investment based on an astute assessment of the railway's role in a local area. This is another example of the way in which reconstruction should progress.

NATIONALISATION OF THE RAILWAY – A CHOICE MADE 77 YEARS AGO

> Out of 214 votes, there were 214 ayes. The bill to nationalise the railway was carried in the midst of such mayhem that all the opponents left the hall.

This took place on March 28, 1906. It is worth reviewing the debates of that time and to note what potential problems the politicians had in mind in deciding to go ahead with nationalisation. In particular, the points that its opponents made should be of interest. The following material is taken from the records of the special committee at that time.

> – Although military reasons and national defence are emphasized, the Minister of War admitted after both the Sino-Japanese and Russo-Japanese wars that he had never experienced any inconvenience in railway transportation. The problems were with the Navy. What risk to national defence could possibly arise by carrying on with the railway in its present condition?

– If the railway has a central principle, it should not be whether it is nationally or privately owned but how to expand and improve its services. To take full advantage of the role of the railway as well as enlarging and promoting its services, national ownership does not seem to be an appropriate form.

– If the railway is operated on a monopoly basis by the government, the pitfall of having no competitors – which always accompanies business activities managed by the government – cannot be avoided. The service between Shimbashi and Yokohama, for example, showed no improvement in its journey time of fifty minutes from 1872 until only recently when a competitive service offering a 27-minute trip between Tokyo and Yokohama prompted the relevant government department to address this matter for the first time.

– Services operated by the government are generally less responsive to user's needs than those operated by the private sector. Increasing capacity and reducing operating costs would also be expected to be better in a privately managed organization.

– The economic benefits of the railway can only be maintained when it develops of its own accord, not under political influence. Does the government intend to push the railway into a situation where its management is affected by the traditional evils of government, grounded in emotional factors?

– Whether the railway is nationally or privately owned should not matter if the railway provides benefits to the nation and its people. For what reason was such emphasis placed on national ownership in the first place?

Although there are differences in expression, many of the points concerning potential problems remain valid today. They are similar to the current discussions about the form of JNR's management, especially with regard to the issue of privatisation.

What was the response of the government to these concerns about nationalisation? Regrettably, the discussions revolved around the pronouncements of Prime Minister Saionji who stated that it had been an estabished principle since the Restoration that the nation itself should manage the railway; to this, there was simply a stream of formal and empty responses.

It was fortunate, however, that the railway was in an expansionary phase at the time and that neither form of management would have had any dire consequences on its operation. But today the situation is different. How can the railway specialise in its activities in an age when it must compete with other modes of transportation? This calls for a careful approach in circumstances that are now not always within its control. The task at hand is far more difficult than it was in 1906. Even the smallest mistake or lack of foresight can have far-reaching effects. The issues should be examined in the light of social and management conditions, particularly in terms of factors which are no longer relevant. According to reports of the situation which existed in the days prior to nationalisation, there were more than forty railway companies widely scattered throughout the country, and this created confusion and much inconvenience. A strong need existed for integrated control.

Decisions should be made only after serious and careful study of all the issues since we are dealing here with a long-range national project for the benefit of future generations.

ABILITIES NEEDED TO ACHIEVE REFORM – THE PATH TOWARD REVOLUTION

The year 1983 mark about 20 years since JNR first started to make a loss. During this period, scores of comments and proposals have been made while efforts to reconstruct JNR have also been made. Nevertheless, JNR continues to decline and its prospects are uncertain with respect to the future of its management and its recovery. This means that something is not as it should be.

> Since accounting constitutes the essential foundation on which a variety of systems and all economic activities are based, care must be taken with it. Generally, there is no other way than to control expenses based on estimated revenues. If control of expenses is relaxed, however, and they come to be governed only by circumstances while revenues are estimated based on these expenses, the inevitable result will be the imposition of a heavy tax burden on the public.

The above is a passage from *The Teachings of Nanshu Saigo* (the Iwanami Library). The historical figure, better known as Takamori Saigo, played a major part in the Meiji Restoration of 1868 when power was transferred from the shogunate to the Meiji Emperor. It may comes as a surprise to hear Saigo, generally regarded as a strong and fearless leader, talking about such matters as accounting. On the other hand, without this kind of proficiency no person could have accomplished something as significant as the Meiji Restoration. The following is a quotation from Mao Tse-tung:

> After a detailed analysis of the nature and circumstances of an assignment, [a person] will feel more sure of himself and do it willingly. If he spends time at the job and gains experience ... then he can draw conclusions for himself as to how to go about the job and do it with much more confidence. Only those who are subjective, one-sided and superficial in their approach will issue orders or directives the moment they arrive on the scene, without considering the circumstances, without viewing things in their totality (their history and their present state) and without grasping the essence of things (their nature and the relations between one thing and another). Such people are bound to trip and fall.[7]

Sir Winston Churchill, the distinguished statesman who led the British people in World War II, observed:

> All bold impulses, impatient desires and sudden flashes of military instinct cannot hasten the course of events ... [For the task at hand] we must take all those far-sighted measures which are necessary.[8]

What is common to all these people is that they were leaders who made decisions that affected the destiny of their country, and that they all had a commanding presence. Although they do not appear to be people who paid much attention to small details, their words show that they handled matters meticulously. Their approach to the affairs of state was based on tremendous care that was not apparent at first glance. Without attention to detail, they could not have accomplished the great things for which they are known.

There are those who would pretend to be of like stature but who fail to grasp the actual nature of problems and are apt to view details with disdain. They feel that they already know everything about the subject in question, and assume that people of high repute deal with things in a grand manner. This type of attitude, however, does not lead to the proper assessment of problems and holds up decisions for their solution, with the result that still greater sacrifices must be made as problems become more serious. This is a waste of national resources. The truly great are those who know that to initiate a revolution and point the way ahead one must be able to grasp the current major trends that underlie the overall view, as well as to assess matters as they really are. In today's world, with its more complicated and interactive social mechanisms of accurately assessing and taking account of prevailing conditions is a precondition for the success of any radical step forward. This attitude and approach are a must for policies that are pursued from now on.

A SENSE OF BALANCE IN ADMINISTRATIVE REFORM

One day in late autumn, I was going by car along the Chugoku Expressway from Hiroshima to Yamaguchi Prefecture. Even though it was a cold day, with snow falling lightly, there were so few vehicles on the road that I wondered whether I was travelling on a main trunk route.

This Expressway runs almost directly through the middle of the Chugoku Mountains, and it takes 40 or 50 minutes to get to many of the cities from their nearest interchange, including Hiroshima City. But apart from the question of inconvenience, this expressway cannot be regarded as an efficient investment. The reason that an expressway with such a low level of traffic was built and maintained with national funds – and at a very high cost – is not just on account of its role as part of the national infrastructure but of the 'pool' accounting system for expressways. Under this system, toll revenues from existing trunk roads with a lot of traffic such as the Tomei and Meishin expressways are made available for roads with little traffic. If this system were applied to JNR, revenues from the Tokaido Shinkansen would be reserved for expenditures within the Shinkansen system and that fund would be used to extend new lines even to areas where there is only a low traffic volume (as in the case of the Chugoku Expressway). However, JNR is not allowed to adopt such a system. Revenues form the Tokaido Shinkansen or lines in metropolitan areas cannot be reinvested in profitable projects but are distributed throughout the entire system. In other words, these funds are meant merely to finance deficits incurred by local lines.

Although both are parts of the national transportation system and of the national finances, the country's road and railway networks get different financial treatment. The fact that the entire road network, including ordinary roads, has been heavily supported by national taxes is not taken into account when revenues from expressway or internal subsidies are considered. Another advantage possessed by the expressway system is that as long as a large source of revenues exists, the efficiency of any investments in roads is not put to the test.

Although both the road and railway systems have their inefficiences, any spare funds are put to positive use in the case of roads but not so in the case of railways. Can the balanced development of the economy or the creation of an efficient transportation system be expected under these conditions? If creating a good transportation system is the goal, all transportation modes must be treated on a similar basis with respect to their administration and finance.

JNR has to make annual payments to the cities, towns and villages along its routes – the amount contributed by JNR to local finances since it fell into the red comes to more than 300 billion yen. This system was originally introduced in the mid-1950s as a way in which JNR, which was profitable at that time, could help local finances which were in difficulties. Now, however, JNR's management is itself in difficulties while local authorities have become rich enough to compete with each other over the splendour of their new offices and modern museums. In spite of such an enormous change in circumstances, JNR is still faced with maintaining local lines at a high cost, and is still having to make payments to cities, towns and villages along its local lines.

On the one hand, efficient management is demanded of JNR, while on the other this state of affairs continues to exist. Can this be regarded as socially sound? Attempting to remedy the situation by dwelling on perceived efficiencies may only create new social distortions: reform calls for a new sense of balance.

GAPS IN THE RECONSTRUCTION PLAN

According to JNR's accounts, the deficit incurred by local lines amounted to 290.2 billion yen in 1980/81, 347.3 billion in 1981/82, 403.7 billion in 1982/83 – an increase of about 50 billion yen every year. In 1984/85 two new changes were made to the local lines. One was the introduction of different fare rates in various areas, and the other was a reduction in the special government subsidy, namely, 29.8 billion yen less than it was the year before.

The reduction in government subsidies and grants was part of a financial turn-around that incorporated such concepts as zero or minus ceilings. As a governmental organization JNR is subject to national financial policies. As far as local lines are concerned, however, grants made to them are of a different character from those of other general subsidies. The cutback in government subsidies, of course, would be no problem if the deficit were to decrease by an equivalent amount, by shifting part of the local line services to the third sector – regional development entities combining the public and private sectors – or to bus services, or if new plans for lines that had been planned could be cancelled. Local lines, however, were built largely for the 'national' benefit and are in service day and night. Hence, the subsidies for local lines cannot be dealt with in the same way as subsidies for private companies. Even under the 'minus ceiling' budget, expenses related to local finances have increased by 18 per cent, about 1.4 trillion yen since 1982/83.

Although some believe that the different fare rates will compensate for the reduction in subsidies, the resulting increase in fare revenues is expected to be only about 5 billion yen annually. While it should be welcomed that the uniform fare system has been abandoned, the actual differences in rates will not make much of a contribution to covering costs.

These changes, though introduced for good reasons, will result in an even more serious lack of funds for the maintenance of local lines. Even if this gap could be bridged to some extent by rationalization and increasing management efficiency, the scale of the gap is a problem. Since drastic measures such as closing lines and shifting to bus services cannot be taken overnight, the question is whether rationalization can make a large enough difference in 1984/85 to compensate for the expected deficit in other areas.

The history of JNR's rationalization is one of cumulative attempts ever since 1954 when measures were first adopted to improve the management of the Kihara and Kururi lines. Every possible effort has been made to rationalize management and improve services in accordance with local conditions in all fields – with the exception of the uniform systems on fares, salaries and labour issues, JNR being a 'national' railway. In view of this history, are there any measures that could reduce costs on a scale of tens of billions of yen in 1984/85? JNR has little or no choice but to bear the financial losses of local lines.

If the government – largely on political grounds, and without offering any form of compensation – takes measures that will enlarge JNR's deficit (which is already seriously large), it is as if the government is forcing JNR to increase its debts. When reducing liabilities is one of the most important tasks in reconstructing JNR's management, how can the government's intention be interpreted if JNR is made to increase its liabilities?

JNR cannot be managed according to a single concept or principle. Diverse standards are necessarily adapted by different people at various times but each of them must be seen as applicable in a given context and under given conditions. Reconstruction plans will be incomplete as long as these requirements exist.

OPERATING ON 'PRIVATE RAILWAY STANDARDS'

When newspapers reported that the site of the former freight yard at Shinagawa Station had been sold for 100 billion yen at public auction and that the National Land Agency was trying to impose restrictions on the sale on the grounds that the price was too high, a reader in Shikoku made the following comment in *Yomiuri Shimbun* (a major Japanese daily):

> I have heard that when JNR, which suffers greatly from the size of its deficits, sold the site of its former freight yard at Shinagawa Station in Tokyo, the National Land Agency objected on the grounds that the price was too high. This is inconceivable. What I worry about is the opposite where, when part of JNR's services are shifted to the private sector or existing sites are sold, they are purchased by bargain seekers at unreasonably low prices, or that the characteristics of public service will be abandoned or changed for the sake of their convenience ... What we need most are measures that help, even slightly, to assist JNR in its recovery.

This issue certainly poses a problem for the National Land Agency, and the perception of ordinary people seems to hit the mark. The situation that JNR currently faces is not so simple as to enable it to recover merely by considering peripheral matters. JNR is so close to collapse that the question arises as to whether or not it can even survive as a national transportation system. Problems arising out of social considerations, should be handled by the government. JNR should recognize that it is at a stage where reconstruction cannot be achieved without making every effort to explore every conceivable avenue that would be to its benefit.

One of the few measures that JNR has left to it concerns the valuable land it owns. This asset should not be treated as a concession to others or that its economic benefits should be exploited by others. The disposal of assets such as land is a once and for all event and its timing should be very carefully considered in recognition of its significance in the process of reconstruction: assets should not be sold off aimlessly as if simply to live off one's capital or property.

One of the standards for evaluating the measures for reconstruction is that of private railways whose operations are seen as the best index or model. However, this view overlooks the problem of JNR's system of fares and charges which bear on its revenues. On local lines, even after JNR's latest fare raise, its fares are still less than half those of private railways in the same areas. The Oigawa Railway, for example, charges 1,270 yen for its service between Kanaya and Senzu (39.5 kilometres), but JNR can charge only 630 yen for that distance even under the local line rate. Another example is the 500 yen fare between Fukui and Higashi-Furuichi (10.9 kilometres) charged by the Keifuku Electric Railway Co., compared to 190 yen by JNR. Some private fares in local areas are more than twice those of JNR, and they have long been accepted by the local people. When discussions on charges on JNR's lines are held, the response is usually to point to a lack of consideration in the treatment of local areas.

With respect to JNR's management, measures are not always implemented as thoroughly as they ought to be, and consequently, however right these measures may be for the purpose of reconstruction, they become rather ineffective and their benefits not all that great. This is like a medicine which, no matter how good it may be, will not work if it is taken in small doses.

THOUGHTS ABOUT THE PROFITS OF BRITISH RAIL

The news that British Rail (BR) made a profit in 1983 was reported even in the general newspapers in Japan; British *Financial Times* praised it as 'a record-breaking operating profit of 55 million pounds'. (This included *the Public Service Obligation* payment based on the government's subsidization scheme).

A national railway provides some services which meet 'social needs' or are in response to national or local policies, and this cannot be the case for ordinary private companies. Receiving an amount equivalent to the costs of such services in the form of compensation and treating this as a part of operating revenues is a natural way to manage a railway from the perspective of corporate accounting, whereby costs and revenues should be similarly treated. The profits of a national railway are those made under such an adjusted accounting system.

For more than a decade, the European Economic Community has followed a basic policy in railway management of clearly distinguishing such costs. Although methods may differ in terms of whether an amount equivalent to these costs is included in revenues or these costs are deducted from expenditures, member countries have consistently promoted the normalization of railway accounting in accordance with this policy and have tried to maintain the functions and services of their railway systems. In an effort to clarify the responsibilities of management, the Deutsche Bundesbahn divides its income statement into three parts: the national field, the national economic field, and the commercial field. In Japan, this has not yet been done.

In order to become efficient the first thing to do is to make clear the goal of our efforts. The goal should be attainable and should enable our efforts and responsibilities to be evaluated. It is very difficult and dispiriting to be enthusiastic for long about a goal that is out of reach.

When a revised draft of its reconstruction plan was issued by JNR, the following comment was made:

> The revised plan forecasts that JNR will make a general operating profit by 1985/86, and that the revenues and expenditures of trunk lines will be on balance. A study of the overall revenues and expenditures, however, reveals that the estimated deficit has been increased from 990 billion yen in the original draft to 1.29 trillion in the revised plan; this means a total deficit of more than 1.7 trillion yen when the 420 billion in capital expenses for the Tohoku and Joetsu Shinkansens are added.

The author of this comment went on to say that this was evidence of JNR's lukewarm attitude toward reconstruction. This is correct in so far as the reconstruction plan for JNR does not provide for an improvement in its overall revenues and expenditures. However, it is unreasonable to hold JNR responsible for a management burden caused by national or local policies, or to attribute the inability to bear this burden to a lack of effort on the part of JNR. With respect to the manner in which the national and local authorities implement policies concerning the national railway, JNR is able to state its view on them but cannot allow for them in its reconstruction plan. Any plan of JNR's is bound to be deficient.

If 'social' services and external directives were excluded from the management of JNR, there would be much less of a problem. Even then, however, the past cannot be erased and some expenditures will continue to occur as a result of past policies. It is almost meaningless and certainly misleading to the public to discuss JNR's efficiency unless those matters are taken into account.

The Tohoku and Joetsu Shinkansen are now up and running, but the capital spent on their construction has placed a heavy burden on JNR's management, and the ordinary lines on parallel routes have already lost some operating revenues. If this were a case involving a private company, some form of compensation would be considered. In the event, can any proper view for the reconstruction of JNR be taken?

It is easy to accuse JNR of having a 'laissez-faire' attitude even though there is still room for more efforts in its operation, but all of JNR's problems cannot be solved by JNR alone. If nothing more is done than to insist on greater efforts by JNR while there are problems which cannot be dealt with on a commercial basis, the situation will get more and more difficult to handle as time is wasted and delay follows on delay.

CUTTING BACK TO 320,000 PERSONNEL

Let us take a look at three organizations now employing about 320,000 personnel. The first is JNR. When JNR revised its reorganization plan in 1981, a goal was set for 1985/86 to reduce the number of its employees to 350,000 – this was to be the foundation to assure sound management. This was again revised in May 1984 down to 320,000. This was because rationalization had progressed more rapidly than expected on account of a decline in the demand for transportation services, and particularly on account of the great changes that took place in the rail freight service system. The original goal of 350,000 employees was therefore reduced in

1984/85, a year earlier than expected. The aim of the latest revision is to continue with this policy with an even more thorough and comprehensive rationalization while not taking on any more new staff.

It is good that rationalization has made more progress than originally planned and that goals can be set still higher: this makes reconstruction that much easier. At the same time, however, the presence of 25,000 or 30,000 employees surplus to requirement will stand in the way of reconstruction.

JNR once had 610,000 employees. In the confusion during the immediate post-war years, JNR gave work to large numbers of people returning from overseas and military service. The number reached a peak in 1947. Since then a reduction in number has been one of the main ways to stabilize JNR's management. The planned cutback to 320,000 employees is the latest in the series since 1947. But while the number of employees has been reduced to about half of what it used to be, traffic is estimated in the revised plan to be 216.8 billion passenger/ton-kilometres in 1985, almost double the figure in 1947. JNR's management conditions, however, continue to worsen, and the current situation is such that even an improvement on this scale does not offer any assurances with respect to the future of reconstruction.

Another organization with a large number of workers is the Nippon Telegraph and Telephone Public Corporation (NTT). The number has increased in line with the rapid expansion of telephone services, from 145,000 when it was established in 1952, to 320,000 in 1984. Although both NTT and JNR now employ the same number of people, this represents a decrease from 610,000 in the case of JNR but an increase from 145,000 in the case of NTT.

Though both NTT and JNR are governmental enterprises, their histories are different. With a monopolistic market, NTT has developed to a point where it gets 4.3 trillion yen in operating revenues and makes 370 billion in profit annually. Unlike JNR, NTT's growth has helped its rationalization of management to be that much smoother and easier.

A third example of a workforce of 320,000 is the Deutsche Bundesbahn (DB). The number of people employed by DB was 317,000 in 1982 and about 520,000 in 1949 (when JNR was established as a public corporation). Like JNR, DB has continued to reduce its workforce and has reached the current number, 320,000, after more than 30 years of cutbacks. Overall traffic increased during that time from 78.5 billion to 108.8 billion passenger/ton-kilometres, a growth of only 39 per cent. DB has made operating losses of about 10.6 trillion yen over the past 10 years, but only about 270 billion remain as an accumulated deficit because the government provided subsidies to help meet the deficits.

The level of 320,000 employees is not an ultimate goal but a stage in the history of each of these organizations: the key point relates to the kinds of strategies and management plans they will develop for the future. They happen just now to match up in terms of the size of their workforce and will move on henceforth toward their own goals.

The *Telegraph and Telephone Public Corporation Reform Bill* has passed the House of Representatives, and the time for NTT's break with the past into a new organization is near. Likewise, JNR's management is reaching a turning point. Wise choices made at this critical stage will open up new prospects for the future.

ONE VIEWPOINT ON THE 1983/84 SETTLEMENT OF ACCOUNTS

The 1983/84 business results of two public corporations were recently made public: JNR's on August 27 and those of the Nippon Telegraph and Telephone Public Corporation (NTT) on August 30. JNR had a deficit of 1.66 trillion yen while NTT made a profit of 380 billion yen.

Capital expenditures amounting to 47 per cent of its operating revenues was identified as one of the problems in the management of JNR, the corresponding ratio for NTT being 40 per cent. This is not a great difference percentage wise; the problem lies in the difference in the content of the capital expenditures. In the case of NTT, depreciation came to 1.3 trillion yen and the interest payments 400 billion: for JNR, depreciation came to 460 billion yen and the interest in the profit and loss account alone one trillion. Interest is a disbursement while depreciation enters a reserve fund, and this has a quite different implication for the two organizations. In ten years, NTT has strengthened its finances with depreciation funds of 10 trillion yen while JNR has paid 4.3 trillion in interest – the amount actually paid by JNR exclusive of governmental subsidies. JNR had 3.2 trillion yen of depreciation in its account but this is merely an accounting formality and does not mean an actual reserve of this amount. Its management has been running a deficit before depreciation since 1971/72.

Hence, the financial structures of the two organizations have become quite different with the passage of time. Although both are governmental corporations, one has acquired 10 trillion yen in internal reserves in a decade while the other has been unable to make any real provision for depreciation for more than thirteen years and has no prospect of escaping from this state of affairs in the near future.

An organization with fixed assets valued at about 13 trillion yen and responsible for the transportation of 6.7 billion passengers a year finds it cannot properly upgrade its facilities. The organization has no way other than borrowing to maintain the infrastructure needed to operate its services. Little in the way of commentary can be found pointing out the critical nature of this situation. Unless business operations are abandoned, the time will come when existing facilities must be upgraded. Long-term debts will not be curtailed though the public calls for restraint in investment. Profits become difficult to estimate and the interest that will have to be paid will result in a worsening of management conditions.

In 1983/84, local lines made a loss of 470 billion yen for a traffic volume which was just 4.3 per cent of JNR's total. The audit report describes this situation as follows:

> While traffic continues to decline every year, the amount of the deficit increases and creates a still heavier burden on the finances of JNR. To permit this situation to remain unchanged places a serious obstacle in the path of JNR's reconstruction.

The audit report calls for the implementation of remedial measures 'as soon as possible'. While all this is true, the audit report of 1971/72 when JNR incurred a deficit (before depreciation) for the first time since becoming a public corporation, suggested that measures with respect to local lines should be taken not only from the point of view of JNR's revenues and expenditures, but also from that of the national economy. The history of this problem since that time shows how difficult it is to decide upon any

fundamental policy, and to carry that policy through to its conclusion. This is all the clearer in those cases where the various
twists and turns in measures undertaken for JNR's reconstruction
have been a waste of time and made conditions worse.

In 1983/84, the capital expenditures borne by JNR for the
Tohoku and Joetsu Shinkansen lines exceeded 360 billion yen.
The audit report describes this in the following manner:

> The policy of *The Management Improvement Plan* whereby capital
> related to expenditures of the two Shinkansens is not to be included in
> the revenues and expenditures of trunk lines, should be considered.

Even taken together with the revenues from adjacent parallel
ordinary lines, however, the revenues from these lines amount to
only 340 billion yen. The plan to construct the Tohoku and Joetsu
Shinkansens was designed by the Construction Council in January
in 1971, when strict compliance with the reconstruction plan was
demanded since seven years had already passed since JNR went
into the red. To decide on a plan to invest as much as 4.4 trillion
yen in new equipment and then to charge JNR with all operational
responsibilities on completion, clearly contravenes the goals of
reconstruction. The Joetsu Line was enlarged from a single to a
double track line in 1967 – 36 years after it had opened its service
– and only 15 years later it was again doubled with the wide-
gauge Shinkansen which expanded capacity more than seven
times. This did not originate from the needs of JNR's management; judging from the conditions in the areas along the line, an
increase in transportation demand corresponding to this capacity
cannot be expected in the near future.

The audit report also admitted a difficulty in that the operating
revenues and expenditures of the Tohoku and Joetsu Shinkansens
and the parallel ordinary lines had deteriorated a lot. The only
good reason for such an investment, therefore, was to develop the
basic infrastructure system of the country generally. Adding an
investment burden arising from national policies to JNR's responsibilities at a time when it was already undergoing reconstruction
– treating these difficult types of lines identically as 'trunk lines' –
only confuses the real issue. With the trend towards analyzing
management according to separate categories or divisions, the
process of reconstruction is undermined by going back to the idea
of lumping everything together.

A WORRISOME TENDENCY

On October 18 1984, the Ministry of Transport declared that it shared the view of the *JNR Restructuring Supervisory Committee* with respect to the form of JNR's management and the method of dealing with its long-term liabilities (as stated in its Second Emergency Proposal). Just as the way in which JNR would be reconstructed was being set out, a serious accident occurred on the Sanyo Honsen Line on October 19, the cause being that the driver was drunk and dozed off at the controls.

If an experienced train driver is so irresponsible as to fail in his basic duties, this may be seen as evidence that a sort of stupor has infected the workplace from top to bottom. Why should this be? The problem cannot be solved until its cause is identified and eliminated.

In response to this accident, it was commonly urged that JNR should be privatised and split up as soon as possible. But even if this were done, the presidents of the new companies would not be able to check on whether workers were drinking on the job for the supervisors would still be responsible for these sorts of matters.

Some seem to expect privatisation and division to have a special effect on every aspect of JNR's current problems. Altering the form of management would certainly lead to changes in operating conditions, but this would not necessasrily solve every problem. A study by Tokyo Shoko Research Ltd. revealed that more than 19,000 private companies went bankrupt in 1983: many of these were small and medium-sized companies which are said to be easy for managers to control, since they can attend to the details of the business.

JNR cannot reject the accusation that the accident on October 19 was due to the unforgivable conduct of people who have the safety of many lives in their keeping. When the pay and pensions of JNR's employees are discussed, however, the recognition that these are 'people who have the safety of many lives in their keeping' disappears, and some seem to take it as a matter of course that their pay and pensions should be lower than those of government officials and employees of other public enterprises, and this because JNR is operating at a loss. The reality, however, is that what is referred to as JNR's deficit includes the costs of various services which are provided as part of government policies. Needless to say, lower than average pay and pensions can

only discourage JNR employees when they reflect on their conditions of work and their standards of living.

JNR continues to maintain local lines while incurring large
deficits every uear. 13 years elapsed from the time when JNR first
went into the red before the government decided to pay subsidies
to compensate for this. Furthermore, the subsidies have covered
only part of the deficit: although exceeding 120 billion yen in
1981/82, the amount of the subsidies has consistently declined
since then to only 85.7 billion by 1984/85.

The deficit incurred by local lines in 1983/84 amounted to 470
billion yen even after deducting the subsidies. Progress in shifting
local lines to bus services has been slow; and in addition, of the
33 lines for which JNR sought approval under the second phase
of this programme, six have been postponed. The growing trend
of putting a greater burden on JNR's management, even in fields
where national or local authorities should be primarily responsible, is hard to understand in the context of reconstruction. It is
also said that the difference in fare rates between trunk and local
lines which has only just been allowed, will be scrapped and that
uniformity will be restored in the fares planned for next year.

JNR's current circumstances make privatisation and division
necessary, but personnel reductions and other improvement measures should be implemented now, even before the form of management is altered. Successful reconstruction cannot be expected
if measures are adopted only with respect to the form of management while other factors continue to be neglected.

DISADVANTAGES OF DIVISION AND HOW TO OVERCOME THEM

> The division of the national electric power company into nine individual
> companies in May 1951 was based on the principles of local monopoly
> and charges based on cost, but the system contains many inconveniences
> today and future restructuring is required ... With regard to cost-based
> charges, this does not fit in with the profit system and the charges of
> each company are extremely distorted ... It was forecast in the begin-
> ning that the service areas created by dividingthe country into nine
> regions would be too small for 'wide-sphere' operation.

This is a quotation from an article entitled 'Now is the Time to
Reorganize the Electric Power Industry Again' in the August
1958 issue of *Diamond* magazine. This was written by Yasuzae-

mon Matsunaga who was one of the strongest proponents of reform in the industry. The article is interesting in that it states the views of a founder of the new system seven years after its establishment: that he should call for a further review of the system points to the complexity of resolving problems arising from dividing an organization, even after so many years later.

The electricity industry had a firm regional management basis from the beginning. Also, the fact that electricity can be instantaneously transmitted from Kyushu in the south of the country to Hokkaido in the far north, makes adjustments among regions comparatively simple. It appears, however, that there are conflicts between pursuing the economies of 'wide-sphere' operation and balancing supply and demand within the service area of each regional company. In spite of Matsunaga's proposal, the system of nine regional companies has been maintained up to the present day, while 'wide-sphere' operation has been strengthened and expanded by co-operative action and the inter-regional transmission of electricity.

Many consider the restructuring of the electricity industry to be a good model for JNR's reconstruction but, as history shows, the act of division itself did not directly lead to greater efficiency in or revitalization of the industry. However, much can be learned from the efforts made and means employed to overcome the operational inconveniences and problems that occurred as a result of the division.

Gaiji Yamaguchi, the manager of carriage and wagon allotment and train operations for the Manchurian Railway from 1936 to 1945, reported on the conditions in those days based on his experience in operating direct services on the Korean, Manchurian and Northern Chinese Railways, as follows:

> With only one or two through-expresses, it was impossible to draw up a timetable that was convenient for all the cities along the line. Decisions therefore had to be made on which cities should be given priority, but often such decisions were not made simply on the grounds of logic among these three railways under different management. . . . Each railway kept advocating only its own position, and this eventually resulted in an unsatisfactory compromise on timetables . . . [Regarding the arrangement of trains for direct service,] differences in transportation capacity among the railways were ironed out by utilizing the wagons belonging to the Manchurian Railway. The number was agreed

upon at a conference attended by the military leaders from each area and representatives of the railways, but the agreement was seldom kept.... Of course, the Manchurian Railway constantly pressed for the return of the wagons and took every possible measure, including sending staff to investigate and negotiate, in a vain effort to improve the situation.... Even with the help of the General Staff Office and Kanto Corps, it was still impossible to resolve the conflicts of interest among the different railways.

This report highlights the circumstances of a situation where decisions were not made on the grounds that interests should be adjusted by negotiation.

The case of the electricity industry indicated that difficulties with respect to 'wide-sphere' operation arise even in transmitting a non-physical product such as electricity. Yet the flexibility to make regional adjustments is incomparably greater with electricity than with railways where there is no way of varying capacity other than by moving physical things in the form of rolling stock on fixed tracks. Regional adjustments would be easier if extra capacity were available, but the more each railway economises its capacity for the sake of efficiency, the more difficult these adjustments become.

Any drastic change is bound to have some disadvantages, and the key point is to what extent these can be overcome. There is a tendency to avoid discussion of disadvantages by attributing them to a lack of enthusiasm – in this case, on the part of JNR. The way to achieve a successful change, however, cannot be mapped out by side-stepping negative factors, but by carefully examining all possible measures.

JNR'S OWN REFORM PLAN

A draft of JNR's own proposals concerning its reform generated a public response which was typified in newspaper editorials such as the following:

They are based on nothing but existing ideas and do no more than try to implement measures by an extension of traditional practices. (*Sankei Shimbun*)

They are far too passive, and the practice of avoiding responsibility and relying on others has not changed. (*Asahi Shimbun*).

Far too self-seeking, vague, and full of wishful thinking; their content lacks credibility. (*Nihon Keizai Shimbun*)

> These proposals are hopelessly indecisive; one cannot but regard
> them as wishy-washy in the extreme. (*Yomiuri Shimbun*)

These responses imply that JNR is surrounded by enemies, and
may indicate the intractability of JNR's problems in the sense that
it is impossible to find answers that everybody would support. The
fact that there was such widespread and severe criticism points to
a deep-rooted distrust of JNR's management – and this prevents
JNR's point of view from being listened to by the public.

When JNR's proposals are examined in detail, however, there
are some points that cannot be brushed aside as being traditional
or customary. Privatisation, for example, is advocated by JNR
itself for the first time. Similarly, there is some merit in the
proposal that the number of personnel should be reduced to
188,000 following improvements in management efficiency, particularly when it is recalled that JNR once had as many as 450,000
employees. Many ideas, however, are based on 'judgments at the
present time' and some practices such as the basic rights of labour
are 'unchanged for the moment.' Although this may result from
the fact that JNR, as the actual operator of the services under
review, regards careful and detailed consideration as necessary,
the proposals do give the impression that JNR is not all that keen
on its own reconstruction.

There is also the problem of timing as reflected in the opinion
that JNR's declaration with respect to its own reform was long
overdue and came at an inopportune moment. If the same statement had been issued by JNR earlier on, when the Special
Government Inspection Committee discussed JNR's reconstruction, it would have been perceived by the public rather differently.

Another problem is that the content of the proposals was not
set out in sufficient detail so that it is difficult to grasp the actual
form of the proposed improvements proposed.

> Precisely what privatisation entails is too vague, and strictly speaking,
> it is doubtful that this would really mean privatisation. (*Sankei
> Shimbun*)

As for JNR's advocacy of decentralization instead of division, the
comment was made:

> If JNR is opposed to division, it should, as the operator of the services,
> provide information that will allow a comparison of the merits and

demerits of division. (*Asahi Shimbun*) The proposed decentralization is not specific and uses only abstract phrases such as 'thorough decentralized control.' (*Mainichi Shimbun*)

JNR should try to meet these points.

Another of the basic proposals concerns local lines. Commentaries on this are confusing. On the one hand, JNR is criticized with respect to the social consequences of separating forty per cent of the national railway network from its operations, and this implies JNR's selfish abandonment of local areas. On the other hand, JNR is also accused of being negative about the very idea of division. Off-loading local lines would impose a great burden on the people living in those service areas; at the same time, JNR's requests for subsidies to operate local line services are regarded as a problem, based on the reasoning that they are normal business operations rather than a matter of social policies. Although the plan to establish regional management is a step forward in co-ordinating rail services with the needs of local communities and formulating the best measures for maintaining local transportation services, the proposal is not one that is easy to accept.

Looking at the future of reconstruction, it is regrettable that commentaries are generally against JNR's position from beginning to end and every statement made by JNR is interpreted in an unhelpful way. In the background is a profound distrust of JNR, and overcoming this is quite a challenge. Without the public trust, a consensus for reconstruction is difficult to reach. Prompt and resolute decisions by JNR might bring about a return of trust provided they are made clear to the public at large.

REVOLUTION AND NOSTALGIA

JNR plans to make several changes in its local organizations in the spring of 1985, aiming at a system that is more efficient and streamlined, as well as more adaptable to the conditions in each area. Among them is a change that is little short of remarkable, namely, to unify the Hokkaido General Office and the Sapporo Railway Control Office into a new Hokkaido General Office – in other words, to abolish the Sapporo Control Office and to transfer its work to the Hokkaido General Office. The *Kotsu Shimbun* once held an interivew with the president of JNR about its reorganization:

> The purpose of local reorganization is to simplify the existing system as well as to get away from uniformity so as to create organizations most suited to the circumstances of each local area. . . . In Hokkaido, it may well be felt that the Sapporo Railway Control Office has simply been enlarged . . . and so I think it is right and proper for the new Hokkaido General Office should take direct charge of the control area of the former Sapporo Railway Control Office and to supervise the control offices of each of the other areas. The Hokkaido General Office has the capacity and ability to do this.

This point of view is clear and consistent with the local reorganization plan; however, the person interviewed here is not the current President Nisugi but former President Isozaki, and this was in July 1970. The Sapporo Railway Control Office was merged into the Hokkaido General Office in August 1970 and the same type of amalgamation will again take place in March 1985 – and for the identical purpose of making the local control system more efficient and simple.

This is reminiscent of a 'time warp'. What significance does it have on JNR's management? The answer is simple. The merger of 1970 was reversed in later years when another reorganization was carried out in Hokkaido in December 1976 whereby the Sapporo Railway Control Office was reinstated and the Hokkaido General Office gave up its direct control of the work sites. Although business conditions such as the relations with the labour unions were cited as reasons, this reversal was driven by the basic instinct of not wanting to work under a system different from that of other areas, together with an attachment to the older system.

An article on November 30, 1976 in the *Kotsu Shimbun* reporting on the revival of the Sapporo Railway Control Office stated:

> Some complaints were made by those outside JNR that the organization and work allocations of the Hokkaido General Office were difficult to understand.

This indicated that there was a strong nostalgia for the Sapporo Railway Control Office among former JNR employees.

It is understandable for one to feel more comfortable in a familiar environment. This emotional response, however, undermined an important management reform which was the right choice to make even in the light of today's standards. In fact, this is why the same measures for reconstruction are about to be implemented again. In thinking of the importance of this fifteen-year period, during which JNR should have made every effort toward its restructuring, one experiences a sense of despair. What benefit did JNR's management get by restoring the previous system and undermining a change that had already been carried out? Were JNR's operations in Hokkaido really saved by this action? JNR is now required to initiate the same change under more urgent circumstances to accomplish better results.

JNR's management has delayed implementing a number of policies with which to cope with its problems on account of a nostalgic adherence to the past. An example is the opposition to closing lines with little traffic – often voiced by those who do not use the services of these lines in the first place. If further reversals are permitted on these grounds, JNR's reconstruction will take as long as the waters of the Yellow River take to clear.

JNR must make changes in a variety of forms, and prospects for the future will open up only when these changes are put into effect. In any case, it is now to be hoped that the newly-revived local control system, where the General Office directly supervises the work sites, will act as a base for efficient management.

THE SANRIKU RAILWAY – AN EXAMPLE OF REVITALIZATION

On the first anniversary of the Sanriku Railway, newspapers expressed admiration at its excellent achievements. This railway drew the attention of the public as it was the first case where a local line had been operated in a third-sector system, a combination of public and private sectors. The results for the first year were better than expected and it was seen as representing a possible solution to the problems facing local lines generally. And indeed, the operational experiences of the Sanriku Railway provide a model on how local lines should be operated in the future. The following excerpts from various papers typify the general response to this achievement:

– The Sanriku Railway has revitalized a line formerly operating in the red and one which JNR had abandoned.
– The results are so good that even the people concerned were

surprised that they had done so much better than expected. The residents in the area are proud of themselves since the line incurred a deficit of about 500 million yen annually in the days of JNR.
– This is truly the fruit of the 'Sanriku system.'

These articles are right, but to attribute these miraculous results to the effects of privatisation alone would be hasty and unwarranted; it is as if we were to claim that the division of the national electric power company into nine companies alone led to the prosperity of the industry. The actual conditions of the Sanriku Railway in its first year need to be identified more precisely.

Privatisation provided an opportunity to revitalize management but it would not be correct to say that the deficit disappeared once the railway's management was changed from JNR to that of a private company. When the so-called third-sector operation was inaugurated, many generous measures were introduced which were not available to local lines managed by JNR, particularly with respect to their financial basis.

The first was that the company was freed from the financial burden of fixed costs, the bane of the railway business. The value of the transportation facilities handed over to the Sanriku Railway by JNR and the Japan Railway Construction Corporation came to about 60 billion yen. The Sanriku Railway was able to use these facilities free of charge, including the new advanced facilities constructed by JRCC: these were built at great cost with the aim of reducing maintenance costs. It is a great advantage to the railway business to be free of fixed costs.

The second concession was a grant in the form of a transfer subsidy. At its inauguration, the new company received from 10 to 30 million yen per kilometre, or over 2.2 billion yen in all. The Sanriku Railway thus started out not only without any debts but with assured funds for its business operations thereafter.

The third concession was that many former JNR personnel were employed at wage levels lower than those of JNR; their pay was calculated so that they would receive the same amount as before but including their pension fund allotments, with the result that the Sanriku Railway obtained a highly experienced labour force at wages that were lower than usual. In other words, it employed lower personnel costs by placing some of the burden on JNR's pension fund.

Hence, the financial structure of the Sanriku system was supported by three tiers of protective measures which are not available to JNR's local lines. The good results should be seen as the outcome of having a free hand in both the planning and execution of activities but in the context of a generous financial structure.

Several things can be learned from the experiences of the Sanriku Railway. One is the idea that the people of the prefecture – particularly those living in the cities, towns and villages along the line – should play an active role in maintaining the railway since it was their own. This attitude, which could not have taken root when the line belonged to JNR, led to a spirit of co-operation throughout the entire region, a factor that was not thought of when demand was initially estimated. It would have been impossible to generate this regional sense of pride in a system where management losses could be shifted to other regions, that is to say, by means of the internal subsidy system.

Another factor which contributed to the good results was the productivity of the employees who were so efficient that they were able to carry out work with fewer people than was initially planned. Many of them were from JNR. Employees of JNR should feel proud that their former colleagues have made such a difference to the efficiency of a private company. Most of JNR's personnel could do much the same, but have no way of doing this within the JNR system. Is it that when they leave JNR, they come to life as though a spell has been broken? The factors which prevent them from doing so within JNR should surely be examined.

The Sanriku Railway is expected to build on the results achieved in its first year when it benefited from a number of favourable conditions, and to go on to further achievements in the years to come when conditions are not likely to be quite so favourable.

THE ULTIMATE DIRECTION OF NATIONAL INTEREST

In January 1985, the *Spanish National Railway* closed down 911 kilometres of its passenger and freight services. This coincided with the end of the subsidies previously received from the government for those lines.

This is an excerpt from an article in the February 1985 issue of *Railway Gazette International*. In addition, passenger services were reported to have been discontinued on a further 1,016 kilometres of the Spanish network. These measures were for a railway with 13,000 kilometres of track all told.

Like JNR, national railways in Europe, have many lines which could not be successfully run on a commerical basis. The underlying reason for this is that these lines were seen as contributing to the 'national welfare', and what has enabled them to survive was the assumption of some responsibility for those lines by the government, in the form of financial compensation. If providing subsidies is in the national interest, the same must also be true for discontinuing them. The case of the *Spanish National Railway* illustrates a chain of events based on the national interest, and what can happen if services lose the government's support.

The circumstances in Spain seem to be quite different from those in Japan. In the 1985/86 budget, the special subsidy to JNR for local lines was again reduced, this time to 69.8 billion yen. When compared with the 126.4 billion yen in 1981/82, subsidies have been reduced over these four years by a total of 56.6 billion or 45 per cent. The reason for this must be either that the conditions of the local lines themselves have changed in terms of their scope and scale, or that government policy has changed.

If more rapid progress had been made in shifting local line services to bus services – a policy promoted by the government as a part of JNR's reconstruction – and if the scale of local lines had been reduced, a decline in government subsidies would have occurred of its own accord. However, the length of local lines in operation has been reduced by only 2.6 per cent between 1981 to 1985. Further, when the shift in services to buses has been completed for the local lines that were first designated, it is estimated that the burden on JNR will be lighter by only about 17 billion yen – and yet the government has discontinued subsidies of about 3.3 times this amount. It is not clear whether this means that the government has lost interest in keeping local lines in being.

The cut in subsidies may have been made simply as part of the government's general financial policies, specifically, the so-called 'minus ceiling' principle. At the same time, however, the budget for roads has been enlarged by nearly 200 billion yen. If the government's policy with respect to local lines has really changed, the 'national interest' should be clarified in terms of its financial

implications for the future as well as the government's responsibilities for the end results. How exactly should the lines, on which
trains are operating daily, be treated? Reducing the burden on
the national coffers while leaving the notion of the national
interest vague will only deepen the existing confusion.

JNR will have no choice other than to continue its operations
and incur still greater debt, as has been the case so far. How can
this assist in its reconstruction? JNR is required to get on with
reconstruction but just as the problems of reconstruction have
reached a critical stage, the government increases JNR's debt for
the sake of overall national policy – an area outside JNR's control.
This cannot be consistent with the priority given by government
to the problem of JNR's reconstruction.

Nevertheless, there are signs that the pursuit of the national
interest does lead to some form of overall co-ordination. A
sentence in the agreement on building the new Shinkansen lines,
negotiated between the government and the ruling Liberal-Demo-
cratic Party in the course of the 1985/86 budget, reads:

> For the commencement of construction, closing down existing parallel
> lines should be accomplished by necessary legislation.

Thus, the problems of the existing parallel lines are to be dealt
with as the Shinkansen lines are being built, and not after their
completion.

REMOVING THE POTENTIAL CAUSES OF COLLAPSE

An expert in the reconstruction of companies, Umeo Oyama,
describes his basic philosophy as follows:

> If every cause of collapse can be examined in detail and removed,
> reconstruction is possible under any set of circumstances.

The policy proposals of the JNR Restructuring Supervisory Committee on the restructuring of JNR, depends for their success on
whether or not they can deal with the factors which have brought
its management close to collapse. The Committee stressed that
assessing the underlying reasons for JNR's difficulties would be a
vital aspect in planning JNR's reconstruction. One factor which
was highlighted was the extent to which internal subsidies had
grown 'beyond reasonable limits', for this not only propped up

inefficient areas of activity unsuited to the railway, but also weakened the managerial base of areas most suited to the railway, where it could compete with other transportation modes.

The following appeared in the readers' column of the July 30 edition of the *Sankei Shimbun*:

> JNR's fares are double those of the Tobu Railway. Feeling that I was merely bearing the brunt of the salaries of JNR's employees, I have decided not to use JNR and use only Tobu from now on.

The fact that those who use JNR in the metropolitan area bear the losses incurred by local lines led to misunderstandings and to JNR's unpopularity. It is necessary to examine whether the conditions of the newly-planned companies – which would absorb all local lines (except specially designated ones) and operate them along the trunk lines – would permit them to be managed within 'reasonable limits' of internal subsides; and whether too they can regain the original advantages of the railway and open up the prospect of establishing a more efficient transportation system.

Although the proposals of the JNR Restructuring Supervisory Committee are significant in that they resolve several complicated issues concerning JNR and put an end to the dispute concerning its reconstruction – which has lasted for more than a decade – it is also true that numerous problems are still unresolved. In addition, the Committee admits that various difficulties will arise in implementing their proposals.

No proposal can perfectly solve JNR's problems. The point is to what extent the disadvantage in any proposal can be overcome when it is implemented, and this calls for an accurate assessment of actual conditions: only then, would 'brainstorming' and hard work do the trick. Situations that may arise in the future cannot be dealt with simply by adopting an optimistic outlook that is without a realistic basis, or by relying on mere effort. The present problems do not allow time to be wasted looking for perfect answers and discussing them only in general terms.

The JNR Restructuring Supervisory Committee declared that JNR will have long-term liabilities of 37.3 trillion yen at the beginning of 1987/88. 14.2 trillion of this would be shouldered by the new companies and 6.4 trillion settled by selling off some assets. JNR would be responsible for a debt of 20.6 trillion yen, while the public would be asked to bear the remaining 16.7 trillion. Commentaries on this in newspapers were on these lines:

> This is such an enormous amount that one can only sigh. The ineffi-
> cient management to date should naturally be held responsible.

Of the total debt of approximately 37 trillion yen, 23 trillion was newly incurred after the Second Special Government Inspection Committee had begun its work. The balance of JNR's long-term liabilities before that time was 9 trillion yen. If the figure of 5.3 trillion yen, representing the combined amount of debt deferred on two separate occasions by inclusion in the liability settlement special accounts, is added to the former balance, the total comes to only slightly more than 14 trillion, much less than the 20 trillion announced by the committee for settlement by JNR.

JNR's history stretches back 130 years. Its accumulated liabilities from the first 108 years can be settled by JNR through its own efforts, including both future actitivies and the disposal of assets. Thus, the amount to be borne by the public is that part of the debt incurred during the seven years after the Second Special Government Inspection started its work – in other words, during the period in which measures for JNR's settlement were under the government's control.

JNR has not been idle during this time. The number of employees will be reduced from 413,000 at the end of 1980/81 to 276,000 by the beginning of 1987/88 – a significant achievement in personnel reduction since the level of services has been maintained at much the same level. However, despite JNR's own efforts in this regard, and the exacting guidance of the government, enormous liabilities have accumulated in rather a short period. This means that the true nature of this problem cannot be attributed to ineffective management on the part of JNR. These liabilities came about by allowing time to be wasted in not taking any drastic measures, and the amount involved shows how serious the consequences can be. There is clearly no more room for delay in adopting the measures that are needed.

The policy announced by the JNR Restructuring Supervisory Committee this time should be implemented to get to the heart of the problem through in-depth discussions and studies, so as to offer a bright future for the railway.

HISTORY OF THE JNR AUDIT COMMITTEE

In August 1985, JNR's Audit Committee published its 1984/85 report. The committee was established as the auditing body of JNR in June 1956, and submitted its first report to the Minister of Transport in August of the following year. Since then audit reports have been prepared annually by the committee at the same time as JNR's publication of its annual financial statements. The latest report was published just after the JNR Restructuring Supervisory Committee released its proposals and at a time when JNR was coming to an end as a public corporation. As an internal body of JNR, the committee has been close to JNR's management and has thus been able to oversee the conditions of the organization. What position the committee would take on this issue was therefore one that attracted much interest.

In the mid-1950s, when the Audit Committee was first established, JNR had recovered from the damage it sustained during the war and had set out to enlarge its capacity and modernize its operations. However, JNR gradually declined through the mid-1960s with its financial deficit growing more and more serious until it reached a stage where its reconstruction plans began to fail time after time. The Audit Committee had witnessed these events at close quarters and had made a number of proposals. Naturally perhaps, a committee in this position would be expected to have opinions different from those of the JNR Restructuring Supervisory Committee. Even if both arrived at similar conclusions, the report of the Audit Committee was expected to make concrete suggestions about such matters as how to resolve problems that stood in the way of JNR's goals along with measures to assist the growth of the organizations that were to be newly formed.

JNR's financial balance in 1984/85 greatly improved for the trunk lines, making a profit of 34.5 billion yen and can be attributed to the management improvement plan for the previous year. The audit report commented:

> The management improvement plan, which has been implemented, made a remarkable impact in 1984/85. The efforts during this period should be highly commended.

There is still no prospect, however, that the overall balance of revenues and expenditures will be improved.

An examination of the revenues and expenditures of local lines (under the separate accounting method) reveals that their operating costs were reduced by 18.2 billion yen compared to the previous year. Here too, the results of management efforts are clearly evident. However, because of the 30.2 billion yen decrease in subsidies, etc., overall losses amounted to 526.4 billion.

In its 'Ten Proposals for Tomorrow's JNR,' the 1983/84 audit report made the following judgment about the local lines:

> Looking ahead to the future of JNR's management, the deficits incurred by service categories that cannot take advantage of the basic characteristics of the railway, will seriously hinder reconstruction.

The report also stated that the national subsidies for these lines should be increased even further. In 1984/85, however, the subsidies were reduced rather than increased. In response, the audit report simply commented:

> [Local lines] should be made thoroughly efficient ... and more effort should be made to implement detailed measures so as to improve the balance of revenues and expenditures.

The problem of local lines has been acknowledged by the Audit Committee as a structural one and cannot be solved by a more efficient management. It was in 1976/77 that the audit report stressed the immediate importance of establishing national measures in concert with JNR's own efforts, and of implementing these measures in a unified and decisive manner. The role of the government in this regard was noticeably vague at the time, and the audit report made no comment on the subject. This is difficult to understand in light of the proposals made by the committee in the past. It is understandable that the report should urge JNR to become more independent, but it should have focused more sharply on the incoherence of the measures taken by the government as well as clarifying the relationship of the government to the reconstruction of JNR.

Many newspapers criticized this audit report, as shown by the following examples:

> This report is unconvincing because it has accepted the report of the JNR Restructuring Supervisory Committee as given in the first place. (*Mainichi Shimbun*)

Even the report of the JNR Restructuring Supervisory Committee has various problems. The audit report should instead have taken a firm and realistic position with respect to these problems. (*Nihon Keizai Shimbun*)

These criticisms reflect people's expectations of and frustration with the audit report. If this is evidence of the limits of such reports, as the editorial in the *Nihon Keizai Shimbun* suggests, then their history dating back 30 years is not one that strikes a rewarding note.

THE NEED TO OFFER UNPROFITABLE SOCIAL SERVICES

There are different views with regard to the types of rail services that should be offered – services which ordinary companies could not normally afford. Social and political considerations have resulted in a variety of opinions as to how JNR should be operated and how its problems should be resolved. Although the JNR Restructuring Supervisory Committee has made its report setting out the direction to be taken in revitalizing JNR, consensus has not been reached on this subject.

According to the committee, the railway companies which will be newly established should be managed on the same basic principle as private companies, namely, profitability. But social necessities on the demand side will not disappear as a result of JNR's privatisation and division. The committee itself has admitted that some services must be maintained even if they are at the expense of profitability.

Setting up of the so-called Three Island Fund reflects this recognition. Operating losses incurred by non-designated local lines in Hokkaido, Shikoku and Kyushu are to be permanently covered by revenues available through this fund. Unprofitable but socially desirable services cannot be entirely separated from a railway system even when it is privatised.

In a survey by the Institute of Transportation Economics on the opinions of well-informed people about the role of the railway, some expressed reservations about the provision of services that were inconsistent with efficient commercial management, but most did not deny the need to meet social demand, although opinions varied as to whether fulfilling such demand should be the responsibility of the railway or the national or local governments. This problem was recognized by the JNR Restructuring Supervisory Committee as an expectation on the part of the public with respect to JNR, and as a fundamental aspect of JNR's constitution which is by nature vulnerable to outside interference. Can it safely be said that while JNR was exposed of these external factors because it is a public corporation, a chartered private company would not?

On the other hand, no funds have been set aside for the new railway companies except on the three islands, and the other companies will be required to meet unprofitable social requirements by means of internal subsidies. While each company will be able to fulfill these needs as they currently exist – given the management conditions assumed by the committee – there is no guarantee that the level of these needs will remain static. With social conditions as changeable as they are, the current situation is unlikely to last very long, and new social demands may also arise. Signs of these changes are already visible, such as the recent report that applications for their discontinuance have been withdrawn for two of the second group of designated local lines.

It is usually observed in cases like this that management as a whole has the capacity to absorb small changes. Each change may well be small, but it should not be forgotten that neglecting small issues, together with overestimating the capacity of management as a whole, has contributed to the gradual deterioration of JNR's management. This must not be repeated.

In most countries in Europe, the definition of public services and compensation for their provision is established by national law. Various countries have adopted different rules according to their individual circumstances, such as the Railway Act in the United Kingdom and former West Germany, the Licence Conditions for the Establishment of the National Railway Company in France, and the National Transportation Act in Canada, but the basic rule common to all of these statutes is that the national or the local authorities should pay for the services which they request from the railway.

Since the problem of social rail services cannot be sidestepped in Japan, at the very least a principle on the relationship between such services and their costs should be made clear by the government. Otherwise, the new companies will respond to these demands according to the principles on which private companies are run, and this would not work to the benefit of society. Unnecessary conflicts or distrust between each company and the region in which it is located will be avoided if each company deals with individual cases according to a common, general rule. This is an important part in establishing a proper relationship between the new railway companies and their regional communities on a permanent basis.

THE BASIS OF FAIR COMPETITON

1985 saw many issues arising one after another in various transportation businesses, suggesting the opening of a new era.

Although ideas concerning JNR's reconstruction kept changing, the JNR Restructuring Supervisory Committee issued its 'Opinions on the Restructuring of the JNR' in July and these were accepted as government policy. A direction has thus at last been given to the debate about reconstruction which has seen so many twists and turns since 1964 when JNR first incurred a deficit.

Privatisation has also been proposed for the airline business. The crash of a Japan Airlines jumbo jet in August 1985 came as a major shock, triggering calls for privatisation. In its interim report issued in December regarding a new system for the airline business, the Air Transport Committee of the Transport Policy Bureau urged the complete deregulation of all the airline business so that future airline companies would be managed on a competitive basis.

The privatisation and division of JNR and the privatisation of Japan Airlines represent a turning point in their history. But in the final analysis, the form of management is only the outer cloak of an administrative system. With strong expectations of improvements in the quality of transportation services, the question is how successfully these will be fulfilled.

There were many businessmen, especially executives, on board the aircraft that crashed, some of whom left heart-rending notes addressed to their families. An article at that time quoted a comment by one of their colleagues explaining why businessmen choose to travel by air in the first place:

> The reasons that businessmen go by air are that the flight takes only one hour and that the fare is only 1,000 yen more than the Shinkansen.

The air fare for a commuter ticket between Tokyo and Osaka is 13,800 yen, just 1,200 yen more than for the Shinkansen. When the Tokaido Shinkansen was opened in 1964, the fare between Tokyo and Osaka including the super-express surcharge was 2,480 yen, 41 per cent of the air fare which was 6,000 yen at that time. It is only recently that the gap between the fares has become small. If this were on account of the costs of operating the Shinkansen, the situation could be understood. But the reality is that the Shinkansen has made larger profits every year while its costs are less than half its revenues. The high rail fare stems not from the operation of the Shinkansen itself, but from external factors.

As a matter of interest, the second-class fare between Paris and Lyon on the TGV – the French version of the Shinkansen – was 167 francs when it opened in 1981, 42 per cent of the fare for the corresponding air flight. The TGV fare was later raised to 211 francs, but is still the same in relation to air fare. While the French National Railway had a deficit of more than 800 billion yen in 1984 and the government paid 600 billion in subsidies, this had no effect on TGV's fare. A rapid and cheap form of mass transportation has thus been made available to the French public without any distortion in its market conditions. In Japan, deficits incurred through factors external to the rail business end up as a burden on those who use Shinkansen. The longer this continues, the more the competition with other modes of transportation is distorted.

The privatisation of Japan Airlines and the privatisation and division of JNR are intended to improve services by promoting competition between transport operators. If one of the operators is denied the conditions for the market fares to work properly, then competition cannot be expected to create a transportation system best suited to society's needs.

It is important to take account of the current trends but care must be taken not to be carried away by them. In welcoming privatisation in principle, efforts must be made to give content to the provision of services which will contribute most to the future of our society.

MOVING TOWARD INNOVATION

> I know not whether rains or storms will come this fall. But as for today, my work lies in the rice fields rooting out all of the weeds.

Shozo Ogiya, who played an active part in the business world until the age of 99, wrote this *tanka* – a Japanese poem of thirty-one syllables – to state his philosophy for coping with the vicissitudes of life. This was how he found himself after going through the ups and downs and changes in circumstances which are part of life on this earth.

Having reached a crucial turning point in its history, JNR now finds itself in the midst of drastic changes in its surroundings. But no interruption of its services is permitted for even a moment, day or night. As an essential condition for the success of new policies, therefore, efforts should be made for the proper provision of basic daily activities, whatever the circumstances. Only thereby can reform be successful and its future assured.

Moves have already been made toward JNR's reconstruction such as drawing up various bills to be enacted. It is interesting to note the extent to which the proposals of the JNR Restructuring Supervisory Committee – which stated that the factors leading to JNR's decline should first be made clear and then dealt with – have been taken on board in the process of defining the management structure of the new railway companies, their specific characteristics and legal status.

Public corporations were seen as the ideal form of public enterprise, incorporating both the efficiency of a private company and the characteristics of a public service provider. They have been successful in some countries on account of the conditions and circumstances of that country – but in Japan they have been unable to do as well as expected. In his address at the 1983 meeting of the Transportation Society, Professor Hiroshi Kato attributed this to the Japanese conditions and outlook under which public corporations have to be managed. If the management of the private companies after the privatisation of JNR are subjected to similar restraints and regulations, and their raison d'être is not clearly identified, the same mistakes will be repeated.

The JNR Restructuring Supervisory Committee pointed out in its proposals that the major cause of the decline of JNR's management was that it had been unable to respond adequately to changing times, and that reforming JNR's management structure by privatisation would permit a more rapid response to changes. But what is it that is distinctive about the way in which the private sector adapts to new circumstances? The key lies in a company's capacity to react rapidly in response to changes in economic and social conditions and this usually means starting up new fields of business activity and giving up fields that are no longer viable. If the goal of JNR's reconstruction is to adopt the methods of private management, this degree of freedom to respond to business conditions should be given to its managers.

The committee's proposals also recognize the drawbacks of uniformity: while an important aspect of railway business is about local variations, uniformity in fares and wages throughout the system has prevented them from taking account of local conditions. Regional and local differences in fares and services must be permitted: this is one of the advantages of separate over centralised or uniform management. For there to be a fair competition with other modes of transportation, fares should be set to reflect direct costs. Demanding that an organization adapt to market conditions while requiring it to maintain an uncompetitive fare system is to be at cross purposes. Another important question is whether internal subsidies can be abolished in the new companies because they make for confusion in regional and individual policies.

A variety of factors led the committee to conclude that there was no alternative to a change in the form of JNR's management. However, to rely solely on this change and to expect problems to be resolved only through the efforts of the new companies, is much too simplistic a view. A foundation has to be built that will enable the new companies to work in a class by itself. If the management of the new companies is subjected to restraints and conditions from the outset, the purpose of privatisation will get lost.

In the process of reform, it must be asked to what extent the new companies will be truly independent – particularly in terms of their primary task of management – and whether measures planned for the foreseeable future, are good enough to eliminate the causes that led to JNR's decline.

UNDERCURRENTS IN TRANSPORTATION CONDITIONS

'Coping with changes' is a challenge that is often made, and an inability to meet the challenge will lead to the eventual downfall of management. But just as the cart should not come before the horse, it is first necesssary to recognize exactly what the change is before trying to find ways to cope with it. It is pointless to discuss the future of the transportation business without identifying and evaluating the changes that have taken place or will take place in traffic conditions.

The general trend of passenger transport is best illustrated by dividing the period from the mid-1960s (when JNR first went into the red) to 1983 into three parts – 1965/66 to 1975/76, 1975/76 to 1980/81, and 1980/81 to 1983/84 – and comparing the changes in passenger-kilometres on each line during each of these periods. This shows that traffic volume decreased during all three periods on 12,000 kilometres of lines, or 60 per cent of the total. At the same time, traffic on 5 per cent of the lines increased during all of three periods, while the remaining 35 per cent experienced an increase during some periods and a decrease during others.

The root of JNR's problems can thus be seen in the decrease in traffic on 60 per cent of its lines, and some trunk lines – totalling as much as 3,600 kilometres – are included in this figure. Does the decline on these trunk lines – in a manner that parallels the decline on most of the local lines – mean that a part of the trunk line system has become similar to the local lines? It would seem that there are forces at work at the heart of the railway business that should be seriously examined. There is, of course, no need to be pessimistic about everything: there are lines on which traffic is increasing, even under current management conditions. As a whole, however, clear-cut policies are still necessary.

The history of the management of the Oigawa Railway, a local railway with 65 kilometres of track running alongside the Oigawa River, is regarded as one of the best examples of efficient management within the private railway industry. In particular, since 1969, every effort has been made to reform the company such as extending profitable services and offering special kinds of services while maintaining local services. Yet despite all this the basic trend of the railway business has proved difficult to change: Taizo Goto, the president of Oigawa Railway, declared:

> Local traffic, which is the source of stable revenues, is sharply declining every year ... [and] there is no hope that transportation activities will become profitable ... We are seriously considering shifting to a 'non-wheel' business.[9]

Due to a decrease in main-line passengers by 53 per cent compared with 1965, the revenues of the Oigawa Railway generated by its railway operations account for only 20 per cent of its overall revenues. But even if the revenues and expenditures of the railway business can be balanced, there is no prospect that services can be maintained since the decrease in traffic volume has not been halted. The experience of the Oigawa Railway indicates that the decline of railways cannot be reversed whatever the efforts that are made. In fact, the history of the railway business shows that there have always been services that tend to decline after a time.

Although the general decline in railway services has long been noted, to regard all aspects of the railway business as being in the same shape would not be accurate. Simply to think that the 'Oigawa method' could revitalize the entire railway also betrays a lack of understanding. Only individual measures, based on an accurate assessment of the conditions in each region and each line, will produce any good results. In other words, the question is whether a way can be found to save the railways through measures based on regional or local conditions.

There is an old saying pointing out the folly of 'marking the side of the boat to help find the sword' – this comes from an allegory in an ancient Chinese book where a person who had dropped his sword into the river marks the side of his boat as a reference point to help him find it again. But needless to say, the boat is being carried along by the current. In this changeable world, one can become divorced from reality as time passes if one is attached to an analysis made at a particular point in time. President Goto has stated that good managers in private companies are flexible and sensitive enough to detect the signs of changes and to take measures in response to them.

THE NATION'S RESPONSE TO THE FORMATION OF JNR'S LIABILITIES

An article based on Hideto Maruyama's lecture, 'Memories of a Former Paymaster in Charge of JNR,' appeared in the March edition of *Transportation General*. As shown in this article, the relationship between the government and JNR is a fundamental aspect of JNR's problems. It was at the time of the fare revision in 1964 that Maruyama first came to deal with JNR's problems as the chief of the Price Bureau of the Economic Planning Agency. Returning to the Ministry of Finance in 1967 as the paymaster in charge of transportation, he took direct charge of JNR's problems. It was at a time when JNR was beginning to fall into the red.

Quite early on Maruyama realized that the issues facing JNR could not be dealt with by JNR's management alone, but would have to be tackled by placing JNR within the nation's overall transportation policy in the context of social and economic developments. It was significant that a paymaster should view JNR's problems from this perspective, since Ministry of Finance officials are inclined to attend to a single year's results, one at a time.

This lecture is a valuable piece of history since it bears the hallmark of a high-rank official who was involved at a practical level with national financial policies relating to JNR. In his lecture, Maruyama stated:

> The comment is often made that the state of JNR would not have reached the current point if its deficit were not accumulated but settled through the national finances every year ... [In this connection,] a suspension of JNR's liabilities took place in 1976/77 to the tune of 2.54 trillion yen, and again in 1980/81 for a further 2.78 billion ... I regard this 5.3 trillion yen as essentially a national debt. Thus, the deficit was not settled every year but periodically on a lump-sum basis up to 1980/81. Since 1981/82, however, circumstances have changed drastically.

Because the accumulated long-term debts of JNR are a result of various factors over a period of many years – including unprofitable services provided by JNR as a governmental organization – the settlement of these debts should be considered in terms of both these factors themselves and the responsibilities of those who created them in the first place. In cases where those actually responsible cannot be identified, it is reasonable to expect the national government to take responsibility by implementing measures to deal with an amount of debt equivalent to the losses carried forward in any given period, since the government has long placed the burden of various obligations on JNR.

The balance of ordinary losses carried forward at the end of 1979/80, 3.3 billion yen, was settled by withdrawing capital reserves for a part of the amount and by transferring the other part to a special account for corresponding long-term liabilities. Although the balance of long-term liabilities still amounted to 7.3 trillion yen after these measures, this should not be regarded as an abnormal debt from the point of view of standard company management practices, because fixed assets at book value amounted to slightly over 11 trillion yen. At the time, the finances of JNR were apparently sound. In other words, most of the 37 trillion yen in long-term liabilities which are currently being questioned was incurred after this time. As Maruyama pointed out, JNR's decline has resulted from the measures taken since 1981/82.

The structure that brought about these deficits existed since before that time so that the problem of dealing with the accumulated deficits cannot be solved unless this structure is put right. Meanwhile, it can be seen that since 1981/82, simply to allow deficits to remain as they are will greatly enlarge the burden on the public in the future, with a succession of debts to compensate for annual losses and thereby creating a vicious circle leading to an endless multiplication of deficits and accumulating liabilities. This shows that in contrast to the approach taken since 1981/82, the administration's judgment was accurate prior to that time in dealing twice with the accumulated deficit as an urgent measure, thereby lightening the burden on the public.

A statement in the 1982/83 report of JNR's Audit Committee reads:

> Although JNR should make every effort to limit the expansion of accumulated liabilities in the future, most of these liabilities are the consequence of a structural problem beyond the realm of corporate profitability within JNR ... Deficits incurred each year, in particular, have been dealt with by creating new liabilities, a method unheard of in Europe. This is a major cause of the current crisis in JNR's finances because it has not only resulted in a downward spiral where losses and debts grow larger in turn, but has also postponed solving the underlying problems.

Unfortunately, there is no evidence that this commentary has had any influence on actual practices since then.

THE SOURCE OF JNR'S ASSETS

We have traced the way in which JNR's liabilities were formed and noted that most of its liabilities were incurred after 1981/82. JNR's liabilities can thus be seen as a relatively new issue in its long history.

The disposal of JNR's assets is being discussed as a method of getting rid of its liabilities. But we should first know how these assets were obtained in the first place as well as the source of their funding.

The railway business in Japan began in 1868 with the construction of a line between Tokyo and Yokohama, and the cost of this was met by issuing public bonds. However, these bonds were later redeemed by using the profits of the railway services. In other words, although the railway was constructed and managed by the government, none of its assets were paid for out of taxes.

JNR entered a new era in 1906 when the railway was nationalised. The fixed capital at that time, 188 million yen, was funded mainly by bonds, while the profits transferred since the commencement of services had amounted to 125 million yen.

In 1909, the way was opened to pay for further investment and the introduction of additional services by using the profits of the railway, by the issue of bonds, or by raising money through loans. Between 1909 and 1944, 2.1 billion yen was raised by issuing bonds and 186 million by means of loans, while the amount transferred from the railway special account to the general (including the temporary special military account) was as much as 4.6 billion yen. Then, from 1945 on, rapid inflation set in and enormous operating losses were incurred.

The year 1949 saw the establishment of a new public corporation to run the national railway business. Although this corporation, JNR, purportedly started as an enterprise supported by government investment, no money was actually set aside for this purpose by the government; on the contrary, JNR shouldered an enormous debt from the beginning. The initial balance sheet listed JNR's own capital as 4.9 billion yen, but this amount was merely the difference between the assets owned by the corporation and its total liabilities, 78 billion yen, at the time when these were transferred to the new management. Thus, what was identified as 'own-capital' would not ordinarily be labelled as capital: it could be regarded as capital accumulated through years of operation, and the investors – if they were to be defined – would mainly be the users of the rail services.

In 1950, the 4 billion yen in subsidies provided for the construction costs of JNR from the collateral fund of the US Aid Special Account was redesignated as an investment of the Japanese government. The government's role as the sole investor in JNR was clarified. After that, for as long as two decades, however, JNR's capital remained at 8.9 billion yen.

Finally, in 1971, an investment of 3.5 billion yen was approved as a special measure for JNR's financial reconstruction. In 1973, in view of the anticipated expansion of investment in equipment under the nationwide Shinkansen network plan, a scheme was put in place in the new reconstruction plan whereby the government would invest 1.5 trillion yen over the following decade. This plan, however, was discontinued in 1975 and the amount invested totalled only 447.1 billion yen, even including investments made in 1971 and 1972. JNR's capital has stood at 456 billion yen since that time.

Over its long history of more than a century, JNR has had no choice but to rely on external loans to finance the cost of new fixed assets, and these loans have ultimately been repaid through fares and charges for rail services. In the current situation, the only way that JNR can repay debts is by selling its assets. Since JNR's transportation system, which now carries 7 billion passengers a year, is at a critical point, its customers will understand that selling its assets is necessary to maintain the system – even though these assets have been built over a long period of time by the customers themselves. In any event, these assets serve a beneficial purpose only if they are used by customers through the services provided to them.

ONE-SIDED DISCUSSIONS ON A MANY-SIDED ISSUE

In the many discussions concerning JNR's reconstruction, a long time has passed without any firm conclusions being reached. There are several reasons for this, but one that stands out is that the problems of JNR are complex and have many aspects while the discussions about these problems tend to be one-sided.

Discussions or proposals based on a narrow point of view only serve to avoid facing the issue at hand rather than finding a solution because they highlight points that are favourable to a particular argument and sidestep those that are inconvenient. Delays then become inevitable since viewpoints of this kind cannot share a common framework in which to discuss the problem. Frustration results from discussions that fail to reach decisive conclusions and from repeated debates – a feature of the recent history of JNR's problems. Solutions are reached not by focusing on a single point or just a few but by thoroughly examining all aspects of the problem and by pursuing consistent measures to deal with the conditions that go to create the problem.

The problems of local lines, for example, are usually discussed only in the context of emphasizing the important role they play as a transportation system in local areas. This is, of course, not wrong in itself since that is the raison d'être of local lines. However, emphasizing this point alone does not result in any progress in finding a solution, because the core of the problems lies elsewhere.

Unprofitability is not the origin of the problems either since local lines have operated at a loss from the start. The reason they have been maintained for such a long time in spite of their unprofitability, is that their losses have been borne by others, and the problems arose when the system of easing the burden of these deficits began to break down. JNR's management has been organised on the basis of an internal subsidy by using the profits of trunk lines to meet the deficits of local lines. This system, however, is no longer satisfactory; it has created a situation which the JNR Restructuring Supervisory Committee described as follows:

> [The internal subsidy system] weakens the managerial foundation of those areas most suited to the railway . . . thus undermining the vitality of management itself.

The question is, in fairness, who should shoulder the burden of maintaining the local lines in the future? Should a system be introduced where feasibility is determined separately for each line, passing costs on to customers in the form of higher fares and reducing costs by more efficient management? Should local lines be supported by subsidies provided by the national or local government? Or should we continue with an internal subsidy system similar to the existing one? In the latter case, as the JNR Restructuring Supervisory Committee has pointed out, the internal subsidy should be 'within reasonable limits', but what is the criterion for this principle? These questions should be answered to avoid repeating the experience of some trunk lines deteriorating at the same time as local lines. Otherwise, it will be impossible to ensure the stability of local lines, a factor that will bear on the way in which new railways will be planned. From the very beginning, the range of JNR's activities was an issue that JNR could not settle on its own: a decision required the support of the government on the basis of a national consensus. When JNR is privatised, profitability will be the main concern of the new management. What will then happen to the 'social needs' which have been so strongly imposed upon JNR's management as a public service provider? Will they simply disappear when the form of management is changed? These points must be clarified in discussions about JNR's reconstruction.

The will of the nation should be the basis on which Japan's new railway system will run, a system which it is hoped will be able to make an effective and long-standing contribution to the well-being of our society.

30TH ANNIVERSARY OF THE JNR AUDIT COMMITTEE – THE DESTINY OF THE RECOMMENDED PROPOSALS

The Audit Committee of JNR was set up in June 1956, and its report for 1985/86 will probably be its last one. Placed as it is inside JNR, the committee has always been able to observe JNR's operations closely and has made numerous suggestions and provided much valuable advice on JNR's problems.

The Audit Committee's first report, issued in August 1957, pointed out that the authority of the president of JNR was extremely limited.

> This stands as a great obstacle in establishing mutual trust between labour and management, and drives the labour unions in political directions ... It is necessary to give the president enough independence to enable him to fulfill his responsibility, as a manager, and to make that responsibility clear.

The audit report in the following year stated:

> Demands concerning JNR's function as a public service provider are extremely strong, and numerous limitations and burdens are imposed on it ... It is important to establish a new concept of management [so that JNR can fulfill its mission] ... which can be achieved by granting independence to management with regard to outside matters and encouraging commercial practices and a sense of responsibility on the inside.

The 1958/59 audit report detected trends which did not augur well for the future of JNR's management, namely, the growth of personnel costs, the increase in loans and the problem of interest payments and the slow-down in the growth of revenues. An understanding of the essence of JNR's problems thus appeared in this audit report many years ago.

The 1962/63 audit report noted:

> To meet the increasing demand for transportation services ... the current second five-year plan needs to be followed by a third and fourth plan.

The 1973/74 audit report proposed a large investment in freight yards on the grounds that they should be automated. In 1974/75, when a 650 billion yen deficit was incurred, the audit report noted that freight services were lagging behind in the development of their infrastructure partly through insufficient investment in equipment in the past.

According to the JNR Reconstruction Administrative Committee, the main reason for the decline of JNR was its inability to cope with the changing times. The fact that the Audit Committee – which was not directly involved in JNR's operations and was able to take an independent view – had consistently made judgments such as these, points to the difficulty of identifying and evaluating changes. It was not until 1981/82 that the Audit Committee first proposed a reduction in investment.

The audit report of 1966/67 noted:

> In contrast to earlier years, it is becoming difficult for the profitable lines to support all the unprofitable ones. The government should be responsible for maintaining unprofitable lines in so far as there is a public demand for these lines. Some financial measures are necessary on the part of the administration to enable these lines to remain open.

The 1974/75 audit report noted the long-term liabilities:

> It is particularly important for the government to identify measures to deal with long-term liabilities such as the extent to which responsibility for payment will be transferred to the public or whether payment will simply be postponed.

The report also stated that measures for dealing with past debts were extremely important to enable future policies to function effectively.

The 1970/71 report stated:

> The desire to construct new lines and the refusal to abolish local lines
> – coupled with the various public burdens with which JNR is charged
> – are the outcome of excessive reliance on the power which JNR had
> when it was a monopoly. Likewise complacency had also not been
> absent within JNR itself in delaying improvements to its basic struc-
> ture. However, today's JNR is not what is used to be.

Although the annual audit report has had its own ups and downs
over its thirty-year history, it has effectively pointed out problems
and proposed measures for dealing with them. It is regrettable
that the Audit Committee's work has been largely ignored for
such a long time; the best time for dealing with many of these
problems has passed, and the extent of the problems is therefore
that much greater.

This illustrates a fundamental and serious aspect of JNR's problems. The last report was expected to include the views of the
Audit Committee about the fate of the numerous suggestions and
proposals it had made in recent years, as well as a summary of its
activities over the last thirty years. The 1985/86 audit report, however, merely repeated the general observation that it is important to
build a foundation for healthy management, and to carry out reforms
as soon as possible. After reading this report, all that remains after
thirty years of effort, is a feeling of emptiness if not despair.

HOW RAILWAY FREIGHT SERVICES CAN SURVIVE

The final changes to JNR's train schedule, which became effective
in November 1986, are said to have been made with the aim of
creating a basis for the new companies to be set up in the spring.
Of these changes, two are especially worthy of note.

The first is the abolition of 492 'collect and delivery' trains. The
shift from the yard system to the direct system began in February
1984, and the abolition of the old system in November means that
the direct shipment system is now fully in place.

The other feature is the introduction of the Super Liner, a
container train with a top speed of 100 kilometres per hour. Its
three round trips per day on the Tokaido and Sanyo lines were
introduced in anticipation that this would also improve the public
image of JNR's freight services.

An important aspect of railway freight services is that marshalling and relaying freight cars take up a lot of time and money. There is a great difference both in time and cost between a system which transports freight directly between regional stations, and a system which relays freight via a number of yards and interim stations. According to one estimate, the cost of a direct service between two stations is about half that of a relay service with collection and delivery at each station.

'Characteristic of mode' is a fashionable concept: in the case of the railway this is seen as rapid and concentrated mass transportation. Railway services provide an advantage over other transportation modes in terms of both convenience and efficiency, but only when they are used and operated in accordance with this characteristic, and the railway can then be regarded as a 'heavy' transportation system. Simply continuing the system of collecting and distributing freight at each station with a locomotive drawing only one or two freight cars will inevitably lead to its collapse due largely to high costs compared with alternative modes including road transport.

Faster train speeds not only provide more rapid delivery; slow moving freight trains require more on-board operators compared to passenger trains over the same distance, and this means higher costs.

A booklet entitled *The Future of Freight Services* was issued by JNR in 1964. Although JNR was still prosperous at the time, signs of decline could be detected in its freight services. After a thorough study with the help of staff in charge of freight services, the results were summarized in this booklet. In a section entitled 'The Future Transportation System,' the first proposal was for a rapid direct system connecting 'base' stations at high speeds. To implement this proposal, the Freight Car Modernization Committee was set up and the development of freight cars which could be run at high speeds was mooted, and 336 high-speed freight cars were first manufactured in 1966/67. Now, a rapid system is again being promoted as the trump card for the salvation of existing freight services. It has been too long in coming.

During the interval, JNR's freight services have declined every year and now stand close to collapse. The business results of freight services have traditionally been judged only from the standpoint of the amount of traffic and revenues; a proper cost analysis has seldom been carried out. Freight management have taken a defensive attitude that simply accepted the conditions as they were and thus caused delay in taking corrective action.

The reason why an idea proposed so many years ago still remains fresh is that the original study was properly carried out at the time – and one based on facts not baseless optimism or makeshift compromises, and that the measures that were put forward were designed to take full advantage of the special characteristics of the railway.

The key to revitalizing the railway freight business lies in attracting customers in terms of their demand for direct and rapid service, while also attempting to reduce costs. A high level of service does not have to mean high cost and could lead to savings. In order to survive in a market where consumer preferences are paramount, railway freight services will need to exploit their own unique qualities.

The introduction of the new train schedule heralds the end of past concepts of freight services. It also points the right direction for the survival of these services in the future.

COMPETITION AND SOLIDARITY IN THE NEW ERA OF RAILWAYS

With the passing of a series of bills relating to JNR's reconstruction, a transformation has taken place in policy on railway services in Japan. The national railway will be replaced by a network of railways owned and operated by private companies.

Railway management was made a public corporation in 1949 after being directly operated by the government for over 40 years. And now, 37 years later, the shift is being made to separate management by special chartered companies, with management by private companies to follow in the near future. In fact, the trend of railway management since the time it was nationalised, has strongly and steadily progressed toward privatisation.

In 1906, when the railway was nationalised, conflicting pros and cons were considered up to the last moment, and the bill was passed in spite of much frenzied opposition. Concern about nationalisation appears in the records of the special committee at that time:

From the point of view of taking full advantage of the functions of the railway, national ownership does not seem to be an appropriate form ... The economic benefits of the railway can only be realized when it is not subject to political influences.

The system is now about to revert to the one which existed before nationalisation, for much the same reasons. This must mean that problems which have been left unsolved will emerge again, however vigorously they may have been kept within bounds for the time being.

This reform will provide an opportunity to clear away various constraints that have bedeviled JNR. The conditions necessary for railway management to carry out normal business functions have been settled, and this represents a major achievement of the change that is taking place.

Because of the broad scope and complexity of JNR's management, it has been difficult to get to the core of its problems. What made the situation worse was to allow these problems to fester without taking any decisive measures in respect to them. Cause and effect became mixed up, one with the other, to create more and more confusion. These issues will be taken in hand in implementing the series of plans to divide and separate the various aspects of JNR's management such as the division of management according to regions, the separation of passenger and freight services, and the case-by-case handling of accumulated liabilities. It will be much easier in the future to get to grips with the conditions of railway management and to tackle problems that are bound to arise.

One of the issues requiring close attention in the future is the extent to which the new companies can function independently as individual management organizations in the context of the new railway system. It is said that many of the advantages of public corporations have not materialised in Japan, and the so-called 'environment peculiar to Japanese society' is often cited in support of this claim. Whether or not the new chartered companies can rid themselves of this 'environment' and make the best choices from the standpoint of effective management, and to what extent they can ensure vitality as private organizations, will determine the success of this reform.

A further element of JNR's reconstruction is that it is being undertaken at some sacrifice on the part of the public as well of its employees. This makes it all the more important that the lessons of JNR's history to date – full of regrets and bitter experiences as it is – would have been learnt by management in the future. The same mistakes must not be repeated.

The management of each new railway company will be more strongly focused on efficiency and profitability, and a competitive spirit will exist among these companies. This should provide the basis for revitalizing the rail services – and this is, after all, the major purpose of reform. On the other hand, there are concerns that limiting the work of each company to its area will also limit the advantages of large-scale operations. Thus, maintaining a cohesive service for the railway should be the common responsibility of all the new companies.

Since these companies would be connected by 20,000 kilometres of track, they should regard this as an advantage and make the most of it by co-operating in carrying out their various functions. Co-operation will be of even greater importance on account of the division of management, and will ultimately bring about increased market opportunities. Competition and co-operation should not be treated as abstract concepts; they must be put into practice as part and parcel of the manager's role in the business.

In an emergency, for example, as when a train schedule is disrupted, the worth of the new business structure will be judged by the public in light of the extent to which the companies can then maintain their services through mutual co-operation. If the trust of the public and of rail users is damaged because of barriers between the companies, the future of the companies themselves will be jeopardised. To avoid this, a broad-based and sensitive approach and a sense of solidarity among the companies will be necessary. Although the management of internal matters calls for decisions on detailed matters, a business cannot be successful without being able to take an overall view of external conditions and events as well.

No system can be so perfect as to solve all problems at one and the same time, and solving one problem may create further problems. The new companies will have to face new (and some old) issues in the future, but these will have to be attended to, not pushed to one side. Refusing to recognize problems does not mean that they will go away. The first thing that must be done is to acknowledge the facts as they are; we can then call on our resources to deal with the facts in so far they constitute a problem.

In the midst of the sweeping changes now taking place, we can hope that in the hands of the new companies, a proper role for the railways can be found for a long time into the future.

NOTES

1 George Long, *Marcus Aurelius and His Times* (New York: Walter J. Black, Inc., 1945)
2 *People and the Country*, November 1980
3 Kamo no Chomei, *Hojoki* ('The Ten Foot Square Hut'), a classical collection of essays written by Kamo in 1212 after he had become a buddhist recluse. (A. L. Salder, trans.)
4 Darrell Huff, *How to lie with Statistics* (New York: W. W. Norton & Company, Inc. 1954.)
5 Alfred P. Sloan, Jr., *My Years with General Motors* (New York: Doubleday & Company, inc., 1963)
6 The Regional Division of the Electric Power Industry
7 *Selected Readings from the Works of Mao Tse-tung* (Peking: Foreign Language Press, 1967)
8 Winston Churchill, *Address on Receiving the Freedom of the City of London* (June 30, 1943)
9 *Transportation and Economics*, February 1986

Chronology

1825.09.27. World's first steam train operation in England
1853.07.18. Russian delegation led by Admiral E. V. Putiatin to Nagasaki brings model steam engine
1854.01.16. US delegation led by Perry arrives offshore Uraga for the second time with model steam engine as a gift from the President to the Shogun
1855.08. Production of Japan's first model steam engine in Sagaclan
1869.11.10. Cabinet decision to construct railway
1870.03.25. Surveys begin in Shiodome area led by hired English construction chief, Edmund Morel
1871.09.02. Completion of Yokohama Station's main building
1871.11. Completion of Shiodome Station's main building
1872.02.23. Promulgation of first regulations on railway
1872.03.08. Setting of fares between Shinagawa and Yokohama
1872.05.04. Promulgation of penal regulations concerning railway crimes
1872.05.07. Temporary operation between Shinagawa and Yokohama
1872.06.15. Permission given to Englishman John Reddie Black to sell newspapers within station grounds (first business in stations)
1872.08.20. Permission given to operate western food restaurant within station grounds
1872.09.12. Ceremony for commencement of railway operation between Shinbashi and Yokohama (29 km)
1872.09.21. Operation of special train on the day of Kawasaki Daishi temple's festival (Lunar calendar used up to this point, excluding world's first railway in England)

1873.09.15. Beginning of freight operation between Shinbashi and Yokohama

1874.05.11. Business begins between Osaka and Kobe

1874.08. Introduction of first and middle class return ticket between Osaka and Kobe

1875.05. Production and operation of coaches and wagons at Kobe workshop; parts imported from England (Japan's first production of rolling stock).

1876.09.05. Service begins between Osaka and Kyoto

1876.12.01. Completion of double line between Shinbashi and Shinagawa

1877.02.14. Transporting of soldiers, etc. for the Seinan War (civil war in Japan) begins

1877.11.26. Completion of Rokugou-gawa Railway Bridge

1878.08.21. Construction between Kyoto and Otsu begins (Japanese responsible for the work)

1878.10.01. Introduction of discount return ticket (between Shinbashi and Yokohama)

1878.12. Handling of public telegraphs begins in stations between Shinbashi and Yokohama

1879.04.14. Hiring of first Japanese engine driver at Shinbashi Office

1880.06.28. Completion of Ousakayama Tunnel

1880.07.15. Service commences between Kyoto and Otsu

1880.11.28. Start of operation between Temiya and Sapporo by Horanai Railway Company

1881.05.07. Doubling of track between Shinbashi and Yokohama is completed

1882.05.01. Start of train-ferry connection using Taiko Kisen for passenger and freight transportation between Otsu and Nagahama (until completion of Tokaido Line)

1883.05.01. Operation begins along the section between Nagahama and Sekigahara

1883.07.28. Opening of line between Ueno and Kumagaya by Nihon Railway Company

1884.04.15. Section between Nagahama and Kanegasaki begins service

1884.05.01. Completion of Nihon Railway Company's line between Ueno and Takasaki

1885.03.01. Operation begins on the line from Shinagawa to Akabane by Nihon Railway Company; beginning of joint traffic

1885.07.16. Nihon Railway Company starts business between Omiya and Utsunomiya

1885.07.16. First selling of lunches, tea, etc. while standing at platforms of Utsunomiya Station

1885.10.15. Service between Takasaki and Yokokawa commences

1886.01.01. First selling of season tickets between Shinbashi and Yokohama

1887.06.01. Delivering parcels arriving at Shinbashi and Yokohama Stations begins

1887.08. First placement of interlocking frame on junction of Yamanote (Nihon Railway Company line) and Tokaido Lines in Shinagawa Station

1887.11.01. Introduction of express trains running from Shinbashi to Yokohama, and from Takasaki to Yokokawa (no special charges)

1888.12.01. Section between Ueda and Karuizawa starts service; beginning of operation between Naoetsu and Karuizawa

1889.04.18. Section between Shizouka and Hamamatsu opens; beginning of full service between Shinbashi and Nagahama

1889.05.10. Toilets installed in trains on the Tokaido Line

1889.07.01. Beginning of full service between Shinbashi and Kobe on Tokaido line

1889.07.01. Revision of train fares (adoption of distance scale rates)

1890.05.04. First operation of electric trains at National Industrial Exhibition (Ueno Park)

1891.04. Kansai Railway Company installs vacuum brakes on all coaches

1891.09.01. Beginning of full service between Ueno and Aomori by Nihon Railway Company

1892.06.21. Promulgation of Railway Construction Law

1892.07.21. Jurisdiction over Railway Agency given to Teishin-syo (Ministry of Communications)

1893.04.01. Opening of section between Yokokawa and Karuizawa (abt-system) (First operation of electric locomotive along this section on 1912.05.11)

1893.06.   Production of first domestic locomotive (later named type 860)

1895.01.31.   Kyoto Electric Railway Company begins business (first electric tramway)

1896.09.01.   Express train service between Shinbashi and Kobe (17 hr. 22 min.)

1896.11.21.   Kansai Railway Company paints coaches according to class (first class, white; middle class, blue; third class, red; Imperial Government Railways (IGR) began colour classification from 1897.11)

1897.03.31.   Sanyo Railway Company introduces porter service in major stations

1897.11.05.   Selling of platform tickets begins

1897.11.   Porter service begins in major stations of IGR

1897.04.   Installation of electric lights on first and second class express coaches

1898.08.   Set up of information booth in Shinbashi Station

1898.08.01.   Beginning of handling express freight delivery

1898.09.22.   Sanyo Railway Company places stewards on non-stop trains (same service by IGR from 1901.12.01. on first and second classes between Shinbashi and Kobe)

1899.03.16.   Abolition of distance scale rates, and implementation of tapering distance rate

1899.05.25.   Sanyo Railway Company couples dining cars onto express trains

1899.08.   Sanyo Railway Company lends mosquito nets to passengers on first and second class night trains during the summer

1900.03.16.   Promulgation of Private Railway Act and Railway Business Law (1900)

1900.04.08.   Sanyo Railway Company couples first class sleepers onto non-stop trains

1900.06.12.   IGR hires 10 women

1900.12.01.   Installation of steam heaters in coaches of express trains running the Tokaido Line

1901.05.27.   Beginning of full service between Kobe and Shimonoseki by Sanyo Railway Company

1901.06.16.   Introduction of season tickets for students

1902.07.   Installation of electric fans in sleepers and dining cars

1902.11.01. First operation of special excursion trains running from Shinbashi to Kyoto for people travelling to view autumn leaves

1903.05.01. Introduction of seasonal platform tickets

1904.08.21. First operation of electric trains between Iidamachi and Nakano by Kobu Railway Company

1906.03.31. Promulgation of Railway Nationalisation Act (purchasing of 17 private railways including Nihon Railway Company, Sanyo Railway Company and Kyushu Railway Company)

1906.04.16. Classification of trains running from Shinbashi to Kobe into super-express, express, and non-stop; introduction of express charges for super-express trains

1906.05.20. Ceremony to celebrate the operation of 5000 miles of railway lines in Nagoya City

1906.05. Construction of pipeline between Karuizawa and Yokakawa

1908.03.07. IGR begins direct management of ferry transportation between Aomori and Hakodate

1908.12.05. Establishment of Tetsudo-in (Railways Agency)

1909.04.01. First operation of steam railcars along Kansai Line

1909.12.16. First operation of electric cars between Karasumori (now Shinbashi), Shinagawa, Ikebukuro, and Ueno, and from Ikebukuro to Akabane

1910.03.11. Joint transportation of freight between the main islands of Japan and Sakhalin begins

1910.06.12. Inauguration of ferry service between Uno and Takamatsu

1911.03.01. Start of international railways in Japan and the Russian railways via Dalian, Korea, and Vladivostok

1911.05.01. Section between Miyanokoshi and Kiso Fukushima begins operation; full service from Iidamachi to Nagoya via Nagano

1912.01.31. Coupling of 'ladies only' coach onto electric trains running the Chuo Line

1912.03.12. Establishment of Japan Tourist Bureau (now known as Japan Travel Bureau, Inc.)

1912.06.15. Operation of first and second class limited express trains between Shinbashi and Shimonoseki; selling of seat reservation tickets

1913.04.01. Start of full service on Hokuriku Main Line
1913.08.01. Completion of double line Tokaido Main Line
1914.12.18. Completion of new Tokyo Central Station, named
Tokyo Station (business from 12.20)
1916.11.17. First installation of electric heaters in second class
coaches of electric trains running from Tokyo to
Yokohama
1917.05.23. Testing of reconstruction to broad gauge along
Yokohama Line
1919.04.10. Promulgation of Local Railway Act (enforcement on
08.15)
1920.05.15. Establishment of Tetsudo-syo (Ministry of Railways)
1922.10.13. Oct. 14 declared as Railway Commemoration Day
1923.05.01. Start of sea transport between Wakkanai and
Otomari (Sakhalin)
1924.07.31. Beginning of full service on Uetsu Line; completion
of railway along Japan Sea coast
1924.12.24. Adoption of colour-light signals in Tokyo Station yard
1925.07.01. Work carried out to replace autocouplers of coaches
(completed on the 10th)
1925.07.16. Work carried out to replace autocouplers of
locomotives; completed on the 17th (Kyushu on the
20th)
1925.07.17. Work carried out to replace autocouplers of wagons;
completed on the same day (Kyushu on the 20th)
1925.08.25. Setting up of railway information booth, a branch
office of Tokyo Station, in Tokyo Matsuya
Gofukuten (kimono fabrics shop)
1925.10.25. Introduction of sight-seeing tickets, including tickets
for railway, ships, buses and accommodation, by
Japan Tourist Bureau
1925.11.01. Beginning of belt line operation of Yamanote Line
with completion of the section between Kanda and
Ueno
1925.12.13. Operation of electric locomotives from Tokyo to
Yokosuka, and from Tokyo to Kozu
1926.04.25. First use of German-made platform ticket vending
machines at Tokyo and Ueno Stations
1926.09.28. Coaches with automatic doors operated on several
trains running from Sakuragicho to Ueno

1927.08.01. Commencement of international joint transport of passengers and baggage between USSR, Estonia, Latvia, Lithuania, Poland, Germany, France, Czechoslovakia, Austria, and Italy, via Siberia

1927.12.30. Underground railway service begins between Ueno and Asakusa

1929.09.15. Names given to limited express trains running from Tokyo to Shimonoseki; first and second trains named 'Fuji' while third and fourth became 'Sakura'

1930.02.01. First operation of Japanese-made petrol-engined railcar between Ogaki and Mino Akasaka of Tokaido Main Line

1930.03.15. First handling of advertisements inside electric trains of Yokosuka Line

1930.10.01. First operation of 'Tsubame,' a super-express train with all classes running from Tokyo to Kobe

1930.12.20. Introduction of Railway Ministry's bus service between Okazaki and Tajimi, and Setokinenbashi and Kozoji

1931.02.01. Coupling of third class sleepers onto trains running from Tokyo to Kobe

1931.05.01. Trial use of 1 tonne containers for transportation of part load cargo

1931.07. Installation of comressed air-brakes on all coaches

1931.09.01. Completion of Shimizu Tunnel, marking the full-scale operation of Joetsu Line

1931.10.01. Start of warehousing business using space under elevated platform of Akihabara Station

1932.02.26. Formation of Rikuun Tosei Iinkai (Land Transportation Control Committee) within Tetsudo-syo

1932.07.01. First installation of escalator in the new elevated Akihabara Station

1932.12.06. Beginning of full service on Nippo Main Line connecting Kobura, Miyakonojo and Kagoshima

1932.09.15. First express train service between Tokyo and Nakano

1934.03.08. First operation of 'kiha-40000' type petrol-engined railcar

1934.12.01. Completion of Tanna Tunnel; unification of Atami
Line and Tokaido Main Line, and new name,
Gotenba Line, given to route between Kozu,
Gotenba, and Numazu

1935.07.15. First use of showers and bathtubs in some first class
sleepers of limited express trains linking Tokyo and
Shimonoseki

1936.08.19. Installation of air-conditioning in dining cars of
limited express train 'Tsubame'

1937.04.05. Promulgation and enforcement of Forwarding
Business Act and Nippon Express Co., Ltd. Act

1938.03.23. Promulgation of Law Concerning Transferring
Money from Railway Special Account to General
Account to use as special military expenses

1939.07.12. Setting up of Tetsudo Kansen Chosakai (Railway
Trunk Lines Research Committee)

1940.02.01. Promulgation of Ordnance on Control of Land
Transportation (Enforcement on 02.25)

1941.07.16. Abolition of third class sleepers and reduction of
coupling dining cars

1942.03.20. Groundbreaking ceremony at Kinomiya for the start
of construction work on Tanna Tunnel for the bullet
train connecting Tokyo and Shimonoseki

1942.06.11. Completion of undersea tunnel between Shimonoseki
and Moji'; opening of line heading to Moji

1942.10.11. Implementation of 24 hour system to train schedule

1943.02.15. Enormous war-time cut-backs in operation of
passenger trains nationwide

1943.07.20. Cabinet decision on national control of workshops
for rolling stock

1943.08.27. Formation of General Headquarters for Railway
Defence

1943.10.01. Revision in train schedule (abolition of limited
express 'Tsubame')

1944.01.28. Organisation of headquarters, branches and offices
for evacuation purposes

1944.04.01. Based on Summary of Emergency Measures for the
Final Battle, complete abolition of first class cars,
sleepers and dining cars, and reduction of express
trains

1944.05.10. Introduction of women guards in Nagoya Railway Office
1944. Completion of moha-63 type electric train
1945.03.20. Abolition of express trains excluding first and second trains between Tokyo and Shimonoseki
1946.02.27. Formation of Federation of Government Railway Workers
1946.07.01. Business selling boxed lunches, bread, etc. inside coaches resumes within express trains running between Tokyo and Moji, and Ueno and Aomori
1946.11.10. Reduction of 16% in distance covered by passenger trains due to lack of coal
1947.04.01. Electrification completed along Joetsu Line between Takasaki and Minakami
1947.10.01. Electrification completed along Joetsu Line between Nagaoka and Ishiuchi
1949.05.20. Electrification achieved along Tokaido Main Line between Numazu and Hamamatsu
1949.06.01. Establishment of public corporation, 'Japanese National Railways'
1949.07.06. Shgimoyama Incident
1949.07.15. Mitaka Incident
1949.07.20. Dismissal of 94,312 employees based on Teiin Ho (Law for the Fixed Level of Personnel in the Public Sector) is concluded
1949.08.17. Matsukawa Incident
1949.09.15. Restaurants in trains re-open
1949.09.15. First operation of limited express 'Heiwa' linking Tokyo and Osaka
1950.01.30. Completion of moha-80 type Shonan electric train
1951.04.24. Accident at Sakuragicho Station
1951.05.23. Formation of National Railway Locomotive Crew Union
1952.04.01. Electrification completed along Takasaki Line between Omiya and Takasaki
1954.09.26. Toya-maru ferry disaster
1955.05.11. Shiun-maru ferry disaster
1956.03.20. Reappearance of third class sleepers
1956.03.28. Elimination of wooden coaches
1956.11.19. Electrification of Tokaido Main Line is achieved

1957.06.20.	Coupling of special coaches for the elderly and children onto trains running on Chuo, Keihin and Tohoku Lines
1957.09.01.	First test use of telephones in limited express trains running the Tokaido Main Line
1957.09.05.	Completion of first AC electrification along Senzan Line between Sendai and Sakunami
1958.05.20.	First installation of CTC system along Ito Line
1958.06.01.	First operation of electric trains for school trips between Shinagawa and Kyoto
1958.10.01.	Introduction of limited express electric train 'Kodama' operating between Tokyo and Kobe (first operation on 11.01), and limited express train 'Hatsukari' connecting Ueno and Aomori (first operation on 10.10)
1958.10.14.	Designation of '0 Mile Post' and 4 other properties as railway monuments
1958.07.15.	Kisei Main Line starts full service
1959.11.05.	First operation of limited express container 'Takara'
1960.02.01.	Implementation of seat reservation system MARS-1
1960.03.25.	First use of A type warning devices within coaches running from Tokyo to Kobe and from Kobe to Himeji
1960.07.01.	Revision of fare classes to 2
1961.10.01.	Drastic revision in train schedule; large increase in the number of limited express trains, express trains, etc.
1962.05.03.	Mikawajima accident
1962.06.10.	Completion of Hokuriku Tunnel
1963.03.30.	Record of 256 km/h by testing Shinkansen train
1963.09.01.	ATS-S begins to be in use
1963.09.29.	Abolition of abt-system railway along Shinetsu Main Line; operation of new line from the 30th
1963.11.09.	Accident at Tsurumi
1964.02.23.	Implementation of MARS-101
1964.10.01.	First operation of Tokaido Shinkansen connecting Tokyo and Shin Osaka
1964.10.05.	JNR bus operation on Meishin Expressway begins
1965.10.01.	Setting up of 'Midori no Madoguchi (reservation counters with on-line computers)' in all major stations nationwide

1966.03.05. First use of radio communication in trains along Joban Line

1966.04.20. ATS installation on all lines is accomplished

1966.04.28. Completion of 4 line elevated railway between Nakano and Ogikubo; mutual use of tracks with the underground begins

1967.08.20. Electrification completed along Joban Line

1967.09.28. Opening of Shin Shimizu Tunnel; Joetsu Line becomes an electrified, double line

1968.08.22. Full electrification of Tohoku Main Line (completion of double track on 08.05)

1968.10.01. Overall nationwide revision in train schedule

1969.04.25. First operation of freight liner

1969.05.10. Introduction of 'Green (first class) Car'

1969.06.10. JNR bus operation on Tomei Expressway begins

1969.09.29. Electrification and doubling of Hokuriku Main Line is completed

1970.05.18. Promulgation of Nation-wide Shinkansen Railway Development Law

1971.04.20. First operation of multiple lines along Joban Line between Ayase and Aniko; 2 lines for rapid transportation and another 2 lines for local transport

1971.04.28. First operation of 'Dream,' a bus running the expressway between Tokyo and Kobe during the night

1971.11.28. Commencement of construction work on Tohoku and Joetsu Shinkansen

1972.03.15. Shinkansen service between Shin Osaka and Okayama begins

1972.03.15. Revision in timetable due to operation of Sanyo Shinkansen

1972.07.15. Inauguration of Sobu Main Line between Tokyo and Kinshicho; Tokyo Underground Station, and Shin Nihonbashi and Bakurocho Stations open for business

1972.07.26. Success in public testing of ML 100 (within technical research institute)

1972.10.14. Holding of 100th anniversary ceremony with the presence of the Emperor and Empress

1972.11.06. Fire in dining car of express train inside Hokuriku
             Tunnel; car totally burnt, 30 lives lost
1972.11.08. First operation of hovercraft between Uno and
             Takamatsu
1973.04.01. Musashino Line starts service, linking Fuchu
             Honmachi and Shin Matsudo
1973.07.10. Electrification of Chuo Main Line is achieved
1974.07.20. Completion of elevated railway, double track and
             electrification of Kosei Line between Yamashina and
             Omi Shiotsu
1975.03.10. Commencement of Shinkansen service between
             Okayama and Hakata
1975.11.26. Sutokensuto (strike by JNR employees for the right
             to strike legally)
1976.11.06. Tariff increase of 50.4% for passenger, 53.9% for
             freight and 42.8% for special charges (average)
1977.12.09. Passing of 'Bill Concerning Partial Revision of JNR
             Fare law and JNR Law;' authorisation of tariff rise
             without prior approval from Diet
1977.12.17. Linear motor car (maglev) succeeds in world's first
             levitated transportation
1978.05.20. Opening of New Tokyo International Airport
1979.05.20. Tariff rise of 8.8% for passenger and 9.0% for freight
1980.04.20. Tariff rise of 4.5% for passenger and 8.9% for freight
1980.11.28. Passing of JNR Rehabilitation Act (1980)
1981.10.01. Sekisho Line begins service
1982.04.20. Tariff increase of 6.1% for passenger and 6.3% for
             freight
1982.05.17. Second Ad Hoc Commission on Administrative
             Reform receives reform proposal regarding the three
             public corporations from its 4th Sub-committee
1982.06.23. Tohoku Shinkansen begins service between Omiya
             and Morioka
1982.11.15. Joetsu Shinkansen begins service between Omiya
             and Niigata
1984.02.   Complete abolition of freight marshalling yards
1985.03.14. Tohoku Shinkansen extended to Ueno
1985.04.20. Tariff increase of 4.3% for passenger and 3.1% for
             freight
1986.09.01. Implementation of 4.8% passenger fare increase

1986.11.28. Passing of 8 bills regarding JNR reform
1986.12.16. Cabinet decision on basic succession plan of 11
            organisations inheriting assets and liabilities of JNR
1987.03.31. Termination of JNR's 115 year history

Reference: Nikon Kokuyu Tetsudo Hyakunen-shi (Hundred
            Years History of the Japanese National Railways)
            Tetsudo Yoran (Summary of Railways)

Railway Maps

RAILWAY MAP

(As of March 31. 1893)

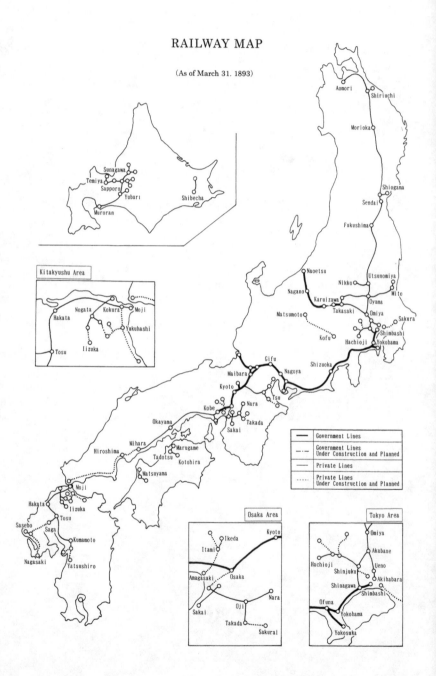

RAILWAY MAP

(As of September 30. 1906)

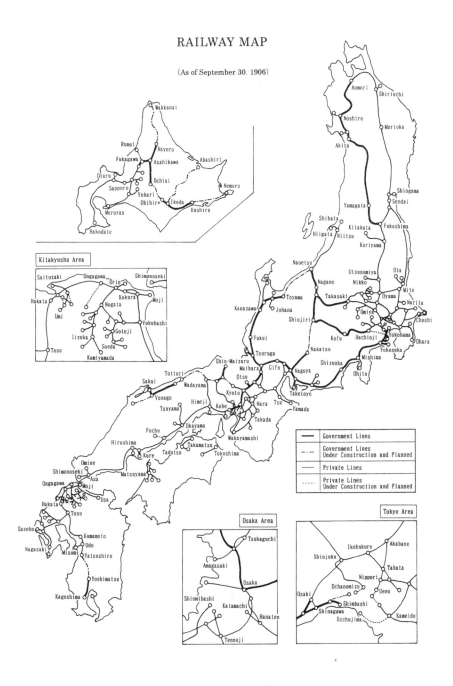

RAILWAY MAP

(1920 ~ 1950)

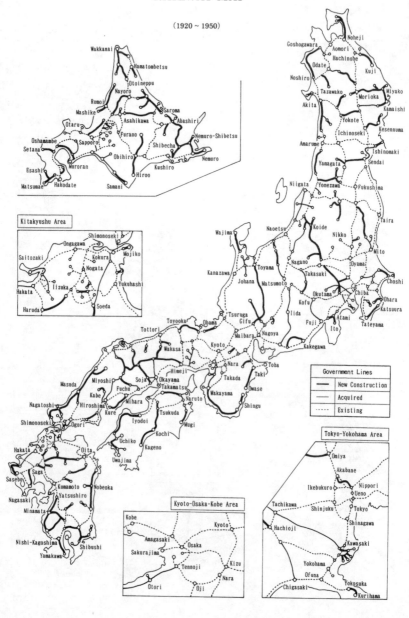

RAILWAY MAP

On Dissolution of JNR Public Corporation

(Electrified) 1987

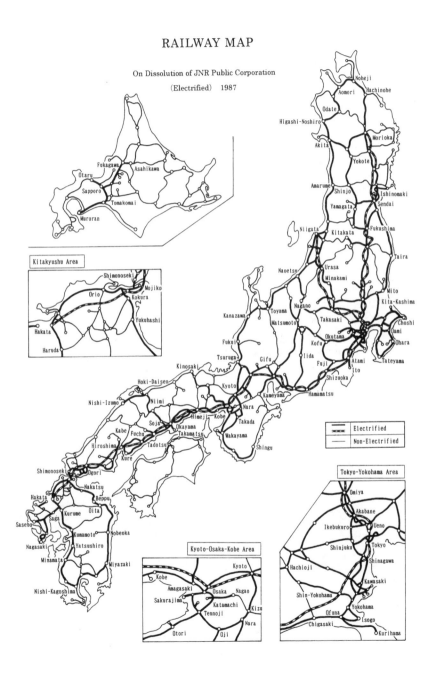

Statistics

× indicates a leap year

1-Route Kilometres (1)

Unit:km

| Fiscal year | Rail | | | Electrified Section | Sea |
	Passenger End of Fiscal year	Freight End of Fiscal year	All End of Fiscal year		Passenger End of Fiscal year
1872	-	-	29.0	-	-
1873	-	-	29.0	-	-
1874	-	-	61.7	-	-
× 1875	-	-	61.7	-	-
1876	-	-	104.8	-	-
1877	-	-	104.8	-	-
1878	-	-	104.8	-	-
× 1879	-	-	117.9	-	-
1880	-	-	123.1	-	-
1881	-	-	161.7	-	-
1882	-	-	184.7	-	-
× 1883	-	-	202.2	-	-
1884	-	-	202.2	-	-
1885	-	-	270.0	-	-
1886	-	-	336.0	-	-
× 1887	-	-	393.5	-	-
1888	-	-	716.5	-	-
1889	-	-	886.1	-	-
1890	-	-	886.1	-	-
× 1891	-	-	886.1	-	-
1892	-	-	886.1	-	-
1893	-	-	897.4	-	-
1894	-	-	934.8	-	-
× 1895	-	-	954.8	-	-
1896	-	-	1,016.7	-	-
1897	-	-	1,065.1	-	-
1898	-	-	1,236.1	-	-
× 1899	-	-	1,205.9	-	-
1900	-	-	1,325.2	-	-
1901	-	-	1,457.0	-	-
1902	-	-	1,709.9	-	-
× 1903	-	-	1,844.2	-	-
1904	-	-	2,001.7	-	-
1905	-	-	2,562.4	-	-
1906	4,258.8	4,269.9	4,977.9	12.1	-
× 1907	7,078.2	7,150.8	7,153.2	12.1	-
1908	7,223.8	7,308.3	7,311.1	12.5	-
1909	7,285.8	7,438.7	7,442.2	47.0	-
1910	7,755.6	7,832.2	7,838.0	48.9	-
× 1911	8,032.1	8,111.9	8,117.7	48.9	-
1912	8,321.7	8,389.8	8,395.9	60.4	535.9
1913	8,723.9	8,801.3	8,807.4	60.4	479.6
1914	9,064.9	9,151.4	9,156.3	82.4	479.6
× 1915	9,168.7	9,261.6	9,268.2	84.4	479.6
1916	9,325.0	9,422.0	9,428.6	84.4	479.6
1917	9,545.1	9,651.9	9,658.5	84.4	479.6
1918	9,653.3	9,772.4	9,780.9	94.1	479.6
× 1919	9,856.9	9,981.9	9,990.5	94.1	479.6
1920	10,313.6	10,427.6	10,436.1	94.1	479.6
1921	10,704.0	10,812.4	10,820.9	94.1	479.6
1922	11,157.7	11,266.0	11,274.6	103.0	479.6
× 1923	11,686.1	11,796.3	11,804.8	103.0	488.8
1924	12,033.8	12,139.3	12,147.8	103.0	688.8
1925	12,482.8	12,582.6	12,593.2	177.6	655.0

Route Kilometres (2)

Fiscal year	Rail			Electrified Section
	Passenger	Freight	All	
	End of Fiscal year	End of Fiscal year	End of Fiscal year	
1926	12,744.7	12,853.2	12,863.8	177.6
× 1927	13,265.3	13,383.4	13,394.1	198.3
1928	13,548.1	13,681.0	13,694.5	212.4
1929	13,986.3	14,132.4	14,151.9	215.4
1930	14,355.6	14,541.6	14,574.9	234.9
× 1931	14,771.0	14,980.7	15,014.0	357.4
1932	15,120.4	15,336.0	15,372.1	435.9
1933	15,607.6	15,811.1	15,844.5	463.2
1934	16,289.3	16,496.1	16,535.1	564.0
× 1935	16,884.3	17,099.2	17,138.2	582.0
1936	17,280.6	17,491.1	17,530.1	611.7
1937	17,682.1	17,895.0	17,934.0	702.0
1938	17,925.3	18,139.7	18,178.7	798.3
× 1939	18,033.8	18,258.5	18,297.5	812.2
1940	18,148.8	18,361.0	18,400.0	812.2
1941	18,241.5	18,456.5	18,495.5	840.4
1942	18,330.4	18,542.4	18,581.4	850.2
× 1943	19,455.1	19,678.5	19,725.5	1,114.5
1944	19,757.1	20,030.5	20,056.3	1,310.2
1945	19,259.8	19,585.5	19,619.8	1,310.2
1946	19,349.8	19,657.5	19,692.0	1,310.2
× 1947	19,419.3	19,712.4	19,752.3	1,443.1
1948	19,428.2	19,719.7	19,759.6	1,497.1
1949	19,428.1	19,725.4	19,765.3	1,638.7
1950	19,436.6	19,746.5	19,786.4	1,658.6
× 1951	19,484.7	19,806.5	19,849.6	1,661.8
1952	19,517.4	19,855.3	19,902.6	1,750.6
1953	19,611.9	19,959.9	20,007.8	1,870.6
1954	19,664.7	19,983.4	20,046.0	1,874.9
× 1955	19,704.5	20,025.1	20,093.1	1,961.2
1956	19,785.7	20,118.4	20,186.4	2,026.5
1957	19,874.8	20,199.6	20,275.5	2,097.0
1958	19,946.6	20,277.5	20,357.0	2,236.6
1959	19,996.8	20,280.5	20,402.1	2,482.5
1960	20,079.2	20,363.8	20,481.9	2,698.8
1961	20,105.0	20,357.9	20,519.3	3,086.7
1962	20,099.1	20,357.7	20,516.3	3,333.5
× 1963	20,243.9	20,448.1	20,664.7	3,540.0
1964	20,352.2	20,525.4	20,741.2	3,848.7
1965	20,376.3	20,482.7	20,754.0	4,228.2
1966	20,411.4	20,509.7	20,783.2	4,433.7
× 1967	20,414.8	20,498.3	20,774.8	4,843.4
1968	20,458.3	20,492.1	20,826.5	5,418.2
1969	20,473.7	20,437.8	20,833.5	5,704.6
1970	20,520.1	20,482.0	20,890.4	6,020.5
× 1971	20,509.6	20,374.2	20,882.9	6,239.3
1972	20,545.4	20,333.6	20,924.2	6,684.8
1973	20,695.6	20,378.6	21,099.1	6,961.4
1974	20,903.8	20,031.7	21,161.0	7,374.8
× 1975	20,963.2	20,088.2	21,271.9	7,628.1
1976	20,963.2	20,038.6	21,276.1	7,813.0
1977	20,992.9	20,026.1	21,306.5	7,813.0
1978	20,975.0	19,713.2	21,306.9	8,032.2
× 1979	21,020.8	19,658.2	21,322.1	8,278.7
1980	21,038.3	19,433.1	21,321.7	8,413.5
1981	21,132.6	19,447.3	21,418.8	8,434.5
1982	21,112.6	17,686.7	21,386.5	8,829.6
× 1983	20,992.1	15,564.7	21,319.2	8,840.1
1984	20,777.1	15,383.6	21,091.0	9,038.4
1985	20,478.7	15,356.7	20,788.7	9,109.4
1986	19,440.6	10,133.9	19,639.4	9,367.3

Unit:km

Sea		Road			
Passenger	*Freight*	*Passenger*	*Freight*	*All*	*Fiscal*
End of	*End of*	*End of*	*End of*	*End of*	*year*
Fiscal year	*Fiscal year*	*Fiscal year*	*Fiscal year*	*Fiscal year*	
655.0	-	-	-	-	1926
655.0	-	-	-	-	× 1927
655.0	-	-	-	-	1928
655.0	-	-	-	-	1929
670.0	-	65.8	65.8	65.8	1930
670.0	-	126.2	108.6	126.2	× 1931
670.0	-	308.0	290.0	308.0	1932
675.2	-	544.0	510.0	544.0	1933
670.0	-	1,161.0	1,103.0	1,161.0	1934
670.0	-	1,765.0	1,745.0	1,766.0	× 1935
670.0	-	1,980.0	1,968.0	1,980.0	1936
670.0	-	2,182.0	2,169.0	2,182.0	1937
670.0	-	2,436.0	2,413.0	2,436.0	1938
670.0	-	2,530.0	2,507.0	2,530.0	× 1939
655.0	1,285.0	2,619.0	2,585.0	2,619.0	1940
655.0	1,285.0	2,743.0	2,699.0	2,743.0	1941
517.8	1,260.0	2,931.0	2,910.0	2,952.0	1942
729.8	2,910.0	3,346.0	3,529.0	3,566.0	× 1943
729.8	2,910.0	3,601.0	4,094.0	4,156.0	1944
132.8	510.0	3,428.0	4,209.0	4,265.0	1945
205.3	626.0	4,109.0	4,680.0	4,732.0	1946
205.8	776.0	4,695.0	5,143.0	5,211.0	× 1947
205.8	775.0	5,224.0	5,258.0	5,744.0	1948
205.8	775.0	5,238.0	5,265.0	5,754.0	1949
205.8	775.0	5,889.0	5,949.0	6,400.0	1950
205.8	775.0	6,909.0	5,614.0	7,424.0	× 1951
205.8	775.0	7,804.0	7,070.0	9,786.0	1952
205.8	775.0	8,864.0	6,985.0	10,652.0	1953
205.8	775.0	9,518.0	6,997.0	11,230.0	1954
205.8	775.0	10,252.0	7,065.0	12,033.0	× 1955
205.8	775.0	11,039.0	6,922.0	12,677.0	1956
205.8	610.0	11,987.0	6,804.0	13,524.0	1957
205.8	610.0	12,591.0	6,731.0	14,054.0	1958
205.8	610.0	12,885.0	6,595.0	14,243.0	1959
205.8	610.0	13,232.0	6,602.0	14,586.0	1960
205.8	610.0	13,554.0	6,353.0	14,858.0	1961
205.8	610.0	13,936.3	5,870.6	15,071.3	1962
205.8	610.0	14,068.0	5,826.1	15,202.0	× 1963
205.0	610.0	14,603.9	5,728.9	15,727.9	1964
205.0	610.0	14,854.0	5,341.5	15,603.8	1965
205.0	610.0	15,100.2	5,220.6	15,687.0	1966
205.0	610.0	15,288.1	5,219.5	15,874.9	× 1967
205.0	610.0	15,662.9	5,236.3	16,249.7	1968
205.0	610.0	15,898.2	5,047.2	16,485.7	1969
205.0	610.0	15,702.7	5,141.4	16,290.2	1970
205.0	610.0	15,434.5	5,132.1	16,022.0	× 1971
205.0	610.0	14,988.2	4,876.7	15,361.7	1972
205.0	610.0	14,953.8	4,865.2	15,327.3	1973
205.0	350.0	14,816.8	3,695.3	15,190.3	1974
205.0	350.0	14,949.7	3,520.6	15,292.2	× 1975
202.0	350.0	14,806.0	3,303.6	15,084.5	1976
202.0	350.0	14,694.7	2,992.2	14,902.2	1977
202.0	350.0	14,456.4	2,594.5	14,663.9	1978
202.0	350.0	14,163.7	1,640.3	14,342.4	× 1979
202.0	350.0	14,030.6	1,333.5	14,188.6	1980
202.0	350.0	13,894.6	1,328.8	14,052.6	1981
132.0	350.0	13,806.9	1,079.3	13,913.9	1982
132.0	350.0	13,640.2	463.0	13,640.2	× 1983
132.0	350.0	13,048.9	462.9	13,048.9	1984
132.0	350.0	12,534.8	450.5	12,534.8	1985
132.0	350.0	11,739.6	-	11,739.6	1986

2-Train Kilometres

Unit:km

Fiscal year	Converted Train kilometers (Commercial)		Fiscal year	Converted Train kilometers (Commercial)		Fiscal year	Converted Train kilometers (Commercial)	
	Passenger	Freight		Passenger	Freight		Passenger	Freight
1890	-	-	1926	97,224,819	57,531,929	1958	277,438,765	130,081,541
× 1891	-	-	× 1927	104,915,400	58,200,196	× 1959	296,028,368	137,155,387
1892		-	1928	112,340,097	58,450,966			
1893			1929	120,034,637	58,821,390			
1894	-	-						
× 1895	-	-				1960	317,153,767	144,137,715
1896	-	-	1930	128,834,943	53,646,633	1961	347,165,416	152,269,133
1897	-	-	× 1931	134,556,761	52,358,169	1962	377,104,755	153,154,409
1898	-	-	1932	138,923,515	53,248,009	× 1963	397,082,238	159,809,822
× 1899	-	-	1933	146,712,337	58,254,605	1964	411,630,533	162,940,566
			1934	159,331,961	64,239,288	1965	431,443,146	165,652,456
1900	-	-	× 1935	172,254,041	70,158,851	1966	448,350,839	167,156,379
1901	-	-	1936	180,095,889	77,158,850	× 1967	455,083,713	177,571,671
1902	-	-	1937	186,655,424	84,385,492	1968	461,670,462	186,047,070
× 1903	-	-	1938	187,136,658	90,971,162	1969	471,550,388	192,320,381
1904	-	-	× 1939	191,367,344	102,896,009			
1905	7,541,850	9,694,606						
1906	13,639,669	16,807,475				1970	482,984,224	196,461,007
× 1907	27,785,327	32,663,395	1940	197,133,633	108,047,182	× 1971	487,655,891	194,979,285
1908	31,632,548	38,249,770	1941	198,230,664	112,722,219	1972	498,406,991	190,955,937
1909	-	-	1942	197,507,239	121,258,166			
			× 1943	186,715,210	138,978,001	1973	509,704,353	189,511,693
1910	36,490,503	35,560,804	1944	177,254,827	137,988,422	1974	508,442,542	184,657,183
× 1911	38,707,281	39,717,119	1945	135,384,395	82,231,915	× 1975	503,640,275	175,590,064
1912	43,072,037	43,822,558	1946	127,328,942	72,499,928	1976	518,044,596	176,368,650
1913	45,087,424	47,293,203	× 1947	122,709,243	83,294,119	1977	520,965,189	172,785,385
1914	45,341,799	45,000,307	1948	132,996,619	92,311,604	1978	517,386,226	159,064,485
× 1915	49,356,004	46,126,914	1949	149,711,234	99,110,699	× 1979	525,603,583	151,320,132
1916	51,340,528	52,531,706						
1917	55,513,893	56,810,174				1980	516,281,450	141,053,282
1918	57,788,380	58,620,866	1950	168,813,235	106,928,346	1981	514,979,747	134,030,551
× 1919	63,651,920	67,292,170	× 1951	188,555,353	116,609,449	1982	513,915,159	127,185,470
			1952	196,649,620	114,572,236	× 1983	512,657,637	115,294,537
1920	67,580,582	61,729,343	1953	206,280,101	122,477,727	1984	515,139,356	101,723,603
1921	69,073,242	59,156,599	1954	220,555,342	121,911,400	1985	527,134,526	94,409,145
1922	76,043,245	59,157,024	× 1955	234,501,676	126,932,322	1986	547,435,159	86,405,697
× 1923	79,441,073	59,404,869	1956	249,550,213	133,875,186			
1924	86,568,665	62,618,729	1957	264,369,402	135,475,658			
1925	90,907,484	61,286,850						

3-Rolling Stock Kilometres (1)

Unit:km

Fiscal year	Passenger				Freight
	Total	Coach	Electric	Railcar	
1890	40,646,237	-	-	-	18,169,622
× 1891	43,004,402	-	-	-	22,465,591
1892	43,636,066	-	-	-	29,824,376
1893	46,297,601	-	-	-	32,583,333
1894	51,668,220	-	-	-	38,523,188
× 1895	58,628,721	-	-	-	42,615,999
1896	65,562,860	-	-	-	39,568,495
1897	69,891,345	-	-	-	50,571,415
1898	79,775,814	-	-	-	62,710,513
× 1899	81,681,246	-	-	-	84,539,829
1900	88,582,787	-	-	-	101,857,269
1901	92,628,933	-	-	-	101,419,487
1902	99,364,371	-	-	-	111,133,144
× 1903	113,566,340	-	-	-	125,069,008
1904	98,373,822	-	-	-	136,901,618
1905	109,463,088	-	-	-	174,739,326
1906	177,366,432	176,699,328	367,104	-	324,889,758
× 1907	356,770,127	355,451,551	1,318,576	-	665,906,221
1908	408,389,447	406,746,090	1,643,357	-	833,771,426
1909	410,464,096	-	-	-	829,100,662
1910	434,875,089	429,598,594	5,276,495	-	904,025,053
× 1911	469,735,297	463,351,871	6,383,426	-	978,075,011
1912	523,459,778	515,452,179	7,542,838	464,761	1,066,980,112
1913	555,582,494	546,929,511	7,967,987	684,996	1,186,058,469
1914	571,479,051	561,776,966	8,645,571	1,056,514	1,152,165,977
× 1915	602,900,045	585,378,683	16,349,148	1,172,214	1,250,026,868
1916	630,673,974	607,979,100	21,540,108	1,154,766	1,477,273,599
1917	699,840,148	676,494,063	22,258,540	1,087,545	1,590,480,359
1918	763,119,678	736,869,207	25,138,810	1,111,661	1,671,527,366
× 1919	862,600,466	828,054,148	33,547,167	999,151	1,855,473,639
1920	926,562,910	888,789,841	36,951,713	821,356	2,247,650,638
1921	981,691,122	937,298,928	43,627,695	764,499	2,274,324,934
1922	1,086,180,444	1,028,339,638	57,067,489	773,317	1,716,331,062
× 1923	1,143,119,634	1,091,778,917	50,672,157	668,560	1,733,719,324
1924	1,267,246,150	1,196,193,085	70,341,956	711,109	1,899,561,383
1925	1,329,323,543	1,246,799,578	81,823,146	700,819	1,911,929,974

3-Rolling Stock Kilometres (2)

Fiscal year	Passenger				Freight
	Total	Coach	Electric	Railcar	
1926	1,414,910,301	1,307,321,756	106,900,838	687,707	1,940,031,128
× 1927	750,995,328	687,147,290	63,379,012	469,026	2,030,341,735
1928	793,709,120	724,555,908	68,752,321	400,891	2,095,800,841
1929	808,768,194	731,707,635	76,607,169	453,390	2,095,282,120
1930	820,370,660	734,346,239	85,441,737	582,684	1,914,713,226
× 1931	802,169,105	720,127,828	81,323,245	718,032	1,895,529,743
1932	794,230,654	708,496,614	85,151,968	582,072	1,890,530,672
1933	828,321,887	728,820,714	97,216,195	2,284,978	2,095,483,612
1934	888,331,190	767,902,317	112,622,518	7,806,355	2,285,579,975
× 1935	960,563,447	823,814,670	124,916,922	11,831,855	2,391,256,989
1936	1,009,836,750	864,267,367	130,786,786	14,782,597	2,645,538,947
1937	1,051,467,874	890,226,132	144,954,595	16,287,147	2,922,091,475
1938	1,086,333,212	913,684,964	158,064,143	14,584,105	3,181,102,793
× 1939	1,181,183,522	993,656,664	174,197,993	13,328,865	3,484,389,376
1940	1,272,617,829	1,076,096,430	185,389,732	11,131,667	3,634,416,748
1941	1,319,780,703	1,119,554,756	195,539,748	4,686,199	3,786,865,649
1942	1,345,113,628	1,144,306,916	197,694,742	3,111,970	4,153,135,444
× 1943	1,317,599,400	1,129,862,312	183,515,554	4,221,534	4,628,317,257
1944	1,205,823,576	1,004,661,243	201,162,333	Added to Coach	4,108,359,301
1945	933,714,960	784,040,135	149,674,825		2,086,791,484
1946	916,661,324	765,847,303	150,628,829	185,192	2,077,901,000
× 1947	987,560,891	808,947,145	178,254,849	358,897	2,312,966,409
1948	1,054,612,372	867,849,141	186,233,213	530,018	2,645,204,510
1949	1,156,005,588	945,543,376	209,637,097	825,115	3,052,024,219
1950	1,221,258,374	954,321,818	263,870,468	3,066,088	3,266,795,725
× 1951	1,339,382,530	1,031,784,794	300,667,260	6,930,476	3,727,481,620
1952	1,376,870,101	1,038,814,405	327,088,224	10,967,472	3,746,086,156
1953	1,450,035,079	1,091,178,584	343,105,567	15,750,928	3,957,603,669
1954	1,522,364,456	1,128,348,273	357,921,753	36,094,430	3,946,583,391
× 1955	1,609,415,045	1,166,580,149	387,416,151	55,418,745	4,165,273,101
1956	1,685,794,892	1,196,923,457	407,277,170	81,594,265	4,468,529,640
1957	1,784,292,862	1,229,347,669	449,444,034	105,500,409	4,525,582,153
1958	1,887,610,763	1,245,445,265	504,757,627	137,407,871	4,388,855,796
× 1959	1,995,421,625	1,263,777,501	559,422,786	172,221,338	4,657,021,881

Fiscal year	Passenger				Freight
	Total	Coach	Electric	Railcar	
1960	2,114,718,250	1,256,334,087	625,903,115	232,481,048	4,918,240,682
1961	2,254,104,848	1,199,687,881	733,987,901	320,429,066	5,170,117,015
1962	2,404,699,453	1,148,619,115	838,577,456	417,502,882	5,172,827,742
x 1963	2,584,270,241	1,132,196,732	953,664,324	498,409,185	5,398,984,115
1964	2,750,065,643	1,122,174,672	1,081,351,753	546,539,218	5,410,872,473
1965	2,965,694,918	1,101,375,301	1,266,211,623	598,107,994	5,272,920,034
1966	3,169,005,120	1,062,335,148	1,451,314,396	655,355,576	5,132,967,250
x 1967	3,251,135,882	1,004,644,548	1,567,877,471	678,613,863	5,364,346,612
1968	3,346,401,112	950,139,450	1,708,014,188	688,247,474	5,210,083,276
1969	3,508,530,937	929,743,586	1,882,434,143	696,353,208	5,286,162,333
1970	3,712,760,000	947,803,351	2,058,685,784	706,270,865	5,447,070,215
x 1971	3,762,870,193	914,588,814	2,132,694,782	715,586,597	5,242,095,814
1972	3,954,435,366	860,877,371	2,386,823,085	706,734,910	4,782,359,368
1973	4,113,691,882	848,151,304	2,589,394,195	676,146,383	4,609,082,322
1974	4,101,798,771	820,417,243	2,619,845,164	661,536,364	4,326,630,354
x 1975	4,124,207,496	693,256,636	2,813,541,152	517,409,708	4,088,084,829
1976	4,256,482,065	698,910,928	2,937,728,278	619,842,859	4,039,860,279
1977	4,296,044,299	699,730,506	2,974,705,379	621,608,414	3,869,294,521
1978	4,252,044,947	671,623,126	2,978,736,112	601,685,709	3,578,819,507
x 1979	4,322,869,372	669,952,953	3,056,878,068	595,846,415	3,441,281,137
1980	4,253,841,064	644,961,254	3,047,854,855	561,024,955	3,076,451,281
1981	4,238,171,995	633,428,074	3,063,055,708	541,688,213	3,049,102,604
1982	4,198,321,533	594,193,065	3,092,442,477	511,685,991	2,878,822,496
x 1983	4,123,252,243	554,030,748	3,103,211,448	466,010,047	2,364,309,486
1984	3,997,696,760	493,905,293	3,084,293,636	419,497,831	1,683,358,578
1985	3,949,346,111	414,016,371	3,168,498,780	366,831,003	1,505,187,151
1986	3,934,647,018	365,334,021	3,211,749,591	357,565,406	1,335,186,391

4-Summary of Statistics on Traffic Volume (1)

Fiscal year	Passenger Carried				Tonnage Carried	
	Total	Rail	Sea	Road	Total	Rail
	Person	*Person*	*Person*	*Person*	*t*	*t*
1872	495,078	495,078	-	-	-	-
1873	1,415,225	1,415,225	-	-	-	-
1874	2,093,560	2,093,560	-	-	-	-
x 1875	2,756,482	4,238,243	-	-	-	-
1876	2,933,260	2,933,260	-	-	-	-
1877	3,096,707	3,096,707	-	-	-	-
1878	3,477,904	3,477,904	-	-	-	-
x 1879	4,337,422	4,337,422	-	-	-	-
1880	5,332,318	5,332,318	-	-	-	-
1881	5,758,734	5,758,734	-	-	-	-
1882	6,003,802	6,003,802	-	-	-	-
x 1883	5,161,206	5,161,206	-	-	-	-
1884	4,100,038	4,100,038	-	-	-	-
1885	2,636,784	2,636,784	-	-	-	-
1886	3,761,473	3,761,473	-	-	426,422	426,422
x 1887	5,919,383	5,919,383	-	-	578,340	578,340
1888	8,404,776	8,404,776	-	-	710,340	710,340
1889	11,365,937	11,365,937	-	-	626,762	626,762
1890	11,265,383	11,265,383	-	-	682,103	682,103
x 1891	11,787,913	11,787,913	-	-	819,415	819,415
1892	12,873,547	12,873,547	-	-	998,122	998,122
1893	14,444,327	14,444,327	-	-	1,093,916	1,093,916
1894	14,883,986	14,883,986	-	-	1,034,591	1,034,591
x 1895	18,764,387	18,764,387	-	-	1,117,660	1,117,660
1896	22,750,749	22,750,749	-	-	1,286,377	1,286,377
1897	27,922,577	27,922,577	-	-	1,583,125	1,583,125
1898	31,449,539	31,449,539	-	-	1,793,706	1,793,706
x 1899	28,308,318	28,308,318	-	-	2,342,920	2,342,920
1900	31,459,945	31,459,945	-	-	2,684,295	2,684,295
1901	31,596,401	31,596,401	-	-	2,556,399	2,556,399
1902	31,401,662	31,401,662	-	-	3,019,278	3,019,278
x 1903	33,478,195	33,478,195	-	-	3,296,581	3,296,581
1904	28,217,193	28,217,193	-	-	3,380,179	3,380,179
1905	31,026,964	31,026,964	-	-	4,473,950	4,473,950
1906	47,895,844	47,566,920	328,924	-	7,770,823	7,742,456
x 1907	102,426,263	101,115,739	1,310,524	-	18,693,127	18,605,219
1908	124,884,512	123,227,543	1,656,969	-	24,063,119	23,900,952
1909	129,989,706	128,306,960	1,682,746	-	24,252,108	24,034,110
1910	140,519,650	138,629,706	1,889,944	-	26,227,314	25,889,578
x 1911	153,106,023	151,077,779	2,028,244	-	30,211,961	29,806,447

Sea	Road	Total	Rail	Sea	Road	Fiscal year
t	*t*	*Passenger km*	*Passenger km*	*Passenger km*	*Passenger km*	
-	-	-	-	-	-	1872
-	-	-	-	-	-	1873
-	-	-	-	-	-	1874
-	-	-	-	-	- x	1875
-	-	-	-	-	-	1876
-	-	-	-	-	-	1877
-	-	-	-	-	-	1878
-	-	-	-	-	- x	1879
-	-	-	-	-	-	1880
-	-	-	-	-	-	1881
-	-	-	-	-	-	1882
-	-	-	-	-	- x	1883
-	-	-	-	-	-	1884
-	-	-	-	-	-	1885
-	-	-	-	-	-	1886
-	-	-	-	-	- x	1887
-	-	-	-	-	-	1888
-	-	-	-	-	-	1889
-	-	458,390,535	458,390,535	-	-	1890
-	-	435,543,618	435,543,618	-	- x	1891
-	-	480,965,249	480,965,249	-	-	1892
-	-	549,794,519	549,794,519	-	-	1893
-	-	649,427,733	649,427,733	-	-	1894
-	-	841,756,563	841,756,563	-	- x	1895
-	-	862,486,188	862,486,188	-	-	1896
-	-	1,003,159,441	1,003,159,441	-	-	1897
-	-	1,083,196,393	1,083,196,393	-	-	1898
-	-	1,011,131,563	1,011,131,563	-	- x	1899
-	-	1,136,848,552	1,136,848,552	-	-	1900
-	-	1,153,830,834	1,153,830,834	-	-	1901
-	-	1,163,893,210	1,163,893,210	-	-	1902
-	-	1,304,252,009	1,304,252,009	-	- x	1903
-	-	1,303,593,732	1,303,593,732	-	-	1904
-	-	1,520,933,843	1,520,933,843	-	-	1905
28,367	-	1,971,017,956	1,971,017,956	-	-	1906
87,908	-	3,787,212,773	3,787,212,773	-	- x	1907
162,167	-	4,414,747,214	4,414,747,214	-	-	1908
217,998	-	0	0	-	-	1909
337,736	-	4,890,360,949	4,890,360,949	-	-	1910
405,514	-	5,443,731,616	5,443,731,616	-	- x	1911

Summary of Statistics on Traffic Volume (2)

Fiscal year	Passenger Carried				Tonnage Carried	
	Total	Rail	Sea	Road	Total	Rail
	Person	Person	Person	Person	t	t
1912	162,793,852	160,711,737	2,082,115	-	33,578,190	33,057,943
1913	169,967,122	167,773,143	2,193,979	-	37,707,233	36,929,936
1914	168,255,623	166,092,421	2,163,202	-	36,604,351	35,837,241
x 1915	174,622,363	172,290,045	2,332,318	-	37,306,054	36,373,475
1916	199,626,204	197,043,320	2,582,884	-	44,115,023	42,774,345
1917	248,837,659	245,234,480	3,603,179	-	51,056,815	49,533,090
1918	292,541,353	288,061,584	4,479,769	-	55,717,366	54,166,740
x 1919	363,367,550	357,881,957	5,485,593	-	62,747,161	60,898,557
1920	411,562,353	405,819,694	5,742,659	-	59,339,820	57,529,853
1921	460,461,514	454,535,924	5,925,590	-	60,148,476	58,312,333
1922	516,315,575	509,808,705	6,506,870	-	67,138,393	65,095,702
x 1923	583,551,759	576,472,225	7,079,534	-	67,828,796	65,818,955
1924	642,474,630	635,454,260	7,020,370	-	73,304,349	71,178,263
1925	683,987,815	677,085,503	6,902,312	-	75,490,232	73,090,274
1926	742,405,952	735,706,451	6,699,501	-	84,900,561	82,231,341
x 1927	797,148,762	789,949,277	7,199,485	-	89,702,740	86,807,056
1928	854,668,940	847,300,471	7,368,469	-	91,447,715	88,527,880
1929	870,422,061	862,939,432	7,482,629	-	88,188,705	85,263,791
1930	831,325,163	824,152,598	7,047,701	124,864	73,597,773	70,883,581
x 1931	794,979,545	787,222,491	6,972,527	784,527	69,017,510	66,576,071
1932	789,240,132	781,149,732	6,879,969	1,210,431	69,692,447	67,394,397
1933	850,755,138	841,315,316	6,757,058	2,682,764	80,599,489	78,064,207
1934	925,103,402	913,564,566	7,404,307	4,134,529	88,346,335	85,355,324
x 1935	999,180,517	985,041,029	7,875,036	6,264,452	92,001,707	88,875,989
1936	1,076,157,992	1,058,630,711	8,582,960	8,944,321	101,253,475	97,599,984
1937	1,179,277,532	1,156,266,149	9,416,186	13,595,197	111,075,805	106,450,207
1938	1,372,549,035	1,344,505,193	11,174,196	16,869,646	123,964,955	118,054,223
x 1939	1,649,027,949	1,613,206,175	13,983,828	21,837,946	138,534,338	131,419,419
1940	1,918,878,280	1,878,332,735	16,309,853	24,235,692	153,589,001	145,745,586
1941	2,212,525,420	2,172,218,725	17,528,464	22,778,231	159,945,774	151,693,683
1942	2,321,899,076	2,279,840,315	16,413,235	25,645,526	163,635,177	158,039,668
x 1943	2,695,091,075	2,648,099,746	13,502,936	33,488,393	184,771,563	178,176,988
1944	3,149,233,330	3,107,390,725	11,576,398	30,266,207	168,997,112	161,063,953
1945	3,010,048,275	2,973,094,369	8,121,433	28,832,473	85,354,083	81,468,947
1946	3,217,342,285	3,176,357,568	10,427,044	30,557,673	94,734,697	91,295,914
x 1947	3,363,404,370	3,310,501,563	11,615,648	41,287,159	112,864,673	109,133,496
1948	3,322,939,082	3,265,884,204	9,180,682	47,874,196	133,483,038	128,035,049
1949	3,113,296,511	3,043,866,975	8,164,365	61,265,171	134,607,255	127,528,690
1950	3,078,687,109	3,001,082,618	7,967,061	69,637,430	142,858,326	135,690,421
x 1951	3,466,570,838	3,366,714,184	8,979,273	90,877,381	170,026,716	162,058,021
1952	3,541,528,986	3,427,461,285	9,423,059	104,644,642	159,908,003	152,739,314
1953	3,681,010,950	3,546,995,420	9,807,419	124,208,111	166,393,068	159,244,838
1954	3,817,662,694	3,663,131,670	10,150,362	144,380,662	162,772,802	156,218,846
x 1955	4,020,655,036	3,849,218,994	10,049,134	161,386,908	166,804,493	160,246,393

Sea	Road	Total	Rail	Sea	Road	Fiscal year
t	t	Passenger km	Passenger km	Passenger km	Passenger km	
520,247	-	5,835,976,195	5,835,976,195	-	-	1912
677,297	-	5,940,017,000	5,940,017,000	-	-	1913
767,110	-	5,831,834,939	5,831,834,939	-	-	1914
932,579	-	6,206,479,201	6,206,479,201	-	- x	1915
1,340,678	-	6,848,344,747	6,848,344,747	-	-	1916
1,523,725	-	8,876,389,331	8,876,389,331	-	-	1917
1,550,626	-	10,572,466,516	10,572,466,516	-	-	1918
1,848,604	-	12,782,396,020	12,782,396,020	-	- x	1919
1,809,967	-	13,492,937,178	13,492,937,178	-	-	1920
1,836,143	-	14,319,431,314	14,319,431,314	-	-	1921
2,042,691	-	15,662,728,955	15,662,728,955	-	-	1922
2,009,841	-	17,170,264,440	17,170,264,440	-	- x	1923
2,126,086	-	18,105,961,846	18,105,961,846	-	-	1924
2,399,958	-	18,740,974,211	18,740,974,211	-	-	1925
2,669,220	-	19,236,767,807	19,236,767,807	-	-	1926
2,895,684	-	20,054,584,323	20,054,584,323	-	- x	1927
2,919,835	-	21,587,102,607	21,587,102,607	-	-	1928
2,924,914	-	21,350,187,867	21,350,187,867	-	-	1929
2,712,508	1,684	19,876,061,387	19,875,113,306	-	948,081	1930
2,435,425	6,014	19,376,292,602	19,122,650,504	247,922,475	5,719,623 x	1931
2,288,498	9,552	19,254,566,650	19,001,523,301	244,632,504	8,410,845	1932
2,509,512	25,770	21,117,256,968	20,822,013,177	277,852,284	17,391,507	1933
2,951,679	39,332	22,935,237,246	22,573,020,205	328,622,989	33,594,052	1934
3,077,922	47,796	24,541,757,662	24,173,052,337	314,247,376	54,457,949 x	1935
3,579,767	73,724	26,638,524,200	26,216,154,565	345,143,882	77,225,753	1936
4,521,307	104,291	29,556,473,624	29,052,146,447	385,074,845	119,252,332	1937
5,771,147	139,585	34,267,159,711	33,632,505,886	480,255,525	154,398,300	1938
6,889,936	224,983	42,903,447,717	42,057,511,112	638,471,220	207,465,385 x	1939
7,542,742	300,673	50,366,033,462	49,338,665,610	781,206,297	246,161,555	1940
7,827,628	424,463	56,580,761,501	55,545,286,529	800,002,487	235,472,485	1941
5,085,076	510,433	61,704,433,673	60,450,556,043	986,783,844	267,093,786	1942
5,662,578	931,997	75,498,923,161	74,073,359,135	1,078,285,076	347,278,950 x	1943
6,110,206	1,822,953	78,523,946,112	77,283,211,279	926,668,449	314,066,384	1944
2,175,349	1,709,787	76,571,874,775	76,034,383,062	230,212,720	307,278,993	1945
2,072,237	1,366,546	88,055,790,117	87,446,935,527	271,380,258	337,474,332	1946
2,686,201	1,044,976	91,882,096,582	91,164,740,525	273,289,994	444,066,063 x	1947
3,321,912	2,126,077	82,758,829,433	81,995,084,882	277,805,560	485,938,991	1948
5,114,307	1,964,258	70,452,642,926	69,664,632,866	226,092,235	561,917,825	1949
5,373,124	1,794,781	69,971,896,073	69,105,562,890	217,951,493	648,381,690	1950
6,287,480	1,681,215	80,112,925,469	79,039,700,830	237,973,967	835,250,672 x	1951
6,260,017	908,672	81,719,897,289	80,479,537,025	266,710,747	973,649,517	1952
6,321,406	826,824	84,984,830,869	83,554,366,337	285,286,531	1,145,178,001	1953
5,856,073	697,883	88,649,254,406	87,038,301,172	307,385,267	1,303,567,967	1954
5,893,406	664,694	92,963,391,928	91,239,005,817	293,363,559	1,431,022,552 x	1955

Summary of Statistics on Traffic Volume (3)

Fiscal year	Passengers Carried				Tonnage Carried	
	Total	Rail	Sea	Road	Total	Rail
	Person	*Person*	*Person*	*Person*	*t*	*t*
1956	4,309,735,265	4,118,793,771	10,610,196	180,331,298	180,075,256	172,891,710
1957	4,533,748,621	4,324,356,423	10,253,418	199,138,780	185,085,747	177,792,036
1958	4,731,487,974	4,514,935,162	10,430,506	206,122,306	174,054,386	167,141,096
X 1959	5,044,336,185	4,812,757,991	10,907,127	220,671,067	188,947,697	181,402,690
1960	5,374,549,750	5,123,900,941	11,377,863	239,270,946	203,336,889	195,294,548
1961	5,553,551,593	5,283,510,206	11,787,449	258,253,938	214,807,128	206,394,813
1962	5,899,177,897	5,609,533,569	11,855,095	277,789,233	210,478,412	201,645,990
X 1963	6,344,003,252	6,040,303,112	12,229,779	291,470,361	215,465,557	206,050,814
1964	6,728,164,970	6,409,838,864	12,459,444	305,866,662	216,176,389	206,606,313
1965	7,042,897,199	6,721,826,779	12,716,490	308,353,930	209,590,541	200,009,886
1966	7,156,189,492	6,841,977,450	12,602,203	301,609,839	205,241,273	195,776,451
X 1967	7,358,608,424	7,047,893,719	13,398,109	297,316,596	213,141,128	202,570,265
1968	7,177,282,408	6,868,497,655	13,788,911	294,995,842	206,532,117	198,808,403
1969	6,842,266,391	6,540,950,165	13,848,638	287,467,588	208,595,757	197,171,071
1970	6,822,477,864	6,534,477,099	13,658,277	274,342,488	210,818,532	198,503,191
X 1971	6,940,189,983	6,658,927,622	14,273,732	266,988,629	205,667,613	193,295,974
1972	7,001,019,697	6,723,786,385	15,082,781	262,150,531	193,978,041	182,450,379
1973	7,142,076,726	6,870,889,122	15,859,753	255,327,851	186,019,805	175,680,748
1974	7,383,855,543	7,112,689,996	15,958,313	255,207,234	167,371,576	157,704,644
X 1975	7,310,940,675	7,048,012,915	15,245,433	247,682,327	150,633,577	141,691,399
1976	7,430,529,463	7,180,348,258	12,656,139	237,525,066	149,379,466	140,913,956
1977	7,307,061,762	7,068,197,681	10,967,594	227,896,487	139,366,391	132,035,630
1978	7,224,195,456	6,996,640,989	10,416,562	217,137,905	140,758,058	133,342,713
X 1979	7,152,857,634	6,930,653,314	10,169,415	212,034,905	144,500,267	136,393,347
1980	7,042,348,110	6,824,812,994	10,160,196	207,374,920	128,639,686	121,619,052
1981	7,005,130,198	6,793,030,370	9,853,716	202,246,112	117,031,301	110,572,047
1982	6,944,641,064	6,742,417,993	9,603,168	192,619,903	103,865,387	97,764,720
X 1983	6,991,328,199	6,796,759,064	9,597,826	184,971,309	91,449,475	86,091,037
1984	7,069,520,764	6,883,837,290	9,249,514	176,433,960	79,284,072	74,928,011
1985	7,121,422,239	6,941,357,751	9,242,920	170,821,568	72,906,244	68,551,661
1986	7,269,376,115	7,103,957,197	9,145,395	156,273,523	65,950,638	61,594,351

| | | | Passenger Kilometres | | | | Fiscal year |
Sea	Road	Total	Rail	Sea	Road	
t	t	Passenger km	Passenger km	Passenger km	Passenger km	
6,672,948	510,598	99,966,533,196	98,081,647,665	307,746,029	1,577,139,502	1956
6,850,207	443,504	103,288,026,584	101,244,411,606	315,888,875	1,727,726,103	1957
6,530,570	382,720	108,347,787,288	106,207,846,272	353,788,068	1,786,152,948	1958
7,120,193	424,814	116,449,784,103	114,189,143,792	369,668,407	1,890,971,904	x 1959
7,632,188	410,153	126,435,971,987	123,983,433,103	400,760,136	2,051,778,748	1960
8,007,573	404,742	134,425,921,649	131,753,765,813	437,158,354	2,234,997,482	1961
8,468,768	363,654	144,056,588,591	141,191,577,360	454,666,270	2,410,344,961	1962
9,070,370	344,373	155,715,641,740	152,710,434,326	484,916,820	2,520,290,594	x 1963
9,291,223	278,853	167,359,987,747	164,176,336,395	527,934,614	2,655,716,738	1964
9,377,193	203,462	177,342,762,843	174,014,429,518	560,080,785	2,768,252,540	1965
9,273,249	191,573	179,080,663,141	175,758,027,589	554,995,813	2,767,639,739	1966
10,390,093	180,770	187,728,208,206	184,314,702,893	583,683,717	2,829,821,596	x 1967
10,555,002	200,664	188,306,644,682	184,807,877,870	618,915,849	2,885,850,963	1968
11,246,239	178,447	185,292,104,792	181,520,314,752	624,531,509	3,147,258,531	1969
12,224,451	90,890	193,566,318,222	189,726,320,818	607,524,073	3,232,473,331	1970
12,299,566	72,073	194,160,092,471	190,321,185,318	640,161,619	3,198,745,534	x 1971
11,467,738	59,924	201,659,795,307	197,829,162,978	653,947,490	3,176,684,839	1972
10,279,924	59,133	211,810,050,144	208,096,973,287	675,294,662	3,037,782,195	1973
9,604,216	62,716	219,222,033,101	215,563,955,811	673,745,744	2,984,331,546	1974
8,894,930	47,248	218,814,008,944	215,289,012,168	625,500,144	2,899,496,632	x 1975
8,416,622	48,888	214,140,178,655	210,740,047,928	543,479,408	2,856,651,319	1976
7,280,919	49,842	202,902,641,614	199,652,946,111	463,762,619	2,785,932,884	1977
7,370,098	45,247	198,908,540,845	195,844,019,959	437,523,523	2,626,997,363	1978
8,063,289	43,631	197,682,141,787	194,690,391,015	430,114,246	2,561,636,526	x 1979
6,987,367	33,267	196,048,706,553	193,143,479,155	403,809,896	2,501,417,502	1980
6,431,380	27,874	194,972,507,465	192,114,619,177	372,203,987	2,485,684,301	1981
6,072,984	27,683	193,532,962,381	190,767,024,041	363,297,931	2,402,640,409	1982
5,339,319	19,119	195,581,607,439	192,905,707,000	349,211,055	2,326,689,384	x 1983
4,356,061		196,823,583,723	194,180,317,217	331,400,138	2,311,866,368	1984
4,354,583		200,095,383,806	197,462,795,695	330,228,375	2,302,359,736	1985
4,356,287		200,822,212,585	198,299,305,315	317,789,836	2,205,117,434	1986

Summary of Statistics on Traffic Volume (4)

Fiscal year	Tonne Kilometres			
	Total	Rail	Sea	Road
1890	42,092,388	42,092,388	-	-
x 1891	49,796,982	49,796,982	-	-
1892	73,292,662	73,292,662	-	-
1893	89,005,211	89,005,211	-	-
1894	118,266,097	118,266,097	-	-
x 1895	125,605,746	125,605,746	-	-
1896	121,537,429	121,537,429	-	-
1897	162,651,234	162,651,234	-	-
1898	216,630,138	216,630,138	-	-
x 1899	286,626,490	286,626,490	-	-
1900	359,666,713	359,666,713	-	-
1901	345,957,220	345,957,220	-	-
1902	394,497,864	394,497,864	-	-
x 1903	450,479,799	450,479,799	-	-
1904	544,200,077	544,200,077	-	-
1905	650,222,681	650,222,681	-	-
1906	1,166,595,970	1,166,595,970	-	-
x 1907	2,356,239,393	2,356,239,393	-	-
1908	2,991,116,673	2,991,116,673	-	-
1909	3,124,807,814	3,124,807,814	-	-
1910	3,477,374,463	3,477,374,463	-	-
x 1911	3,838,769,862	3,838,769,862	-	-
1912	4,400,543,924	4,400,543,924	-	-
1913	4,993,049,063	4,993,049,063	-	-
1914	4,876,875,516	4,876,875,516	-	-
x 1915	5,411,063,037	5,411,063,037	-	-
1916	6,832,885,169	6,832,885,169	-	-
1917	8,229,518,135	8,229,518,135	-	-
1918	9,170,471,477	9,170,471,477	-	-
x 1919	10,290,360,157	10,290,360,157	-	-
1920	9,690,946,221	9,690,946,221	-	-
1921	9,628,026,503	9,628,026,503	-	-
1922	10,406,704,378	10,406,704,378	-	-
x 1923	10,451,457,315	10,451,457,315	-	-
1924	11,522,957,565	11,522,957,565	-	-
1925	11,815,633,194	11,815,633,194	-	-
1926	12,456,213,913	12,456,213,913	-	-
x 1927	13,037,882,307	13,037,882,307	-	-
1928	13,405,536,406	13,405,536,406	-	-
1929	13,209,877,596	13,209,877,596	-	-
1930	11,423,056,119	11,423,036,856	-	19,263
x 1931	11,217,821,295	11,088,188,176	129,568,733	64,386
1932	11,149,900,320	11,029,459,478	120,330,841	110,001
1933	12,616,879,798	12,476,183,153	140,397,667	298,973
1934	14,125,843,053	13,959,279,453	166,076,922	486,678
x 1935	14,763,743,989	14,593,369,818	169,770,420	603,751
1936	16,493,957,334	16,296,692,354	196,345,535	919,445
1937	19,169,679,838	18,916,876,209	251,453,133	1,350,496
1938	22,224,043,455	21,907,303,995	314,887,301	1,852,159
x 1939	25,644,890,167	25,285,541,077	356,229,565	3,119,525

Fiscal year	Total	Rail	Sea	Road
		Tonne Kilometres		
1940	28,328,864,774	27,947,635,342	376,387,946	4,841,486
1941	30,275,301,782	29,871,576,217	396,413,156	7,312,409
1942	34,386,930,677	33,945,534,566	432,701,020	8,695,091
x 1943	43,388,464,920	42,795,444,701	578,297,372	14,722,847
1944	41,894,910,659	41,234,533,777	633,046,224	27,330,658
1945	19,146,798,064	18,981,267,286	140,854,326	24,676,452
1946	19,137,971,058	18,968,638,195	148,021,027	21,311,836
x 1947	22,456,191,107	22,239,310,525	200,113,863	16,766,719
1948	26,694,594,151	26,405,250,646	269,956,436	19,387,069
1949	30,372,547,159	29,875,105,882	480,696,874	16,744,403
1950	33,786,850,985	33,308,552,028	446,694,835	31,604,122
x 1951	40,429,557,800	39,882,577,447	519,550,262	27,430,091
1952	39,815,849,102	39,250,512,687	547,875,716	17,460,699
1953	41,594,011,346	40,993,053,359	585,581,430	15,376,557
1954	40,429,470,709	39,893,526,387	524,213,127	11,731,195
x 1955	43,124,875,498	42,564,362,539	549,285,924	11,227,035
1956	47,559,163,489	46,923,309,144	625,477,227	10,377,118
1957	48,848,947,892	48,216,189,507	624,028,195	8,730,190
1958	45,906,694,463	45,291,262,306	607,436,791	7,995,366
x 1959	50,340,773,996	49,668,310,059	663,398,520	9,065,417
1960	54,293,564,802	53,592,214,878	692,725,161	8,624,763
1961	58,255,767,408	57,535,861,985	710,163,490	9,741,933
1962	57,033,119,663	56,285,187,010	739,568,836	8,363,817
x 1963	59,960,716,064	59,155,107,838	797,605,915	8,002,311
1964	59,689,538,605	58,880,941,511	802,332,269	6,264,825
1965	57,186,345,858	56,408,268,955	773,112,340	4,964,563
1966	55,709,948,116	54,955,779,062	749,546,513	4,622,541
x 1967	59,399,092,745	58,547,369,189	846,946,111	4,777,445
1968	59,834,340,588	58,964,197,734	866,062,674	4,080,180
1969	61,106,598,193	60,166,561,664	936,882,763	3,153,766
1970	63,461,745,060	62,435,317,643	1,024,787,226	1,640,191
x 1971	62,283,786,699	61,250,157,273	1,032,452,431	1,176,995
1972	59,535,131,363	58,560,517,138	973,713,691	900,534
1973	58,252,563,207	57,404,928,032	846,746,067	889,108
1974	52,383,754,694	51,582,805,677	800,006,377	942,640
x 1975	47,314,400,438	46,577,354,890	736,231,300	814,248
1976	46,224,914,153	45,526,015,505	698,132,426	766,222
1977	41,195,920,378	40,587,276,499	607,875,602	768,277
1978	41,040,562,402	40,412,576,178	627,284,494	701,730
x 1979	42,976,327,348	42,284,286,738	691,501,207	539,403
1980	37,559,625,458	36,960,834,013	598,408,531	382,914
1981	33,956,024,793	33,397,940,080	557,767,825	316,888
1982	30,782,811,566	30,246,153,609	536,307,552	350,405
x 1983	27,569,700,744	27,085,660,640	483,791,627	248,477
1984	23,134,562,968	22,720,720,365	413,842,603	-
1985	22,046,746,222	21,625,475,953	421,270,269	-
1986	20,577,676,879	20,145,578,998	432,097,881	-

5-Net Revenues from Transport Operations (1)

	Passenger/Freight Total					
	Total	Rail	Sea	Daily Average		
				Total	Rail	Sea
1872	169,053	169,053	-	463	463	-
1873	419,284	419,284	-	1,149	1,149	-
1874	540,757	540,757	-	1,482	1,482	-
× 1875	329,869	329,869	-	901	901	-
1876	587,074	587,074	-	1,608	1,608	-
1877	711,858	711,858	-	1,950	1,950	-
1878	1,078,779	1,078,779	-	2,956	2,956	-
× 1879	858,426	858,426	-	2,345	2,345	-
1880	1,050,605	1,050,605	-	2,878	2,878	-
1881	1,290,499	1,290,499	-	3,536	3,536	-
1882	1,365,585	1,365,585	-	3,741	3,741	-
× 1883	1,209,547	1,209,547	-	3,305	3,305	-
1884	992,110	992,110	-	2,718	2,718	-
1885	661,847	661,847	-	1,813	1,813	-
1886	927,606	927,606	-	2,541	2,541	-
× 1887	1,266,341	1,266,341	-	3,460	3,460	-
1888	1,732,626	1,732,626	-	4,747	4,747	-
1889	2,928,339	2,928,339	-	8,023	8,023	-
1890	4,091,743	4,091,743	-	11,210	11,210	-
× 1891	3,993,642	3,993,642	-	10,912	10,912	-
1892	4,572,770	4,572,770	-	12,528	12,528	-
1893	5,201,873	5,201,873	-	14,252	14,252	-
1894	6,052,323	6,052,323	-	16,582	16,582	-
× 1895	7,734,201	7,734,201	-	21,132	21,132	-
1896	7,975,170	7,975,170	-	21,850	21,850	-
1897	9,532,879	9,532,879	-	26,117	26,117	-
1898	11,019,515	11,019,515	-	30,190	30,190	-
× 1899	13,586,907	13,586,907	-	37,123	37,123	-
1900	15,561,340	15,561,340	-	42,634	42,634	-
1901	16,176,953	16,176,953	-	44,320	44,320	-

Unit:yen

	Passenger/Freight Total					
	Total	Rail	Sea	Daily Average		
				Total	Rail	Sea
1902	17,846,898	17,846,898	-	48,896	48,896	-
× 1903	19,660,811	19,660,811	-	53,718	53,718	-
1904	20,132,432	20,132,432	-	55,157	55,157	-
1905	23,226,659	23,226,659	-	63,635	63,635	-
1906	34,950,628	34,783,281	167,347	95,755	95,297	458
× 1907	67,712,953	66,877,406	835,547	185,008	182,275	2,283
1908	78,993,935	77,604,441	1,389,494	216,422	212,615	3,807
1909	80,955,891	79,384,862	1,571,029	221,797	217,493	4,304
1910	88,294,256	86,390,309	1,903,947	241,902	236,686	5,216
× 1911	98,449,250	96,349,952	2,099,298	268,987	263,251	5,736
1912	105,824,524	103,683,686	2,140,838	289,930	284,065	5,865
1913	111,585,116	109,344,274	2,240,842	305,713	299,573	6,140
1914	108,666,572	106,422,467	2,244,105	297,717	291,568	6,149
× 1915	116,743,548	114,325,826	2,417,722	318,971	312,366	6,605
1916	137,855,223	134,634,948	3,220,275	377,686	368,863	8,823
1917	177,414,233	173,164,997	4,249,236	486,066	474,424	11,642
1918	235,169,285	229,644,041	5,525,244	644,299	629,161	15,138
× 1919	301,046,309	293,355,582	7,690,727	822,531	801,518	21,013
1920	345,799,786	337,070,400	8,729,386	947,397	923,481	23,916
1921	390,591,389	381,760,840	8,830,549	1,070,113	1,045,920	24,193
1922	420,715,937	411,394,947	9,320,990	1,152,646	1,127,109	25,537
× 1923	437,251,118	427,579,497	9,671,621	1,194,675	1,168,250	26,425
1924	463,270,036	453,374,314	9,895,722	1,269,233	1,242,121	27,112
1925	471,669,156	460,573,689	11,095,467	1,292,244	1,261,846	30,398

Net Revenues from Transport Operations (2)

Fiscal year	Passenger/Freight Total			
	Total	Rail	Sea	Road
1926	478,978,122	467,595,295	11,382,827	-
x 1927	495,752,605	483,062,336	12,690,269	-
1928	519,163,526	506,024,226	13,139,300	-
1929	510,285,139	496,979,793	13,305,346	-
1930	450,903,434	439,233,129	11,641,877	28,428
x 1931	427,061,128	416,095,952	10,795,946	169,230
1932	418,649,254	408,093,702	10,302,263	253,289
1933	464,719,898	452,572,126	11,610,362	537,410
1934	507,142,606	492,777,443	13,321,046	1,044,117
x 1935	534,298,088	519,736,963	12,899,280	1,661,840
1936	585,956,494	569,666,194	13,905,255	2,385,045
1937	654,908,343	635,505,189	16,354,512	3,048,642
1938	755,556,139	731,306,161	20,384,366	3,865,612
x 1939	907,297,172	876,524,459	25,496,263	5,276,450
1940	1,022,423,651	987,542,473	28,591,490	6,289,688
1941	1,106,131,711	1,070,446,324	29,420,153	6,265,234
1942	1,423,238,707	1,373,799,420	39,576,798	9,862,489
x 1943	1,687,863,604	1,626,389,969	48,152,819	13,320,816
1944	1,881,176,779	1,800,679,093	60,082,943	20,414,743
1945	2,072,168,377	2,024,883,443	21,483,685	25,801,249
1946	6,067,553,593	5,945,440,773	51,119,182	70,993,638
x 1947	26,213,765,650	25,572,567,163	312,308,854	328,889,633
1948	71,925,452,069	69,475,237,132	1,208,356,256	1,241,858,681
1949	109,565,597,366	105,395,507,775	2,375,945,598	1,794,143,993
1950	139,493,157,724	133,978,732,331	3,157,334,823	2,357,090,570
x 1951	178,426,497,164	171,370,394,800	4,004,425,520	3,051,676,844
1952	212,335,895,801	203,462,189,090	5,255,829,988	3,617,876,723
1953	245,954,940,779	235,905,801,252	5,978,360,856	4,070,778,671
1954	246,019,580,314	236,148,148,836	5,498,658,907	4,372,772,571
x 1955	255,322,281,243	245,223,316,523	5,407,050,322	4,691,914,398
1956	280,001,960,381	268,832,380,625	6,079,331,999	5,090,247,757
1957	325,172,492,793	314,304,306,742	5,248,884,447	5,619,301,604
1958	326,125,288,243	314,767,415,349	5,219,710,305	6,138,162,589
x 1959	356,439,630,313	344,138,819,627	5,695,823,071	6,604,987,615
1960	393,685,943,239	380,561,313,963	6,052,183,019	7,072,446,257
1961	488,199,428,076	473,594,294,001	6,604,310,023	8,000,824,052
1962	510,708,693,638	494,986,316,790	6,984,927,867	8,737,448,981
x 1963	549,939,401,695	532,566,237,339	7,264,090,186	10,109,074,170
1964	578,696,936,368	560,446,749,257	7,632,928,193	10,617,258,918
1965	610,374,351,469	591,042,953,233	7,790,152,073	11,541,246,163
1966	768,427,095,901	746,428,777,108	8,918,405,904	13,079,912,889
x 1967	827,644,883,300	804,002,017,307	9,941,935,746	13,700,930,247
1968	882,778,095,715	858,336,881,565	10,351,398,727	14,089,815,423
1969	1,005,055,358,829	976,991,741,188	11,593,049,375	16,470,568,266
1970	1,100,747,086,129	1,069,707,561,215	12,499,677,263	18,539,847,651
x 1971	1,109,629,955,659	1,077,090,845,777	13,628,180,280	18,910,929,602
1972	1,161,160,419,421	1,127,076,374,122	13,348,488,927	20,735,556,372
1973	1,230,325,923,282	1,195,334,758,177	12,428,896,622	22,562,268,483
1974	1,365,694,700,102	1,325,728,648,381	13,224,987,443	26,741,064,278
x 1975	1,556,672,087,007	1,512,741,671,157	13,776,176,482	30,154,239,368
1976	1,806,961,359	1,758,962,436	15,031,399	32,967,524
1977	2,130,667,100	2,079,962,044	15,920,425	64,784,631
1978	2,259,452,014	2,206,486,982	16,669,134	36,295,898
x 1979	2,508,950,522	2,453,439,049	18,795,276	36,716,197
1980	2,572,019,705	2,515,195,322	18,298,693	38,525,690
1981	2,714,828,461	2,657,327,402	18,045,203	39,455,856
1982	2,820,875,713	2,763,240,546	17,194,284	40,440,883
x 1983	2,821,215,021	2,765,031,190	15,389,427	40,794,404
1984	2,948,885,150	2,893,438,077	13,941,186	41,505,887
1985	3,127,948,270	3,071,926,137	13,773,446	42,248,687
1986	3,194,492,959	3,140,726,837	13,411,489	40,354,633

Net Revenues from Transport Operations (3)

Fiscal year	Net Revenues from Passenger Service			
	Total	Rail	Sea	Road
1872	169,053	169,053	-	-
1873	419,284	419,284	-	-
1874	540,757	540,757	-	-
× 1875	329,869	329,869	-	-
1876	587,074	587,074	-	-
1877	711,858	711,858	-	-
1878	1,078,779	1,078,779	-	-
× 1879	858,426	858,426	-	-
1880	1,050,605	1,050,605	-	-
1881	1,290,499	1,290,499	-	-
1882	1,365,585	1,365,585	-	-
× 1883	1,209,547	1,209,547	-	-
1884	992,110	992,110	-	-
1885	661,847	661,847	-	-
1886	927,606	927,606	-	-
× 1887	1,266,341	1,266,341	-	-
1888	1,732,626	1,732,626	-	-
1889	2,928,339	2,928,339	-	-
1890	3,312,945	3,312,945	-	-
× 1891	3,163,597	3,163,597	-	-
1892	3,497,428	3,497,428	-	-
1893	3,958,523	3,958,523	-	-
1894	4,462,757	4,462,757	-	-
× 1895	5,925,712	5,925,712	-	-
1896	6,328,847	6,328,847	-	-
1897	7,468,162	7,468,162	-	-
1898	8,209,482	8,209,482	-	-
× 1899	9,854,931	9,854,931	-	-
1900	11,061,548	11,061,548	-	-
1901	11,256,214	11,256,214	-	-
1902	12,188,530	12,188,530	-	-
× 1903	13,325,520	13,325,520	-	-
1904	12,678,137	12,678,137	-	-
1905	14,442,790	14,442,790	-	-
1906	20,609,815	20,454,863	154,952	-
× 1907	38,236,128	37,573,791	662,337	-
1908	42,871,124	41,868,780	1,002,344	-
1909	43,552,465	42,448,518	1,103,947	-
1910	46,810,263	45,533,079	1,277,184	-
× 1911	52,027,947	50,674,259	1,353,688	-

Net Revenues from Transport Operations (4)

Fiscal year	Net Revenues from Passenger Service			
	Total	Rail	Sea	Road
1912	55,680,105	54,306,013	1,374,092	-
1913	57,341,102	55,975,342	1,365,760	-
1914	55,994,467	54,671,971	1,322,676	-
× 1915	58,677,373	57,282,341	1,395,032	-
1916	66,333,655	64,773,111	1,560,544	-
1917	86,880,046	84,725,517	2,154,529	-
1918	123,161,138	119,899,610	3,261,528	-
× 1919	165,846,901	161,546,479	4,300,422	-
1920	208,474,348	203,887,083	4,587,265	-
1921	219,165,134	214,519,192	4,645,942	-
1922	237,256,753	232,174,781	5,081,972	-
× 1923	255,078,339	249,470,408	5,607,931	-
1924	264,430,260	258,810,661	5,619,599	-
1925	267,558,498	261,787,479	5,771,019	-
1926	271,875,938	265,985,340	5,890,598	-
× 1927	277,794,075	271,312,358	6,481,717	-
1928	292,221,829	285,337,862	6,883,967	-
1929	286,181,589	279,030,319	7,151,270	-
1930	261,214,734	255,086,230	6,103,098	25,406
× 1931	245,732,153	239,971,712	5,601,493	158,948
1932	239,201,868	233,387,259	5,578,393	236,216
1933	261,377,427	254,533,956	6,347,330	496,141
1934	282,163,434	274,096,342	7,089,177	977,915
× 1935	300,304,169	291,635,214	7,122,595	1,546,360
1936	325,964,032	316,001,496	7,791,039	2,171,497
1937	360,827,559	349,543,030	8,541,213	2,743,316
1938	416,592,462	402,581,232	10,570,220	3,441,010
× 1939	527,139,164	508,448,801	14,077,699	4,612,664
1940	624,690,015	602,135,285	17,134,369	5,420,361
1941	697,713,420	674,897,460	17,705,095	5,110,865
1942	935,325,820	899,745,957	27,982,300	7,597,563
× 1943	1,138,637,757	1,098,523,640	30,208,869	9,905,248
1944	1,352,677,047	1,304,875,601	35,710,690	12,090,756
1945	1,737,127,371	1,704,222,482	15,005,699	17,899,190
1946	5,028,021,829	4,954,310,095	28,081,643	45,630,091
× 1947	18,504,692,392	18,121,350,007	158,652,487	224,689,898
1948	42,244,368,205	41,114,941,015	415,339,762	714,087,428
1949	68,573,143,459	66,762,088,326	667,106,325	1,143,948,808
1950	73,699,012,029	71,455,565,832	696,131,319	1,547,314,878
× 1951	91,475,966,730	88,389,625,707	931,856,115	2,154,484,908
1952	109,772,236,375	105,900,563,678	1,095,820,965	2,775,851,732
1953	126,756,570,567	122,302,925,328	1,272,134,089	3,181,511,150
1954	131,610,528,291	126,788,261,040	1,270,814,983	3,551,452,268
× 1955	135,393,440,722	130,339,184,633	1,206,313,121	3,847,942,968

Net Revenues from Transport Operations (5)

Fiscal year	Net Revenues from Passenger Service			
	Total	Rail	Sea	Road
1956	148,102,357,352	142,596,981,909	1,300,923,081	4,204,452,362
1957	173,242,582,772	167,086,309,022	1,396,054,387	4,760,219,363
1958	183,389,638,337	176,640,374,354	1,481,362,108	5,267,901,875
× 1959	198,983,178,949	191,761,240,053	1,547,345,148	5,674,593,748
1960	224,209,789,319	216,446,224,189	1,685,314,452	6,078,250,678
1961	280,796,918,118	271,966,646,352	2,082,576,979	6,747,694,787
1962	308,599,784,152	298,970,026,130	2,175,700,862	7,454,057,160
× 1963	338,430,358,537	327,289,585,294	2,333,392,611	8,807,380,632
1964	369,707,383,753	357,902,350,474	2,443,483,470	9,361,189,809
1965	412,145,866,143	399,101,706,921	2,498,923,613	10,545,235,609
1966	548,386,129,800	533,255,502,624	2,961,800,547	12,168,826,629
× 1967	591,587,182,004	575,690,471,060	3,121,564,184	12,775,146,760
1968	643,442,235,101	627,095,476,527	3,267,293,733	13,079,464,841
1969	760,167,148,989	740,694,636,997	4,023,282,983	15,449,229,009
1970	846,298,135,189	824,458,895,765	4,232,387,118	17,606,852,306
× 1971	859,561,495,193	836,966,406,214	4,576,917,380	18,018,171,599
1972	921,631,802,000	897,040,414,000	4,781,237,000	19,810,151,000
1973	992,228,261,000	965,645,521,000	4,964,096,000	21,618,644,000
1974	1,125,151,453,000	1,094,324,845,000	5,309,210,000	25,517,398,000
× 1975	1,315,125,363,000	1,280,880,876,000	5,489,351,000	28,755,136,000
1976	1,529,024,232	1,491,967,829	5,728,210	31,328,193
1977	1,823,709,103	1,784,394,049	6,307,024	33,008,030
1978	1,949,925,190	1,908,760,462	6,694,885	34,469,843
× 1979	2,154,996,336	2,112,546,272	7,053,448	35,396,616
1980	2,242,441,213	2,197,585,285	7,270,037	37,585,891
1981	2,403,463,097	2,357,593,770	7,135,558	38,733,769
1982	2,541,503,909	2,494,480,020	7,165,028	39,858,861
× 1983	2,579,683,639	2,532,292,689	6,707,777	40,683,173
1984	2,750,413,644	2,701,927,196	7,016,205	41,470,243
1985	2,942,238,877	2,892,675,728	7,314,462	42,248,687
1986	3,026,894,605	2,979,477,179	7,062,492	40,354,633

Net Revenues from Transport Operations (6)

Fiscal year	Net Revenues from Freight Service			
	Total	Rail	Sea	Road
1872	-	-	-	-
1873	-	-	-	-
1874	-	-	-	-
× 1875	-	-	-	-
1876	-	-	-	-
1877	-	-	-	-
1878	-	-	-	-
× 1879	-	-	-	-
1880	-	-	-	-
1881	-	-	-	-
1882	-	-	-	-
× 1883	-	-	-	-
1884	-	-	-	-
1885	-	-	-	-
1886	-	-	-	-
× 1887	-	-	-	-
1888	-	-	-	-
1889	-	-	-	-
1890	778,798	778,798	-	-
× 1891	830,045	830,045	-	-
1892	1,075,342	1,075,342	-	-
1893	1,243,350	1,243,350	-	-
1894	1,589,566	1,589,566	-	-
× 1895	1,808,489	1,808,489	-	-
1896	1,646,323	1,646,323	-	-
1897	2,064,717	2,064,717	-	-
1898	2,810,033	2,810,033	-	-
× 1899	3,731,976	3,731,976	-	-
1900	4,499,792	4,499,792	-	-
1901	4,920,739	4,920,739	-	-
1902	5,658,368	5,658,368	-	-
× 1903	6,335,291	6,335,291	-	-
1904	7,454,295	7,454,295	-	-
1905	8,783,869	8,783,869	-	-
1906	14,340,813	14,328,418	12,395	-
× 1907	29,476,825	29,303,615	173,210	-
1908	36,122,811	35,735,661	387,150	-
1909	37,403,426	36,936,344	467,082	-
1910	41,483,993	40,857,230	626,763	-
× 1911	46,421,303	45,675,693	745,610	-

Net Revenues from Transport Operations (7)

Fiscal year	Net Revenues from Freight Service			
	Total	Rail	Sea	Road
1912	50,144,419	49,377,673	766,746	-
1913	54,244,014	53,368,932	875,082	-
1914	52,671,925	51,750,496	921,429	-
× 1915	58,066,175	57,043,485	1,022,690	-
1916	71,521,568	69,861,837	1,659,731	-
1917	90,534,187	88,439,480	2,094,707	-
1918	112,008,147	109,744,431	2,263,716	-
× 1919	135,199,408	131,809,103	3,390,305	-
1920	137,325,438	133,183,317	4,142,121	-
1921	171,426,255	167,241,648	4,184,607	-
1922	183,459,184	179,220,166	4,239,018	-
× 1923	182,172,779	178,109,089	4,063,690	-
1924	198,839,776	194,563,653	4,276,123	-
1925	204,110,658	198,786,210	5,324,448	-
1926	207,102,184	201,609,955	5,492,229	-
× 1927	217,958,530	211,749,978	6,208,552	-
1928	226,941,697	220,686,364	6,255,333	-
1929	224,103,550	217,949,474	6,154,076	-
1930	189,688,700	184,146,899	5,538,779	3,022
× 1931	181,328,975	176,124,240	5,194,453	10,282
1932	179,447,386	174,706,443	4,723,870	17,073
1933	203,342,471	198,038,170	5,263,032	41,269
1934	224,979,172	218,681,101	6,231,869	66,202
× 1935	233,993,919	228,101,754	5,776,685	115,480
1936	259,992,462	253,664,698	6,114,216	213,548
1937	294,080,784	285,962,159	7,813,299	305,326
1938	338,963,677	328,724,929	9,814,146	424,602
× 1939	380,158,008	368,075,658	11,418,564	663,786
1940	397,733,636	385,407,188	11,457,121	869,327
1941	408,418,291	395,548,864	11,715,058	1,154,369
1942	487,912,887	474,053,463	11,594,498	2,264,926
× 1943	549,225,847	527,866,329	17,943,950	3,415,568
1944	528,499,732	495,803,492	24,372,253	8,323,987
1945	335,041,006	320,660,961	6,477,986	7,902,059
1946	1,039,531,764	991,130,678	23,037,539	25,363,547
× 1947	7,709,073,258	7,451,217,156	153,656,367	104,199,735
1948	29,681,083,864	28,360,296,117	793,016,494	527,771,253
1949	40,992,453,907	38,633,419,449	1,708,839,273	650,195,185
1950	65,794,145,695	62,523,166,499	2,461,203,504	809,775,692
× 1951	86,950,530,434	82,980,769,093	3,072,569,405	897,191,936
1952	102,563,659,426	97,561,625,412	4,160,009,023	842,024,991
1953	119,198,370,212	113,602,875,924	4,706,226,767	889,267,521
1954	114,409,052,023	109,359,887,796	4,227,848,924	821,320,303
× 1955	119,928,840,521	114,884,131,890	4,200,737,201	843,971,430

Net Revenues from Transport Operations (8)

Fiscal year	Net Revenues from Freight Service			
	Total	Rail	Sea	Road
1956	131,899,603,029	126,235,398,716	4,778,408,918	885,795,395
1957	151,929,910,021	147,217,997,720	3,852,830,060	859,082,241
1958	142,735,649,906	138,127,040,995	3,738,348,197	870,260,714
× 1959	157,456,451,364	152,377,579,574	4,148,477,923	930,393,867
1960	169,476,153,920	164,115,089,774	4,366,868,567	994,195,579
1961	207,402,509,958	201,627,647,649	4,521,733,044	1,253,129,265
1962	202,108,909,486	196,016,290,660	4,809,227,005	1,283,391,821
× 1963	211,509,043,158	205,276,652,045	4,930,697,575	1,301,693,538
1964	208,989,552,615	202,544,398,783	5,189,084,723	1,256,069,109
1965	198,228,485,326	191,941,246,312	5,291,228,460	996,010,554
1966	220,040,966,101	213,173,274,484	5,956,605,357	911,086,260
× 1967	236,057,701,296	228,311,546,247	6,820,371,562	925,783,487
1968	239,335,860,614	231,241,405,038	7,084,104,994	1,010,350,582
1969	244,888,209,840	236,297,104,191	7,569,766,392	1,021,339,257
1970	254,448,950,940	245,248,665,450	8,267,290,145	932,995,345
× 1971	250,068,460,466	240,124,439,563	9,051,262,900	892,758,003
1972	239,528,617,000	230,035,959,000	8,567,252,000	925,406,000
1973	238,097,662,000	229,689,236,000	7,464,801,000	943,625,000
1974	240,543,247,000	231,403,802,000	7,915,778,000	1,223,667,000
× 1975	241,546,722,000	231,860,794,000	8,286,825,000	1,399,103,000
1976	277,928,065	266,994,607	9,303,190	1,630,268
1977	306,990,195	295,567,995	9,613,401	1,808,798
1978	309,492,625	297,726,520	9,974,248	1,791,856
× 1979	353,954,186	340,892,777	11,741,828	1,319,581
1980	329,578,492	317,610,037	11,028,656	939,799
1981	311,365,363	299,733,632	10,909,645	722,087
1982	279,371,804	268,760,526	10,029,256	582,022
× 1983	241,531,383	232,738,501	8,681,651	111,231
1984	198,471,506	191,510,881	6,924,981	35,644
1985	185,709,393	179,250,409	6,458,984	
1986	167,598,654	161,249,658	6,348,997	

6-Balance Sheet

Fiscal year	Total	Fixed Assets	Investments	Working Stocks	Floating Assets	Others
1926	2,689,863	2,647,453	-	28,815	13,595	-
× 1927	2,908,564	2,858,794	-	27,430	22,340	-
1928	3,110,155	3,062,615	-	23,913	23,627	-
1929	3,286,643	3,246,725	-	23,162	16,756	-
1930	3,384,283	3,347,392	-	23,409	13,482	-
× 1931	3,462,978	3,413,786	-	15,704	33,488	-
1932	3,564,384	3,503,893	-	17,242	43,249	-
1933	3,683,833	3,613,169	-	22,889	47,775	-
1934	3,814,528	3,728,485	-	27,706	58,337	-
× 1935	3,940,277	3,850,508	-	30,147	59,622	-
1936	4,091,788	3,987,210	-	25,250	72,328	7,000
1937	4,262,842	4,127,215	2,000	29,690	66,937	37,000
1938	4,457,986	4,283,604	2,000	42,738	52,644	77,000
× 1939	4,749,418	4,502,169	2,000	40,337	87,912	117,000
1940	5,057,011	4,765,123	4,000	58,718	62,170	167,000
1941	5,346,978	4,986,421	16,000	82,284	35,273	227,000
1942	5,843,418	5,284,241	23,492	79,044	64,641	392,000
× 1943	6,764,517	5,930,862	26,492	94,938	204,225	508,000
1944	7,856,106	6,762,014	35,617	99,961	195,514	763,000
1945	8,707,353	6,970,691	44,742	322,638	605,282	764,000
1946	15,105,885	10,876,668	53,867	1,743,216	1,668,134	764,000
× 1947	34,079,948	19,208,234	62,992	8,381,529	5,663,193	764,000
1948	73,398,351	44,521,500	62,992	16,604,923	11,444,936	764,000
1949	87,752,198	59,236,404	62,992	12,176,842	13,562,790	2,713,170
1950	97,202,874	63,110,802	13,492	11,064,905	20,418,154	2,595,521
× 1951	125,505,382	85,180,125	80,492	20,983,154	19,205,025	56,586
1952	141,073,041	100,142,413	192,492	19,434,273	21,257,500	46,363
1953	165,902,671	124,296,516	192,492	17,862,122	23,524,495	27,046
1954	185,891,135	144,065,610	384,000	16,743,830	24,671,071	26,624
× 1955	1,306,641,095	1,265,991,274	484,000	15,735,759	24,401,328	28,734
1956	1,333,109,420	1,276,248,188	684,000	17,943,471	38,231,437	2,324
1957	1,380,924,103	1,328,863,974	984,000	22,258,122	28,815,683	2,324
1958	1,425,363,836	1,365,635,499	1,391,999	19,351,092	38,671,576	313,670
× 1959	1,499,867,221	1,413,276,756	1,891,999	19,171,904	65,526,562	-
1960	1,576,690,543	1,460,004,207	2,416,999	22,027,835	91,849,420	392,082
1961	1,714,406,619	1,573,650,950	2,916,999	26,078,234	111,340,215	420,221
1962	1,901,619,732	1,749,331,663	3,616,999	32,487,422	115,791,169	392,479
× 1963	2,102,093,513	1,938,426,262	22,669,023	31,796,611	108,804,230	397,387
1964	2,254,725,698	2,021,013,926	29,890,559	36,167,379	98,453,162	69,200,673
1965	2,446,758,494	2,194,172,126	38,152,666	35,270,327	109,630,591	69,532,784
1966	2,685,470,231	2,361,633,777	47,317,666	35,778,999	165,332,611	75,407,178
× 1967	2,907,560,432	2,539,294,237	55,860,166	34,234,594	198,078,438	80,092,997
1968	3,094,439,452	2,741,461,896	64,140,166	35,753,404	165,655,896	87,428,090
1969	3,326,648,324	2,944,444,934	75,204,666	36,822,543	181,072,698	89,103,483
1970	3,566,112,591	3,147,237,920	83,640,666	30,690,193	213,334,496	91,209,316
× 1971	3,912,186,529	3,366,374,742	91,098,666	34,825,869	299,937,595	119,949,657
1972	4,356,935,056	3,707,880,179	92,804,666	39,409,702	399,837,472	117,003,037
1973	4,886,160,302	4,284,347,346	94,708,466	49,337,720	351,233,892	106,532,878
1974	5,424,246,334	4,778,828,183	97,188,466	54,020,706	328,760,393	165,448,586
× 1975	5,937,752,402	5,271,520,608	99,192,633	51,887,671	330,052,472	185,099,018
1976	6,362,233,836	5,715,773,490	101,381,203	46,897,820	309,629,522	188,551,801
1977	7,099,244,539	6,309,616,596	103,166,203	51,661,032	452,635,345	182,165,363
1978	7,986,508,518	7,149,852,726	107,084,203	47,291,716	498,766,257	183,513,616
× 1979	9,012,174,554	8,005,738,992	111,218,203	53,358,661	653,392,158	188,466,540
1980	9,921,458,615	8,875,406,413	114,925,203	53,102,663	693,190,628	184,833,708
1981	10,822,025,493	9,744,448,930	119,610,203	54,440,143	696,011,309	207,514,908
1982	11,391,052,860	9,556,520,459	122,425,203	48,408,976	708,790,948	954,907,274
× 1983	11,800,680,782	9,832,873,555	125,739,203	51,693,800	801,491,737	988,882,487
1984	12,100,970,938	9,917,115,672	132,136,203	46,306,683	874,461,421	1,130,950,959
1985	11,902,759,220	9,829,488,400	133,136,203	50,856,862	689,777,691	1,199,500,064
1986	12,490,327,107	9,885,903,826	140,037,703	73,118,596	1,218,879,456	1,172,387,526

Unit:1,000 yen

		Capital and Liabilities					Fiscal year
Total	Capital	Capital Reserve	Accumulated Profit	Long Term Liabilities	Short Term Liabilities	Others	
2,689,863	1,220,627	-	-	1,468,043	1,193	-	1926
2,908,564	1,351,010	-	-	1,555,994	1,560	-	× 1927
3,110,155	1,481,690	-	-	1,627,399	1,066	-	1928
3,286,643	1,580,498	-	-	1,704,668	1,477	-	1929
3,384,283	1,639,594	-	-	1,743,226	1,463	-	1930
3,462,978	1,672,757	-	-	1,789,565	656	-	× 1931
3,564,384	1,724,882	-	-	1,838,540	962	-	1932
3,683,833	1,802,811	-	-	1,879,615	1,407	-	1933
3,814,528	1,891,897	-	-	1,921,314	1,317	-	1934
3,940,277	1,995,965	-	-	1,942,297	2,051	-	× 1935
4,091,788	2,118,446	-	-	1,971,179	2,163	-	1936
4,262,842	2,262,225	-	-	1,993,792	6,825	-	1937
4,457,986	2,454,246	-	-	2,000,056	3,684	-	1938
4,749,418	2,731,327	-	-	2,011,928	6,163	-	× 1939
5,057,011	3,022,717	-	-	2,027,065	7,229	-	1940
5,346,978	3,210,979	-	-	2,126,417	9,582	-	1941
5,843,418	3,646,848	-	-	2,182,781	13,789	-	1942
6,764,517	4,186,497	-	-	2,557,819	20,201	-	× 1943
7,856,106	4,507,309	-	-	3,280,571	68,226	-	1944
8,707,353	3,308,837	-	-	4,162,093	1,236,423	-	1945
15,105,885	4,916,823	-	-	9,347,695	841,367	-	1946
34,079,948	4,916,823	- △	18,592,574	32,955,536	4,806,575	9,993,588	× 1947
73,398,351	4,916,823	- △	40,306,470	53,580,066	13,927,608	41,280,324	1948
87,752,198	4,916,823	-	118,662	71,632,429	9,631,527	1,452,757	1949
97,202,874	8,916,823	-	4,977,687	71,632,429	10,948,047	727,888	1950
125,505,382	8,916,823	508,503	2,115,349	88,632,429	23,301,219	2,031,059	× 1951
141,073,041	8,916,823	1,122,700	595,025	104,497,370	22,884,315	3,056,808	1952
165,902,671	8,916,823	2,049,389	1,175,154	127,047,345	22,655,598	4,058,362	1953
185,891,135	8,916,823	3,268,990 △	1,912,124	146,598,775	23,531,098	5,487,573	1954
1,306,641,095	8,916,823	1,124,305,712 △	19,890,207	169,592,708	18,872,642	4,843,417	× 1955
1,333,109,420	8,916,823	1,130,624,494 △	35,710,878	197,932,652	27,250,996	4,095,333	1956
1,380,924,103	8,916,823	1,133,675,328 △	13,078,516	216,252,657	31,286,911	3,870,200	1957
1,425,363,836	8,916,823	1,137,030,327 △	2,903,905	254,007,865	24,197,062	4,115,664	1958
1,499,867,221	8,916,823	1,140,794,811	561,489	305,279,295	39,500,281	4,814,522	× 1959
1,576,690,543	8,916,823	1,145,229,697	6,029,736	361,987,813	49,293,437	5,233,037	1960
1,714,406,619	8,916,823	1,150,925,744	52,456,708	423,041,056	72,538,620	6,527,667	1961
1,901,619,732	8,916,823	1,154,028,645	102,158,579	540,744,810	88,026,931	7,743,944	1962
2,102,093,513	8,916,823	1,160,338,644	159,536,691	689,021,062	78,545,743	5,734,550	× 1963
2,254,725,698	8,916,823	1,167,222,579	129,517,635	831,308,525	108,969,087	8,791,049	1964
2,446,758,494	8,916,823	1,174,566,116	6,525,199	1,110,175,910	137,047,931	9,526,515	1965
2,685,470,231	8,916,823	1,180,621,945 △	53,597,405	1,368,899,070	166,284,391	14,345,407	1966
2,907,560,432	8,916,823	1,187,790,067 △	147,717,754	1,643,459,972	203,267,027	11,844,297	× 1967
3,094,439,452	8,916,823	1,199,811,715 △	282,101,318	1,930,624,141	223,437,751	13,750,340	1968
3,326,648,324	8,916,823	1,210,547,299 △	413,691,304	2,249,133,762	256,146,022	15,595,722	1969
3,566,112,591	8,916,823	1,223,927,784 △	565,396,845	2,603,705,656	274,758,786	20,200,387	1970
3,912,186,529	12,416,823	1,267,444,866 △	799,622,048	3,087,088,136	322,703,745	22,155,007	× 1971
4,356,935,056	78,016,823	1,287,728,778 △	1,141,126,396	3,719,139,918	386,684,207	26,491,726	1972
4,886,160,302	273,016,823	1,316,566,334 △	1,595,521,283	4,367,919,979	448,288,276	75,890,173	1973
5,424,246,334	386,016,823	1,347,706,409 △	2,246,319,206	5,538,131,837	316,299,062	82,411,409	1974
5,937,752,402	456,016,823	1,383,682,716 △	3,161,022,359	6,779,299,949	383,502,622	96,272,649	× 1975
6,362,233,836	456,016,823	859,562,915 △	974,225,089	5,458,196,506	455,642,152	107,040,529	1976
7,099,244,539	456,016,823	905,703,361 △	1,808,162,603	6,886,600,596	517,103,209	141,983,153	1977
7,986,508,518	456,016,823	905,703,361 △	2,694,896,767	8,461,873,207	602,040,591	255,771,303	1978
9,012,174,554	456,016,823	905,703,361 △	3,516,710,331	10,149,234,867	605,430,459	412,499,375	× 1979
9,921,458,615	456,016,823	381,451,806 △	1,178,819,556	9,077,021,476	611,121,335	574,666,731	1980
10,822,025,493	456,016,823	381,451,806 △	2,264,710,605	10,829,373,173	693,269,234	726,625,062	1981
11,391,052,860	456,016,823	381,451,806 △	3,642,499,842	12,723,504,893	652,334,920	820,244,261	1982
11,800,680,782	456,016,823	381,451,806 △	5,302,899,026	14,661,130,503	721,367,058	883,613,619	× 1983
12,100,970,938	456,016,823	381,451,806 △	6,953,294,908	16,504,753,072	762,493,853	949,550,292	1984
11,902,759,220	456,016,823	381,451,806 △	8,801,074,419	18,240,885,760	609,073,340	1,016,405,911	1985
12,490,327,107	456,016,823	381,451,806 △	10,162,110,432	19,745,083,420	953,660,072	1,116,225,418	1986

△   indicates a deficit.

Statistics

7-Profit and Loss Statement

Fiscal Year	Total	Costs					Non-operating Costs	Profit/Loss
			Oprrating Costs					
		Subtotal	Cost of Railway Activities	Interest etc.	Depreciation Cost	Retirement Cost		
1926	353,176	341,978	270,839	71,139	-	-	11,198	130,907
× 1927	368,277	356,617	281,988	74,629	-	-	11,660	138,168
1928	393,381	381,251	300,708	80,543	-	-	12,130	135,876
1929	399,027	387,137	304,143	82,994	-	-	11,890	118,990
1930	382,553	371,066	284,824	86,242	-	-	11,487	75,587
× 1931	365,088	354,520	266,634	87,886	-	-	10,568	68,453
1932	364,875	353,965	265,082	88,883	-	-	10,910	61,079
1933	385,579	375,975	282,200	93,775	-	-	9,604	88,675
1934	417,771	405,914	314,126	91,788	-	-	11,857	100,897
× 1935	435,000	423,288	329,537	93,751	-	-	11,712	109,986
1936	452,709	437,626	354,420	83,206	-	-	15,083	145,462
1937	504,015	490,485	406,692	83,793	-	-	13,530	166,149
1938	568,504	554,140	470,007	84,133	-	-	14,364	200,443
× 1939	658,091	636,696	552,844	83,852	-	-	21,395	266,326
1940	766,339	749,317	666,309	83,008	-	-	17,022	277,771
1941	883,279	864,135	780,467	83,668	-	-	19,144	243,879
1942	1,012,159	994,768	908,497	86,271	-	-	17,391	429,907
× 1943	1,198,736	1,180,003	1,091,084	88,919	-	-	18,733	513,264
1944	1,524,772	1,499,142	1,397,006	102,136	-	-	25,630	340,331
1945	2,969,259	2,932,251	2,809,715	122,536	-	-	37,008 △	741,451
1946	9,924,744	9,871,300	9,624,792	246,508	-	-	53,444 △	4,080,750
× 1947	40,759,408	40,674,284	39,696,109	898,234	-	79,941	85,124 △	13,407,886
1948	107,618,998	103,299,083	97,603,314	2,161,231	613,000	2,921,538	4,319,915 △	21,713,895
1949	117,464,445	115,219,340	110,584,031	2,666,558	1,318,886	649,865	2,245,105 △	2,257,540
1950	141,515,323	140,107,733	115,812,588	3,180,673	20,556,406	558,066	1,407,590	4,977,687
× 1951	186,639,176	186,494,857	162,904,409	3,472,534	19,268,380	849,534	144,319 △	267,829
1952	220,320,325	220,313,816	185,357,148	4,504,219	30,388,227	64,222	6,509 △	1,653,651
1953	251,807,933	251,750,855	212,324,596	6,813,044	32,561,633	51,582	57,078	436,301
1954	256,304,603	256,294,852	214,289,710	8,442,152	33,489,024	73,966	9,751 △	3,488,957
× 1955	281,413,147	281,402,622	222,068,538	9,678,609	46,996,716	2,658,759	10,525 △	18,349,746
1956	304,123,388	304,048,906	238,922,413	11,643,120	48,387,992	5,095,381	74,482 △	15,303,632
1957	318,646,465	318,199,713	249,946,180	13,569,757	48,682,284	6,001,492	446,752	22,632,362
1958	334,658,078	333,059,232	260,384,336	15,554,615	51,057,268	6,063,013	1,598,846	10,174,611
× 1959	370,524,105	365,003,342	287,495,206	17,777,789	52,231,465	7,498,882	5,520,763	3,465,394
1960	403,909,764	399,299,119	311,912,339	24,014,945	53,755,164	9,616,671	4,610,645	5,468,247
1961	463,132,087	458,804,305	347,513,523	22,925,175	78,577,079	9,788,528	4,327,782	46,426,972
1962	483,519,321	477,538,476	377,433,740	25,197,205	64,548,020	10,359,511	5,980,845	49,701,871
× 1963	515,698,387	514,369,308	408,246,816	25,168,061	67,610,069	13,274,220	1,329,079	57,378,112
1964	633,971,519	632,560,555	484,267,163	38,582,282	98,835,441	10,875,669	1,410,964 △	30,019,056
1965	762,505,879	757,088,449	539,615,536	64,568,894	136,171,319	16,732,700	5,417,430 △	122,992,436
1966	856,141,431	854,729,197	604,945,837	83,470,230	145,373,492	20,939,638	1,412,234 △	60,122,604
× 1967	951,992,598	950,759,732	674,330,066	101,215,580	152,962,638	22,251,448	1,232,866 △	94,120,349
1968	1,054,233,587	1,052,573,631	758,578,321	119,498,951	161,186,083	13,310,276	1,659,956 △	134,383,564
1969	1,179,594,156	1,176,314,656	842,598,684	138,260,602	170,207,309	25,248,061	3,279,500 △	131,589,986
1970	1,303,220,890	1,300,592,665	946,378,556	152,215,179	175,349,030	26,649,900	2,628,225 △	151,705,540
× 1971	1,424,320,161	1,420,727,208	1,056,560,320	163,185,472	165,772,657	35,208,759	3,592,953 △	234,225,203
1972	1,599,406,238	1,594,402,945	1,175,752,187	198,275,554	180,355,180	40,020,024	5,003,293 △	341,504,348
1973	1,847,607,132	1,840,708,150	1,383,769,799	227,760,671	189,539,822	39,367,858	6,898,982 △	454,394,887
1974	2,237,926,313	2,232,879,542	1,722,612,187	269,784,579	202,729,572	37,753,204	5,046,771 △	650,797,922
× 1975	2,747,911,591	2,744,430,680	2,058,971,722	405,496,357	234,804,197	45,158,404	3,480,911 △	914,703,151
1976	2,919,267,960	2,915,617,438	2,294,259,330	316,034,403	256,386,224	48,937,481	3,650,522 △	914,050,500
1977	3,218,539,477	3,214,687,890	2,492,895,488	401,948,501	270,096,900	49,747,001	3,851,587 △	833,937,514
1978	3,475,539,074	3,471,380,176	2,651,167,921	477,708,280	288,711,399	53,792,576	4,158,898 △	886,734,164
× 1979	3,747,784,290	3,744,589,028	2,818,309,746	552,484,586	317,942,514	55,852,182	3,195,262 △	821,813,564
1980	4,007,992,562	3,964,263,021	3,090,053,083	476,422,366	341,496,400	56,291,171	43,729,541 △	1,005,375,780
1981	4,331,996,880	4,325,426,840	3,303,667,091	602,977,833	358,852,318	60,129,598	6,570,040 △	1,085,891,048
1982	4,783,893,119	4,774,928,350	3,446,614,598	798,868,539	430,785,655	98,659,558	8,964,769 △	1,377,789,238
× 1983	5,150,620,715	5,140,079,185	3,574,006,271	978,545,154	463,087,505	124,440,254	10,541,530 △	1,650,395,882
1984	5,219,010,588	5,209,127,570	3,531,798,933	1,092,586,315	464,537,604	120,204,718	9,883,018 △	1,650,395,882
1985	5,582,431,164	5,572,839,523	3,763,724,448	1,219,890,063	462,440,115	126,784,898	9,591,641 △	1,847,779,511
1986	5,326,576,990	5,305,237,304	3,311,845,007	1,325,319,801	461,001,899	207,070,598	21,339,686 △	1,361,036,013

△ indicates a deficit

Unit:1,000yen

Total	Receipts				Non-operating Receipts	Fiscal Year
	Receipts from operation					
	Subtotal	Passenger	Freight	Miscellaneous		
484,083	484,083	271,249	205,079	7,755	-	1926
506,445	506,445	278,953	220,286	7,206	-	× 1927
529,257	529,132	292,624	228,016	8,492	125	1928
518,017	517,795	286,047	223,265	8,483	222	1929
458,140	458,140	261,131	189,161	7,848	-	1930
433,541	433,541	245,350	180,366	7,825	-	× 1931
425,954	425,954	239,018	178,717	8,219	-	1932
474,254	473,571	261,118	203,231	9,222	683	1933
518,668	518,668	282,789	225,315	10,564	-	1934
544,986	544,534	300,310	233,509	10,715	452	× 1935
598,171	598,171	326,398	259,987	11,786	-	1936
670,164	670,164	362,316	294,438	13,410	-	1937
768,947	768,947	415,903	339,388	13,656	-	1938
924,417	924,417	529,744	377,291	17,382	-	× 1939
1,044,110	1,039,495	623,425	396,208	19,862	4,615	1940
1,127,158	1,122,778	698,478	402,000	22,300	4,380	1941
1,442,066	1,441,920	899,480	517,255	25,185	146	1942
1,712,000	1,711,671	1,100,025	584,903	26,743	329	× 1943
1,865,103	1,865,101	1,297,502	544,220	23,379	2	1944
2,227,808	2,227,808	1,784,091	426,207	17,510	-	1945
5,843,994	5,843,994	4,901,654	901,046	41,294	-	1946
27,351,522	27,351,522	18,736,887	7,440,632	1,174,003	-	× 1947
85,905,103	72,171,350	41,968,697	29,361,890	840,763	13,733,753	1948
115,206,905	111,658,536	68,504,252	41,095,724	2,058,560	3,548,369	1949
146,493,010	143,184,336	73,855,376	66,364,101	2,964,859	3,308,674	1950
186,371,347	183,928,559	91,553,620	86,759,817	5,615,122	2,442,788	× 1951
218,666,674	218,224,721	109,818,604	102,596,697	5,809,420	441,953	1952
252,244,234	252,064,772	126,441,157	119,230,363	6,393,252	179,462	1953
252,815,646	252,709,645	132,085,384	114,660,214	5,964,047	106,001	1954
263,063,401	262,965,120	135,521,410	120,113,625	7,330,085	98,281	× 1955
288,819,756	287,870,448	148,157,775	131,959,927	7,752,746	949,308	1956
341,278,827	333,874,696	173,305,235	152,115,918	8,453,543	7,404,131	1957
344,832,689	335,845,830	183,389,637	142,735,650	9,720,543	8,986,859	1958
373,989,499	367,794,496	198,983,180	157,456,451	11,354,865	6,195,003	× 1959
409,378,011	407,468,586	224,209,789	169,476,154	13,782,643	1,909,425	1960
509,559,059	505,390,413	280,796,918	207,402,510	17,190,985	4,168,646	1961
533,221,192	529,120,331	308,599,785	202,108,910	18,411,636	4,100,861	1962
573,076,499	568,701,060	338,430,357	211,509,044	18,761,659	4,375,439	× 1963
603,952,463	600,239,354	369,707,383	208,989,553	21,542,418	3,713,109	1964
639,513,443	634,104,604	412,145,866	198,228,486	23,730,252	5,408,839	1965
796,018,827	793,938,848	548,386,130	220,040,966	25,511,752	2,079,979	1966
857,872,249	856,091,459	591,587,182	236,057,701	28,446,576	1,780,790	× 1967
919,850,023	916,489,551	643,442,235	239,335,860	33,711,456	3,360,472	1968
1,048,004,170	1,044,041,471	760,167,149	244,888,210	38,986,112	3,962,699	1969
1,151,515,350	1,145,696,428	846,298,135	254,448,951	44,949,342	5,818,922	1970
1,190,094,958	1,178,173,557	859,561,495	250,068,460	68,543,602	11,921,401	× 1971
1,257,901,890	1,244,256,920	921,631,802	239,528,617	83,096,501	13,644,970	1972
1,393,212,245	1,379,056,789	992,228,262	238,097,662	148,730,865	14,155,456	1973
1,587,128,391	1,571,414,527	1,125,151,454	240,543,246	205,719,827	15,713,864	1974
1,833,208,440	1,820,932,353	1,315,125,364	241,546,723	264,260,266	12,276,087	× 1975
2,005,217,460	1,993,110,156	1,529,024,232	277,928,064	186,157,860	12,107,304	1976
2,384,601,963	2,368,996,459	1,823,709,104	306,990,195	238,297,160	15,605,504	1977
2,588,804,910	2,570,160,590	1,949,925,190	309,492,625	310,742,775	18,644,320	1978
2,925,970,726	2,902,103,113	2,154,996,334	353,954,186	393,152,593	23,867,613	× 1979
2,999,616,782	2,963,678,619	2,242,441,213	329,578,492	391,658,914	35,938,163	1980
3,246,105,831	3,173,016,097	2,403,463,097	311,365,364	458,187,637	73,089,734	1981
3,406,103,881	3,313,019,348	2,541,503,909	279,371,804	492,143,634	93,084,534	1982
3,490,221,531	3,298,907,283	2,579,683,639	241,531,382	477,692,261	191,314,248	× 1983
3,568,614,706	3,389,788,515	2,750,413,645	198,471,505	440,903,365	178,826,191	1984
3,734,651,653	3,552,752,912	2,942,238,878	185,709,393	424,804,642	181,898,740	1985
3,965,540,977	3,605,077,142	3,026,894,305	167,598,654	410,584,183	360,463,835	1986

8-Capital Expenditure

Unit:yen

Fiscal year	Investments	Fiscal year	Investments	Fiscal year	Investments
×1875	951,783	×1915	31,930,721	×1955	52,489,672,201
1876	123,568	1916	34,574,044	1956	58,698,766,865
1877	29,631	1917	57,491,203	1957	98,724,408,363
1878	74,048	1918	85,721,501	1958	87,287,499,247
×1879	443,992	×1919	143,075,773	×1959	107,587,842,703
1880	726,728	1920	170,569,599	1960	116,405,704,177
1881	497,974	1921	205,925,131	1961	207,092,572,895
1882	743,813	1922	216,471,816	1962	251,819,250,599
×1883	897,203	×1923	192,105,465	×1963	291,403,543,450
1884	701,367	1924	196,151,127	1964	259,260,227,916
1885	1,039,832	1925	193,249,383	1965	331,176,436,998
1886	2,394,508	1926	207,328,571	1966	339,279,132,847
×1887	5,167,670	×1927	218,479,669	×1967	362,270,206,513
1888	6,184,720	1928	212,581,238	1968	396,277,380,523
1889	2,986,006	1929	199,119,622	1969	399,794,624,273
1890	1,148,950	1930	116,640,909	1970	401,452,468,215
×1891	1,499,798	×1931	94,988,510	×1971	446,078,232,164
1892	1,208,971	1932	102,384,414	1972	559,326,622,933
1893	705,599	1933	121,564,076	1973	787,759,688,622
1894	4,288,241	1934	130,898,034	1974	790,138,993,630
×1895	3,390,247	×1935	88,843,962	×1975	787,946,435,744
1896	5,722,110	1936	151,804,101	1976	751,580,974,214
1897	14,382,269	1937	169,358,454	1977	906,329,589,197
1898	12,159,839	1938	181,672,782	1978	1,181,904,618,191
×1899	12,319,057	×1939	227,173,138	×1979	1,231,364,627,064
1900	19,451,026	1940	267,101,076	1980	1,259,063,194,674
1901	15,987,665	1941	296,673,387	1981	1,284,663,440,762
1902	18,849,773	1942	302,345,617	1982	1,077,468,869,998
×1903	16,990,373	×1943	583,696,387	×1983	889,249,088,522
1904	8,568,186	1944	831,101,820	1984	811,318,674,631
1905	5,304,974	1945	686,481,378	1985	569,497,331,722
1906	11,955,321	1946	3,765,101,438	1986	699,355,780,096
×1907	178,030,800	×1947	8,581,589,217		
1908	360,818,731	1948	20,951,479,313		
1909	36,281,325	1949	16,163,071,286		
1910	38,150,897	1950	24,363,973,074		
×1911	51,043,399	×1951	38,734,278,649		
1912	61,311,645	1952	44,544,817,977		
1913	43,895,040	1953	55,255,556,169		
1914	41,893,950	1954	52,339,916,872		

Investments made by Japan Railway Construction Public Corporation

Unit:100million yen

Fiscal year	Investments	Fiscal year	Investments	Fiscal year	Investments
×1963	6	×1971	1,008	×1979	3,312
1964	77	1972	1,237	1980	3,696
1965	177	1973	1,567	1981	2,839
1966	298	1974	2,012	1982	1,371
×1967	439	×1975	2,364	×1983	1,288
1968	498	1976	2,247	1984	1,037
1969	648	1977	3,014	1985	1,385
1970	771	1978	3,220	1986	983

Note: Investments concerning Japan Railway Construction Corporation are the construction
costs of Japanese National Railways (excluding administration costs, interest, etc.).

9-Sectional Profit and Loss Satement
Main Lines

Fiscal Year	Km Under Operation	Traffic Volume		Operating Income				
		Passenger km	Tonne km	Total	Passenger	Freight	Miscellaneous	Subsidies
	km	100million Passenger km	100million Tonne km	100million yen	100million yen	100million yen	100million yen	100million yen
1972	10,673.8	1,817	565	11,463	8,431	2,235	797	-
1973	10,722.3	1,918	555	12,787	9,105	2,234	1,448	-
1974	13,426.5	2,045	511	14,909	10,564	2,315	2,030	-
×1975	13,481.7	2,049	462	17,340	12,400	2,327	2,613	-
1976	13,472.1	2,006	452	18,781	14,445	2,677	683	976
1977	13,471.0	1,901	403	22,279	17,261	2,956	762	1,300
1978	13,477.5	1,868	401	24,155	18,472	2,978	853	1,852
×1979	12,552.8	1,847	413	26,725	20,301	3,330	924	2,170
1980	12,547.6	1,835	361	26,892	21,132	3,098	980	1,682
1981	12,644.7	1,830	327	28,857	22,698	2,931	1,103	2,125
1982	13,354.6	1,821	297	30,245	24,047	2,631	1,230	2,337
×1983	13,329.4	1,845	268	30,274	24,458	2,296	1,336	2,184
1984	13,350.7	1,862	225	31,455	26,105	1,898	1,479	1,973
1985	13,409.7	1,898	216	33,231	27,998	1,781	1,762	1,690
1986	13,396.2	1,909	202	33,851	28,877	1,619	2,145	1,210

Provincial Lines

Fiscal Year	Km Under Operation	Traffic Volume		Operating Income				
		Passenger km	Tonne km	Total	Passenger	Freight	Miscellaneous	Subsidies
	km	100million Passenger km	100million Tonne km	100million yen	100million yen	100million yen	100million yen	100million yen
1972	11,224.3	168	30	770	588	151	31	-
1973	11,314.7	170	28	775	601	138	36	-
1974	9,137.7	117	13	534	432	78	24	-
×1975	9,193.4	110	11	564	463	75	26	-
1976	9,204.2	107	10	817	532	85	28	172
1977	9,235.7	100	9	1,048	646	96	30	276
1978	9,229.6	95	9	1,166	683	99	31	353
×1979	10,169.5	104	17	1,908	895	196	39	778
1980	10,174.3	100	15	2,337	916	189	40	1,192
1981	10,174.3	95	13	2,451	949	175	45	1,282
1982	10,170.7	90	11	2,451	969	157	48	1,277
×1983	10,128.6	88	8	2,275	932	118	51	1,174
1984	9,905.8	83	6	1,995	984	87	52	872
1985	9,544.5	80	5	1,840	1,002	76	56	706
1986	8,408.7	77	4	1,767	989	57	69	652

Total	Operating Costs		Operating Loss		Non-operating Profit / Loss		Current Net Loss		Fiscal Year
	Cost of Railway Act	Interest etc							
100million yen	100million yen	100million yen	100million yen		100million yen		100million yen		
13,013	9,320	3,693	△	1,550		73	△	1,477	1972
15,132	11,040	4,092	△	2,345		56	△	2,289	1973
19,516	14,741	4,775	△	4,607		93	△	4,514	1974
24,089	17,613	6,476	△	6,749		77	△	6,672	×1975
25,452	19,638	5,814	△	6,671		79	△	6,592	1976
28,098	21,337	6,761	△	5,819		108	△	5,711	1977
30,342	22,655	7,687	△	6,187		120	△	6,067	1978
31,909	23,365	8,544	△	5,184		170	△	5,014	×1979
33,619	25,667	7,952	△	6,727	△ 116		△	6,843	1980
36,471	27,351	9,120	△	7,614		609	△	7,005	1981
40,275	28,644	11,631	△	10,030		762	△	9,268	1982
43,352	29,869	13,483	△	13,078		1,678	△	11,400	×1983
43,760	29,632	14,128	△	12,305		1,524	△	10,781	1984
46,666	31,650	15,016	△	13,435		1,589	△	11,846	1985
44,387	27,862	16,525	△	10,536		3,184	△	7,352	1986

Total	Operating Costs		Operating Loss		Non-operating Profit / Loss		Current Net Loss		Fiscal Year
	Cost of Railway Act	Interest etc							
100million yen	100million yen	100million yen	100million yen		100million yen		100million yen		
2,610	2,147	463	△	1,840		12	△	1,828	1972
2,911	2,463	448	△	2,136		15	△	2,121	1973
2,371	2,075	296	△	1,837		14	△	1,823	1974
2,829	2,491	338	△	2,265		10	△	2,255	×1975
3,128	2,774	354	△	2,311		5	△	2,306	1976
3,421	3,018	403	△	2,373		9	△	2,364	1977
3,714	3,255	459	△	2,548		21	△	2,527	1978
4,839	4,181	658	△	2,931		35	△	2,896	×1979
5,276	4,553	723	△	2,939		37	△	2,902	1980
5,977	4,974	1,003	△	3,526		53	△	3,473	1981
6,600	5,087	1,513	△	4,149		76	△	4,073	1982
7,136	5,144	1,992	△	4,861		121	△	4,740	×1983
7,388	4,962	2,426	△	5,393		129	△	5,264	1984
8,019	5,200	2,819	△	6,179		131	△	6,048	1985
7,647	4,526	3,121	△	5,880		200	△	5,680	1986

△ indicates a deficit

10-Number of Staff

Fiscal Year	Number	Fiscal Year	Number
1894	9,893	1940	339,610
× 1895	10,964	1941	384,559
1896	14,000	1942	401,772
1897	17,079	× 1943	470,556
1898	17,774	1944	524,664
× 1899	18,612	1945	518,134
1900	20,882	1946	573,086
1901	22,414	× 1947	610,543
1902	23,702	1948	604,243
× 1903	23,662	1949	490,727
1904	23,461	1950	473,473
1905	28,878	× 1951	442,153
1906	59,647	1952	447,385
1907	88,266	1953	446,837
1908	89,868	1954	442,782
1909	90,131	× 1955	442,512
1910	95,627	1956	442,573
× 1911	103,418	1957	443,879
1912	109,983	1958	444,757
1913	112,087	× 1959	448,996
1914	114,964	1960	448,390
× 1915	112,102	1961	451,356
1916	115,282	1962	452,688
1917	125,888	× 1963	455,797
1918	139,043	1964	461,931
× 1919	158,595	1965	462,436
1920	163,826	1966	469,693
1921	168,371	× 1967	467,791
1922	180,860	1968	466,351
× 1923	188,783	1969	466,873
1924	195,555	1970	459,677
1925	195,876	× 1971	450,338
1926	200,500	1972	441,054
× 1927	206,431	1973	432,894
1928	210,883	1974	430,269
1929	210,472	× 1975	430,051
1930	204,564	1976	429,216
× 1931	198,678	1977	428,928
1932	198,848	1978	426,697
1933	201,538	× 1979	420,815
1934	209,456	1980	413,594
× 1935	218,352	1981	401,362
1936	227,689	1982	386,677
1937	253,247	× 1983	358,045
1938	272,175	1984	326,025
× 1939	309,916	1985	276,774
		1986	223,947

11-Locomotives

Unit:Car

Fiscal year	Total	Steam	Diesel	Electric
1872	10	10	-	-
1873	10	10	-	-
1874	22	22	-	-
×1875	32	32	-	-
1876	34	34	-	-
1877	38	38	-	-
1878	38	38	-	-
×1879	38	38	-	-
1880	36	36	-	-
1881	45	45	-	-
1882	47	47	-	-
×1883	48	48	-	-
1884	46	46	-	-
1885	50	50	-	-
1886	57	57	-	-
×1887	64	64	-	-
1888	78	78	-	-
1889	97	97	-	-
1890	117	117	-	-
×1891	123	123	-	-
1892	133	133	-	-
1893	142	142	-	-
1894	167	167	-	-
×1895	171	171	-	-
1896	183	183	-	-
1897	258	258	-	-
1898	310	310	-	-
×1899	334	334	-	-
1900	373	373	-	-
1901	391	391	-	-
1902	431	431	-	-
×1903	484	484	-	-
1904	467	467	-	-
1905	599	599	-	-
1906	1,357	1,357	-	-
×1907	1,924	1,924	-	-
1908	2,031	2,031	-	-
1909	2,173	2,174	-	-
1910	2,231	2,231	-	-
×1911	2,305	2,295	-	10
1912	2,381	2,369	-	12
1913	2,500	2,488	-	12
1914	2,611	2,599	-	12
×1915	2,680	2,668	-	12
1916	2,727	2,715	-	12
1917	2,827	2,815	-	12
1918	2,933	2,921	-	12
×1919	3,118	3,099	-	19
1920	3,306	3,284	-	22
1921	3,518	3,494	-	24
1922	3,671	3,642	-	29
×1923	3,847	3,797	-	50
1924	3,981	3,916	-	65
1925	3,907	3,830	-	77
1926	3,965	3,876	2	87
×1927	4,114	4,022	2	90
1928	4,200	4,101	2	97
1929	4,222	4,122	3	97
1930	4,189	4,088	4	97
×1931	4,016	3,892	5	119

Fiscal year	Total	Steam	Diesel	Electric
1932	4,094	3,953	10	131
1933	4,064	3,913	10	141
1934	3,986	3,811	10	165
×1935	4,124	3,938	13	173
1936	4,235	4,053	13	169
1937	4,245	4,054	13	178
1938	4,443	4,247	13	183
×1939	4,735	4,536	13	186
1940	5,095	4,882	13	200
1941	5,200	4,961	13	226
1942	5,365	5,115	11	239
×1943	5,794	5,522	11	261
1944	6,236	5,935	9	292
1945	6,204	5,899	9	296
1946	6,287	5,958	9	320
×1947	6,283	5,933	-	350
1948	5,973	5,612	-	361
1949	5,692	5,334	-	358
1950	5,458	5,102	-	356
×1951	5,444	5,072	-	372
1952	5,468	5,066	3	399
1953	5,486	5,035	3	448
1954	5,474	4,982	6	486
×1955	5,425	4,897	6	522
1956	5,387	4,784	20	583
1957	5,406	4,713	31	662
1958	5,334	4,514	73	747
×1959	5,256	4,321	157	778
1960	4,974	3,974	218	782
1961	4,926	3,808	280	838
1962	4,867	3,601	335	931
×1963	4,841	3,471	359	1,011
1964	4,786	3,335	383	1,068
1965	4,944	3,164	469	1,311
1966	4,924	2,915	607	1,402
×1967	4,932	2,644	787	1,501
1968	4,815	2,266	931	1,618
1969	4,881	1,893	1,247	1,741
1970	4,866	1,601	1,447	1,818
×1971	4,679	1,194	1,624	1,861
1972	4,679	809	1,952	1,918
1973	4,415	459	1,952	2,004
1974	4,373	179	2,134	2,060
×1975	4,270	15	2,204	2,051
1976	4,272	15	2,190	2,067
1977	4,271	15	2,207	2,049
1978	4,143	5	2,160	1,978
×1979	4,066	5	2,125	1,936
1980	3,970	5	2,109	1,856
1981	3,840	5	2,075	1,760
1982	3,759	5	2,051	1,703
×1983	3,607	5	1,989	1,613
1984	3,480	5	1,931	1,544
1985	2,833	5	1,540	1,288
1986	1,800	6	820	974

11-Coaches,Railcars and Electric Railcars

Unit:Car

Fiscal year	Total	Coach Railcar	Electric Railcar	Fiscal year	Total	Coach · Railcar	Electric Railcar
1872	58	58	-	1932	10,418	9,149	1,269
1873	58	58	-	1933	10,629	9,254	1,375
1874	144	144	-	1934	10,813	9,410	1,403
×1875	146	146	-	×1935	10,958	9,508	1,450
1876	156	156	-	1936	11,193	9,640	1,553
1877	160	160	-	1937	11,533	9,936	1,597
1878	166	166	-	1938	11,914	10,288	1,626
×1879	173	173	-	×1939	12,286	10,645	1,641
1880	178	178	-	1940	12,738	11,037	1,701
1881	203	203	-	1941	13,149	11,344	1,805
1882	240	240	-	1942	13,268	11,440	1,828
×1883	299	299	-	×1943	13,563	11,600	1,963
1884	303	303	-	1944	13,818	11,637	2,145
1885	313	313	-	1945	12,978	11,028	1,950
1886	284	284	-	1946	13,200	11,160	2,040
×1887	307	307	-	×1947	14,070	11,706	2,364
1888	398	398	-	1948	13,930	11,606	2,324
1889	524	524	-	1949	14,009	11,527	2,482
1890	534	534	-	1950	14,051	11,394	2,657
×1891	614	614	-	×1951	14,108	11,437	2,671
1892	637	637	-	1952	14,335	11,625	2,710
1893	654	654	-	1953	14,358	11,596	2,762
1894	685	685	-	1954	14,683	11,831	2,852
×1895	712	712	-	×1955	15,094	12,003	2,969
1896	803	803	-	1956	15,664	12,056	3,256
1897	878	878	-	1957	16,430	12,495	3,661
1898	974	974	-	1958	17,055	12,753	3,976
×1899	1,005	1,005	-	×1959	17,441	13,181	4,170
1900	1,075	1,075	-	1960	18,173	13,421	4,534
1901	1,092	1,092	-	1961	19,356	13,902	5,322
1902	1,296	1,296	-	1962	20,450	15,206	6,001
×1903	1,434	1,434	-	×1963	20,987	14,227	6,574
1904	1,498	1,498	-	1964	22,079	14,234	7,511
1905	1,612	1,612	-	1965	24,041	14,636	9,084
1906	3,405	3,377	28	1966	24,794	14,494	9,979
×1907	4,989	4,963	26	×1967	25,189	14,350	10,678
1908	5,268	5,240	28	1968	25,711	14,214	11,444
1909	5,433	5,391	42	1969	26,548	14,224	12,174
1910	5,664	5,620	44	1970	26,886	14,082	12,679
×1911	5,893	5,827	66	×1971	26,562	13,660	12,902
1912	6,148	6,076	72	1972	27,101	13,183	13,918
1913	6,453	6,367	86	1973	28,142	13,152	14,990
1914	6,699	6,575	124	1974	28,437	12,381	16,056
×1915	6,836	6,706	130	×1975	28,553	12,051	16,502
1916	6,875	6,750	125	1976	28,757	12,014	16,743
1917	6,911	6,759	152	1977	28,904	12,061	16,843
1918	7,126	6,936	190	1978	29,047	11,800	17,247
×1919	7,528	7,288	240	×1979	29,249	11,787	17,462
1920	8,072	7,782	290	1980	28,910	11,214	17,696
1921	8,575	8,208	367	1981	29,162	11,018	18,144
1922	9,298	8,883	415	1982	28,444	10,209	18,235
×1923	9,493	9,031	462	×1983	27,726	9,542	18,184
1924	10,053	9,411	642	1984	27,243	8,945	18,298
1925	10,302	9,568	734	1985	26,456	7,913	18,543
1926	10,064	9,242	822	1986	24,414	6,143	18,271
×1927	10,772	9,851	921				
1928	11,179	10,203	976				
1929	11,495	10,457	1,038				
1930	11,576	10,448	1,128				
×1931	10,766	9,547	1,219				

11-Freight Wagons

Fiscal year	Loading Capacity	Number of Wagon	Fiscal year	Loading Capacity	Number of Wagon
	t	*car*		*t*	*car*
1872	-	75	1932	864,737	65,903
1873	-	75	1933	873,998	66,824
1874	-	157	1934	892,442	68,545
×1875	-	203	×1935	919,470	71,060
1876	-	255	1936	955,270	74,444
1877	-	320	1937	972,112	76,672
1878	-	363	1938	1,047,307	81,878
×1879	-	413	×1939	1,148,767	88,983
1880	-	445	1940	1,298,237	98,622
1881	-	527	1941	1,371,519	102,922
1882	-	503	1942	1,452,985	107,535
×1883	-	626	×1943	1,828,201	115,937
1884	-	691	1944	1,018,674	122,667
1885	-	713	1945	1,801,252	120,217
1886	-	759	1946	1,767,648	118,473
×1887	-	953	×1947	1,655,744	109,576
1888	-	1,036	1948	1,739,194	110,095
1889	-	1,199	1949	1,744,577	111,155
1890	-	1,271	1950	1,702,952	108,522
×1891	-	1,678	×1951	1,742,993	112,441
1892	-	1,746	1952	1,704,025	109,998
1893	-	1,844	1953	1,696,374	110,501
1894	-	2,105	1954	1,699,409	110,764
×1895	-	2,228	×1955	1,671,929	111,172
1896	-	2,321	1956	1,674,126	113,855
1897	20,070	2,877	1957	1,758,905	118,145
1898	21,571	3,187	1958	1,744,974	111,977
×1899	24,869	3,602	×1959	1,775,746	112,971
1900	27,923	4,086	1960	1,861,172	118,729
1901	33,003	4,825	1961	1,987,509	126,157
1902	36,571	5,292	1962	2,075,347	130,793
×1903	38,908	5,793	×1963	2,176,580	136,731
1904	43,775	5,886	1964	2,200,028	143,197
1905	56,787	8,398	1965	2,275,887	142,258
1906	144,742	20,227	1966	2,270,528	138,451
×1907	234,588	32,617	×1967	2,429,133	142,742
1908	239,504	32,568	1968	2,511,985	147,591
1909	250,629	34,306	1969	2,654,952	158,323
1910	262,402	34,750	1970	2,638,714	151,619
×1911	297,178	37,952	×1971	2,541,660	142,988
1912	337,635	41,079	1972	2,415,611	135,912
1913	371,706	43,283	1973	2,111,360	128,762
1914	396,591	44,431	1974	2,236,043	125,139
×1915	414,776	44,482	×1975	2,171,647	120,597
1916	435,258	45,158	1976	2,074,015	115,018
1917	474,493	47,275	1977	1,989,125	109,890
1918	524,098	49,254	1978	1,852,949	101,012
×1919	579,315	51,778	×1979	1,831,724	99,846
1920	606,359	52,941	1980	1,821,572	99,562
1921	624,159	53,237	1981	1,796,206	98,001
1922	675,346	56,186	1982	1,584,361	84,923
×1923	703,440	57,628	×1983	1,222,462	63,510
1924	723,960	58,679	1984	937,545	48,006
1925	755,937	60,361	1985	803,807	39,519
1926	787,144	62,647	1986	480,568	19,356
×1927	828,539	64,986			
1928	860,469	66,716			
1929	893,342	68,324			
1930	896,266	69,309			
×1931	868,945	66,127			

Bibliography

Tetsudo-Sho (Ministry of Railway): *Nihon Tetsudo-Shi* (Railway History in Japan), Vol. 1–3, 1921, Tetsudo-Sho

Nihon Kokuyu Tetsudo (The Japanese National Railways): *Nihon Rikuun Junen-Shi*, Vol.4, 1951, Nihon Kokuyu Tetsudo

Nihon Kokuyu Tetsudo: *Nihon Rikuun Nijunen-Shi*, Vol. 2 Nenpyo, 1956, Nihon Kokyuy Tetsudo

Nihon Kokuyu Tetsudo: *Nihon Kokuyu Tetsudo Hyakunen-Shi*, Vol.18, 1969–1972, Nihon Kokuyu Tetsudo

Ishikawa, Tatsujiro: *Kokutetsu Kino to Zaisei no Kozu*, 1975, Kotsu Nihonsha

Ishikawa, Tatsujiro: Nichiyo Hyoron, *Kotsu Shinbun*, 1980–1986, Kotsu Kyoryokukai

Ishikawa, Tatsujiro (et al), JNR kara JR e, Zaimu-Hen. *Unyu to Keizai* Vol.48, No.10, 1988, Unyu Chosakyoku

Imashiro, Mitsuhide: Restructuring of the Japanese National Railways and Its Problems, Outcome of the Privatisation of the Japanese National Railways. *MODERN BUSINESS AND MANAGEMENT: Some Aspect of Japanese Enterprise*, Institute of Business Research, Daito Bunka University, March 1992

Imashiro, Mitsuhide: *The History of Railway Construction in Japan 1870–1960*, March 1995 Research Papers No. 21, Institute of Business Research Daito Bunka University

Kotsu Tokei Kenkyujo (Institute of Transportation Statistics): *Kokuyu Tetsudo Tetsudo Tokei Ruinen Hyo*, 1995, Kotsu Tokei Kenkyujo

Kotsu Tokei Kenkyujo: *The Japanese National Railways 1872–1985 A Statistical Summary*, 1996, Kotsu Tokei Kenkyujo

Index